2/21

PROJECT
BLUE BOOK
EXPOSED

PROJECT
BLUE BOOK
EXPOSED

Kevin D. Randle

MARLOWE & COMPANY
NEW YORK

Copyright page

Published by
Marlowe & Company
632 Broadway, Seventh Floor
New York, NY 10012

Library of Congress Card Catalog Number: 97-72378

ISBN 1-56924-746-3

Manufactured in the United States of America.
First Edition.

CONTENTS

To Carl Sagan:

who prevented the destruction of the Project Blue Book files at great personal cost. Thanks, Dr. Sagan.

1934–1996

INTRODUCTION

In the beginning, the Army Air Forces created what would eventually become Project Blue Book. It was a priority project that was classified. Its mission was to determine what the flying saucers were and if they posed a threat to the security of the United States. For twenty-two years the Air Force collected the data, kept it hidden under security regulations, and denied that anything of importance had been found.

In the mid-1970s, the Air Force declassified the files so that private researchers, or anyone else interested in Project Blue Book, could take a look at them. Within weeks of the low-key announcement, I found myself at Maxwell Air Force Base, home of the Air Force Archives, with an assignment from a magazine to study the files. I also had lists of cases to review and questions to be answered from the editor of the magazine and Coral and Jim Lorenzen, the leaders of the now defunct Aerial Phenomena Research Organization.

Since that time, the files have been sanitized by Air Force officers who attempted to remove the names of the witnesses, microfilmed, and relocated to the National Archives. The ninety-six rolls of microfilm are available for purchase by individuals for thirty-four dollars a roll. Now, each of us can own a complete set of the Air Force files for a relatively small amount of money.

These files, that the Air Force suggested told the story of misidentifications, illusion, delusion, hoax, and fraud, and that reveal there has been no threat to national security, also tell many other stories. They tell of bungled investigations, shadings of the truth, and an attitude of disbelief. They tell the story of an attempt to dupe the public with what was believed to be a solid and impressive investigation paid for by and denied to, the taxpayer. That simply isn't the truth.

That myth, of reliable investigation, might have grown as a result of Captain Edward Ruppelt's fine book about his days as the chief of the Air Force UFO office, *The Report on Unidentified Flying Objects*. It tells an exciting story of late-night phone calls, flights around the country to investigate puzzling reports, and briefings to the leaders of the military in Washington, D.C.

It is also a very misleading book in that only for a short period, from the late summer of 1951 to the very beginning of 1953, or about eighteen months, was the investigation solid. Before that, and after it, Blue Book was an investigation in name only. By the time Blue Book ended in 1969, the officers assigned did little more than telephone witnesses to try to convince them they had seen a natural phenomena, artificial satellites, Venus, plasmas, or had misidentified conventional aircraft. The truth had taken a backseat to solving cases.

There is no doubt, and Ruppelt reinforces it in his book, that during the summer of 1947, the military was in a panic over the sudden appearance of flying saucers. If the objects were real, and even if they were piloted by Soviets, they posed a genuine threat to national security. If they were genuine, and not Soviet, the threat could be even higher. Something was invading our airspace and the Army Air Forces was powerless to stop it.

As time passed and the summer ended without the alien invasion fleet appearing, the officers at the highest levels in the Pentagon began to relax. They still needed to know what was happening, but, with each passing day, it became clearer that an invasion was not being planned. They could set up a project to see if they could learn about the flying saucers.

Twenty-two years later, in 1969, they closed it, but not before gathering thousands of reports. Now, for the first time, I have looked at these reports and have found that things were not quite as Ed Ruppelt and the others would have us believe. I found that investigations were not carried out as we had been led to believe. I learned that the files held many interesting things, which we were told didn't exist.

For the first time, we get to really see what is in Blue Book and how the data was manipulated to provide a skewed picture of the situation. We can see that had the Air Force done the job they were supposed to be doing, our perception of the UFO phenomenon would be quite different. We probably wouldn't be arguing about the existence of UFOs, we would be trying to find out how they operated so that we could do the same thing.

While there is no smoking gun in the Project Blue Book files, no one case that screams that UFOs are extraterrestrial, there is a great deal of interesting evidence from eyewitness testimony to radar cases that are unexplained to the rational mind. There are photographic cases that provide strong evidence, and hints of other evidence that somehow is just not available.

One thing should be mentioned here. There is no reference to the UFO crash at Roswell, New Mexico, in this book because there are no references to it in the Project Blue Book files. Or rather, there is a single reference in a single file dated July 10, 1947, and it is part of a three-paragraph newspaper story. The middle paragraph mentions that the officers at Roswell had received a "blistering rebuke" for their claim of having captured one of the flying saucers. That is all that I was able to find about Roswell.

But there were lots of other interesting cases. I made some of my selection of which cases to use based on the fame of the original sighting, how much had been reported on it before, and how it was different than we had been led to believe. I selected others because they hadn't been reported but they demonstrated one of the many points to be made. These cases suggested something about the Air Force's handling of the situation and their drive to explain all sightings regardless of the facts.

And, I tried to make the evaluations based on the information in the case files. But, I also did some independent research to provide a contrast for what the Air Force did and what was possible. Yes, I used the telephone, but I also have visited some of the sites, have met some of the witnesses in person, and tried to go beyond the preliminaries. An investigation can take a number of avenues, all of which are acceptable.

What has been found in the Blue Book files is substantially different than what we have been told. The evidence for that is in the Blue Book files. I think they lead in the direction of extraterrestrial visitation. Others may disagree about the aliens, but will certainly agree all is not as we have been told.

So, here now is the evidence, as it appeared in Project Blue Book. See what you think.

IN THE BEGINNING . . .

A BRIEF HISTORY OF PROJECT BLUE BOOK

Like all things in the UFO field, it is not easy to put together a simple history of Project Blue Book because it was never a single project and it was almost always wrapped in secrecy. There were forerunners to it that were also classified, and good evidence that it coexisted with other projects that were also tasked to investigate UFOs. There is even a suggestion that an official UFO investigation survived the declared end of Project Blue Book in December 1969.

The first document to relate to the beginnings of Project Blue Book was written and signed on September 23, 1947. Lieutenant General Nathan F. Twining, then the commander of the Air Materiel Command, suggested to the commanding general of the Army Air Forces, General Carl Spaatz, through Brigadier General George Schgulen, that "the phenomenon reported is something real and not visionary or fictitious." He recommended that "Headquarters, Army Air Forces, issue a directive assigning a priority, security classification and Code Name for a detailed study of the matter."

On December 30, 1947 (the Air Force having come into official existence on December 17, or just two weeks earlier), Major General L. C. Craigie approved the recommendation for the classified research project. Project Sign was created as a 2A classified project, the highest being 1A. Although the general public was aware that a project had been created, they knew it as "Project Saucer," rather than Project Sign.

Although the project did not exist in the summer of 1947, the complete Project Blue Book files do include cases from that period. The first recorded sighting is from early June and from Hamburg, New York. The case is missing, but according to the Index, was a misidentification of an aircraft. The next case was from Seattle, Washington, and is also missing. It is listed as "Insufficient Data." In fact, the first several cases are listed as missing.

Data was gathered during the summer of 1947 and into the fall. That work included a thick file on the Kenneth Arnold sighting, which is credited with the invention of the term "flying saucer" and with bringing to public attention the idea of craft from other worlds.

A variety of officers inside the Army Air Forces and the then fledgling Air Force investigated the reports. Fourth Air Force intelligence, for example, was responsible of investigating the report and photographs made near Maury Island on June 21, 1947. Although eliminated as a hoax, the case is important because the two investigating officers were killed in a plane crash after they left to return home. The crash had nothing to do with flying saucers or the investigation. It was a tragic accident that has, since that time, taken on an exaggerated importance.

According to the available documentation, Project Sign began its work officially on January 22, 1948, and the first major investigation was into the crash of a Kentucky National Guard aircraft flown by Captain Thomas Mantell. He had been chasing an unknown object near the Godman Army Air Field when the accident took place.

By the summer of 1948, dozens of seemingly inexplicable cases had been reported to the Air Technical Intelligence Center (ATIC) at Wright Field in Dayton, Ohio. It wasn't until a DC-3 was "buzzed" by a flying saucer in July 1948 that the situation began to crystallize. On the twenty-fourth, a rocket-shaped object with two rows of square windows and flames shooting from the rear flashed past the aircraft piloted by Captains Clarence S. Chiles and John B. Whitted. At least one of the passengers also saw something that reminded him of a streak of light. An hour earlier, a ground maintenance crewman at Robins Air Force Base in Georgia claimed to have seen the same object.

Some of the officers at Sign, convinced they now had proof that the flying saucers were extraterrestrial, put together what they called an estimate of the situation. They concluded that flying saucers came from other planets, wrote a report containing the best evidence they had, and shipped it up to General Hoyt S. Vandenberg, then Air Force chief of staff. According to Captain Edward Ruppelt, who would eventually head Project Blue Book, Vandenberg wasn't impressed with the evidence. He rejected the report, ordered it declassified and destroyed.

Dr. Michael Swords, who had an opportunity to review drafts of Ruppelt's original work before the publication of his book, made some interesting observations about the estimate of the situation. In an article published in the *International UFO Reporter*, Swords outlined these deletions made from Ruppelt's classic work, *The Report on Unidentified Flying Objects*. To illustrate what had been left out of the book as published, he used italics to show the deleted material. That text as originally published was printed in a normal typeface.

In intelligence, if you have something to say about some vital problem you write a report that is known as an "Estimate of the Situation." A few days after the DC-3 was buzzed, the people at ATIC decided that the time had arrived to make an Estimate of the Situation. The situation was UFOs; the Estimate was that they were interplanetary!

It was a rather thick document with a black cover and it was printed on legal-sized paper. Stamped across the front were the words TOP SECRET.

It contained the Air Force's analysis of many of the incidents I have told you about plus many similar ones. All of them had come from scientists, pilots, and other equally credible observers, and each one was an unknown.

It concluded that UFOs were interplanetary. As documented proof, many unexplained sightings were quoted. The original UFO sighting by Kenneth Arnold; the series of sightings from the secret Air Force Test

Center, MUROC AFB; the F-51 pilot's observation of a formation of
spheres near Lake Mead; the report of an F-80 pilot who saw two round
objects diving toward the ground near the Grand Canyon; and a report
by the pilot of an Idaho National Guard T-6 trainer, who saw a violently
maneuvering black object.

As further documentation, the report quoted an interview with an Air
Force major from Rapid City AFB (now Ellsworth AFB) who saw twelve
UFOs flying a tight diamond formation. When he first saw them they
were high but soon they went into a fantastically high-speed dive, leveled
out, made a perfect formation turn, and climbed at a 30-to 40-degree
angle, accelerating all the time. The UFOs were oval-shaped and brilliant
yellowish-white.

Also included was one of the reports from the AEC's Los Alamos
Laboratory. The incident occurred at 9:40 A.M. on September 23, 1948.
A group of people were waiting for an airplane at the landing strip in Los
Alamos when one of them noticed something glint in the sun. It was a
flat, circular object, high in the northern sky. The appearance and relative
size was the same as a dime held edgewise and slightly tipped, about 50
feet away.

The document pointed out that the reports hadn't actually
started with the Arnold Incident. Belated reports from a weather
observer in Richmond, Virginia, who observed a "silver disk"
through his theodolite telescope; an F-47 pilot and three pilots in
his formation who saw a "silvery flying wing," and the English
"ghost airplanes" that had been picked up on radar early in 1947
proved the point. Although reports on them were not received
until after the Arnold sighting, these incidents had all taken place
earlier.

When the estimate was completed, typed, and approved, it
started up through channels to higher-command echelons. It drew
considerable comment but no one stopped it on its way up.

General Vandenberg, at the Pentagon, eventually received the Estimate, but was apparently less than impressed. According to Ruppelt,

at that point, "it was batted back down. The general wouldn't buy interplanetary vehicles. The report lacked proof."

A group of military officers and civilian technical intelligence engineers was then called to the Pentagon to defend the Estimate. According to the work done by Michael Swords, these were likely Lawrence H. Truettner, A. B. Deyarmond, and Alfred Loedding. Swords noted, parenthetically, that "Truettner and Deyarmond were the authors of the Project Sign report that contained many of these same cases and sympathies; Loedding was a frequent Pentagon liaison in 1947 and considered himself the 'civilian project leader' of Sign."

The military participants were probably the official project officer, Captain Robert Sneider, as well as Colonels Howard McCoy or William Clingerman, who would have had to sign off on the Estimate.

Swords noted that the defense was unsuccessful, and not long after the visit to the Pentagon, everyone named was reassigned. Swords writes, "So great was the carnage that only the lowest grades in the project, civilian George Towles and Lieutenant H. W. Smith, were left to write the 1949 Project Grudge document about the same cases."

Swords pointed out that Donald Keyhoe had mentioned the existence of the Estimate a number of times and was told that it was a myth. According to Swords, "The famous Armstrong Circle Theatre fiasco of 1958, where Keyhoe was cut off [the air] in mid-sentence, was partly due to the fact that he was about to mention this document."

After Vandenberg "batted" the report back down, after the staff was reduced, and after the fire went out of the investigation, Project Sign limped along. It was clear to everyone inside the military, particularly those who worked around ATIC, that Vandenberg was not a proponent of the extraterrestrial hypothesis. Those who supported the idea risked the wrath of the number one man in the Air Force. They had just had a practical demonstration of how devastating that wrath could be. If an officer was not smart enough to pick up the clues from what had just happened, then that officer's career could be severely limited.

Project Blue Book files show this to be the case. When Sign evolved into Project Grudge and then into Blue Book, a final report about Sign was written. Those inside Sign originally believed that UFOs were extraterrestrial until Vandenberg said he didn't find their reasoning adequate. Then, those inside Sign, those who were left, decided that other answers must be the correct ones. UFOs, flying saucers, were not extraterrestrial.

A report entitled *The Findings of Project Sign*, was eventually written. It outlined the motivation behind Project Sign, who the players were, and then the results of their research. In the Summary, it was noted that the data in the report were "derived from reports of 243 domestic and thirty (30) foreign incidents. Data from these incidents is being summarized, reproduced and distributed to agencies and individuals cooperating in the analysis and evaluation. . . . The data obtained in reports received are studied in relation to many factors such as guided-missile research activity, weather and other atmospheric sounding balloon launchings, commercial and military aircraft flights, flights of migratory birds, and other considerations, to determine possible explanations for sightings."

The authors of the report wanted to make the situation clear. They wrote,

Based on the possibility that the objects are really unidentified and unconventional types of aircraft a technical analysis is made of some of the reports to determine the aerodynamic, propulsion, and control features that would be required for the objects to perform as described in the reports. The objects sighted have been grouped into four classifications according to configuration:

1. Flying disks, i.e., very low aspect ration aircraft.
2. Torpedo—or cigar-shaped bodies—with no wings or fins visible in flight.
3. Spherical—or balloon-shaped—objects.
4. Balls of light.

The authors reported,

Approximately twenty percent of the incidents have been identified as conventional aerial objects to the satisfaction of personnel assigned to Project "Sign" in this Command. It is expected that a study of the incidents in relation to weather and other atmospheric sounding balloons will provide solutions for an equivalent number. . . . Elimination of incidents with reasonably satisfactory explanations will clarify the problem presented by a project of this nature.

The possibility that some of the incidents may represent technical developments far in advance of knowledge available to engineers and scientists of this country has been considered. No facts are available to personnel at this Command that will permit an objective assessment of this possibility. All information so far presented on the possible existence of space ships from another planet or of aircraft propelled by an advanced type of atomic power plant have been largely conjecture.

In other words, they had eliminated the reasons for the existence of the project. They were to determine the nature of the objects reported and if they were a threat to national security. In fact, the national-security aspect of the UFO investigations would become the biggest and most important part of the investigation.

They provided a number of recommendations, writing, "Future activity on this project should be carried on at the minimum level necessary to record, summarize, and evaluate the data received on future reports and to complete the specialized investigations now in progress." They then added a phrase that too many UFO researchers have overlooked in the past. They write, "When and if a sufficient number of incidents are solved to indicate that these sightings do not represent a threat to the security of the nation, the assignment of special project status to the activity could be terminated."

This is a theme that would be repeated in one official UFO investigation after another. They would mention this aspect again and again. Each of the investigations, from Sign forward, had national security as its main concern. If national security wasn't threatened, then the question of reality of the flying saucers and their exact nature became unimportant. And, as time passed, it became more likely to all those military investigators that no threat to the nation was posed.

The authors also wrote, "Reporting agencies should be impressed with the necessity for getting more factual evidence on sightings such as photographs, physical evidence, radar sightings, and data on size and shape."

The conclusions drawn by the report are very interesting. "No definite and conclusive evidence is yet available that would prove or disprove the existence of these unidentified objects as real aircraft of unknown and unconventional configuration. It is unlikely that positive proof of their existence will be obtained without examination of the remains of crashed objects. Proof of the nonexistence is equally impossible to obtain unless a reasonable and convincing explanation is determined for each incident."

They then write, "Many sightings by qualified and apparently reliable witnesses have been reported. However, each incident has unsatisfactory features, such as shortness of time under observation, distance from observer, vagueness of description or photographs, inconsistencies between individual observers, and lack of descriptive data, that prevents conclusions being drawn."

This one paragraph would also become important in understanding the UFO investigations of the future. Time and again those in the government would suggest that there were no good photographs, that eyewitness testimony was unreliable, and that the sightings were of nothing more spectacular than a fuzzy object in the distance seen for only a few seconds. Those arguing against the reality of the phenomenon would often make these same claims.

The reason for the recommendation for a continuation of the project had nothing to do with research into the phenomenon. The authors write, "Evaluation of reports of unidentified objects is a necessary activity of military intelligence agencies. Such sightings are inevitable, and under wartime conditions rapid and convincing solutions of such occurrences are necessary to maintain morale of military and civilian personnel. In this respect, it is considered that the establishment of procedures and training of personnel is in itself worth the effort expended on this project."

About a year earlier, the personnel assigned to Sign had concluded that flying saucers were extraterrestrial. Now, using the same cases and the same evidence, those who survived that earlier housecleaning were claiming that there was nothing to the UFO phenomenon. More importantly, they were saying there was no threat to national security, but that the project should be continued for training purposes.

On December 16, 1948, just a year after its beginning, Project Sign became Project Grudge. With the new name came a new attitude. All reports were investigated on the premise that they were simply misidentifications of natural phenomena or aircraft, or they were outright hoaxes. Flying saucers didn't exist so there could be no proof found that they did exist.

Just a year later, on December 27, 1949, the Air Force announced that Project Grudge, the official investigation into the flying saucer sightings, was being closed. The final report would be available to reporters as soon as it was completed.

That final report contained the case studies of 237 of the best reports. A number of experts, including Dr. J. Allen Hynek, who would become a scientific consultant to Project Blue Book and found the Center for UFO Studies (CUFOS), were able to explain some of the sightings as astronomical phenomena. Captain A. C. Trakowski, of the Air Forces's Cambridge research facility, reviewed the various balloon records to determine if sightings could be explained by balloons. The Grudge report was an in-depth study.

And, when all was said and done, the Grudge report had explained all but 23 percent of the sightings. But the Psychology Branch of the Air Force's Aeromedical Laboratory attempted to eliminate that 23 percent. The officials there wrote, "There are sufficient psychological explanations for the reports of unidentified flying objects to provide for plausible explanations for reports not otherwise explainable. . . ."

But the point that seems to have gotten lost is that nearly a quarter of the sightings reported to the Air Force during the existence of their study did not have mundane explanations. So, when they failed to find a solid explanation, they invented the psychological category. As those at the Aeromedical Laboratory suggested, some people just had spots in front of their eyes.

But even though the Air Force had announced that it had closed Project Grudge, such was not the case. Grudge continued to function at a low level with a single investigator, Lieutenant Jerry Cummings. When a series of spectacular sightings were made at the Army's Signal Corps Center at Fort Monmouth, New Jersey, Cummings, and Lieutenant Colonel N. R. Rosengarten, who was the chief of ATIC's Aircraft and Missiles Branch, were sent to investigate. They then returned to personally brief the chief of Air Force intelligence, Major General C. P. Cabell.

The meeting didn't go well as Cabell, other military officers, and representatives of Republic Aircraft complained about the quality of the work being done by the investigators for Grudge. There was a threat to national security, though no one was sure exactly what that threat might be. Cummings and Rosengarten were ordered back to Wright-Patterson Air Force Base with orders to reorganize the UFO project.

But Cummings didn't have much of a chance to do anything. He was routinely discharged from the Air Force before the work was completed. Lieutenant Colonel Rosengarten then asked Ed Ruppelt, an intelligence officer at ATIC, to reorganize Grudge.

Ruppelt began to file the reports and cross-reference them. He found that many were missing (as evidenced by the overall index that was created). He put together a staff who had no firm beliefs for or against the idea that flying saucers were real. And, he subscribed to a clipping service so that he would be able to learn of sightings that were not reported to the military. He hoped to gain some insights into the UFO problem by gathering data and statistics about them. Ruppelt, trained as an aeronautical engineer, was bringing that training to bear on solving the riddle of the flying saucers.

In 1950 and 1951 combined, there were 379 sightings reported to the UFO project. Of those, all but 49 were explained to the satisfaction of the project officers. Other sightings, from 1947 to 1949, were periodically reviewed, and new solutions were attached to the old cases.

In March 1952, Grudge had its status upgraded. Now it was the Aerial Phenomena Group and the code name was changed once again. It was now known as Project Blue Book.

But just as Ruppelt was getting things organized, the situation changed. Instead of getting two or three UFO reports a week, they began to come in at a rate of two or three a day. In his book he wrote that the clippings that had been coming in a thick envelope once a week or once a month began to arrive in boxes much more often.

July 1952 would be the big month for the UFO project. On two consecutive weekends, UFOs were spotted over Washington, D.C. Fighters were scrambled, people on the ground saw the lights in the sky, and airline pilots alerted about the lights saw them as well. The sightings were front-page news throughout the country, forcing the military to response to reporters' questions and the public's interest.

At a hastily called press conference, Major General John A. Samford told reporters that the sightings might be the result of temperature inversions. Samford hadn't meant that as a complete answer, but the news media seized it and ran with it.

More importantly, Ruppelt, who did investigate, to some extent, the sightings, pointed out that Air Force personnel were pressured by their superiors to change their stories. Lights that had been inexplicable became stars seen through the haze hanging over the city. Skeptics suggested the radar returns were the result of the inversion layers over the city on those days. It made no difference that the men watching the radar scopes, and one of the military officers who witnessed some of the sightings, were experts and could tell weather phenomena from solid targets. The sightings were explained, in the public arena, as temperature inversion. Curiously, the Blue Book files listed them as "unidentified."

Press and public interest increased dramatically when newspapers bannered the Washington National sightings at the end of July. During August the sightings throughout the country continued, as they did in September. By the end of 1952, the Air Force had added more than fifteen hundred sightings to the files. More importantly, over three hundred of them were unidentified. The situation had become intolerable.

Part of the solution was the creation of the Robertson Panel. In September 1952, as the UFO reports were still flooding Project Blue Book, H. Marshall Chadwell, then Assistant Director of Scientific Intelligence, sent a memo to General Walter Bedell Smith, then Director of Central Intelligence (DCI) for the CIA. He wrote,

"Recently an inquiry was conducted by the Office of Scientific Intelligence to determine whether there are national security implications in the problem of 'unidentified flying objects,' i.e. flying saucers; whether adequate study and research is currently being directed to this problem in its relation to such national security implications; and further investigation and research should be instituted, by whom, and under what aegis."

Chadwell continued, writing, "[P]ublic concern with the phenomena indicates that a fair proportion of our population is mentally conditioned to the acceptance of the incredible. In this fact lies the potential for the touching-off of mass hysteria. . . . In order to minimize risk of panic, a national policy should be established as to what should be told to the public regarding the phenomena."

Those words should have a chilling effect on anyone who reads them. What Chadwell is saying, in his best Big Brother voice, is that American citizens are gullible, believe incredible things, and can be manipulated into mass hysteria. The government, with its more learned and stable members, should decide what can be or should not be told to the public about flying saucers.

It is also clear from the tone of the document what Chadwell already believes. Tales of flying saucers are incredible. These things simply cannot exist and therefore do not exist.

In December 1952, just weeks before the group would actually meet, Chadwell decided to form a scientific advisory board. It was decided that Dr. H. P. Robertson, who had accompanied Chadwell to Wright-Patterson Air Force Base to review the UFO evidence in the Project Blue Book files, would chair the investigation.

Under the auspices of the CIA, the panel convened on January 14, 1953. They reviewed the best of the UFO cases including both the films that had been taken by private citizens in the past two years. They examined the radar cases and the photographic cases. In fact, there are indications that it was the movies that had brought the various scientists to the table.

On Friday afternoon, with the evidence presented including briefings by Ruppelt and Hynek, Robertson was given, or took, the task of writing the final report. By the next morning, in an age that had no copy machines, fax machines, word processors, or computers, Robertson finished his draft of the report. Not only that, Lloyd Berkner had already read it. As had Chadwell, who had taken it to the Air Force Directorate of Intelligence to have it approved. Before the committee assembled on Saturday morning, the report was, in essence, finished and approved.

One other thing must be understood to keep the Robertson Panel in perspective. Their first concern was to determine if UFOs posed a threat to national security. That was a question they could answer. They decided, based on the number of UFO reports made through official intelligence channels through the years, that UFOs did, after a fashion, pose a threat.

Ed Ruppelt mentioned it in his analysis of the Robertson Panel. Too many reports at the wrong time *could* mask a Soviet attack on the United States. Although hindsight shows us this threat was of little importance, especially when the sorry state of Soviet missile research in 1952 is considered, it was a major concern to those men in the intelligence field in the early 1950s. A sudden flood of UFO reports, not unlike what had happened during the summer of 1952, could create havoc in the message traffic so that critical messages of a imminent attack would be hidden or lost.

With that as a concern, the Robertson Panel, who had seen nothing to suggest that UFOs were anything other than misidentifications, hoaxes, and weather and astronomical phenomena (and who obviously wanted to see nothing else), needed to address this concern. That was the motivation behind some of the Panel's recommendations. These recommendations then, were born of a need to clear the intelligence-reporting channels, and not of a need to answer the questions about the reality of the UFO phenomena.

According to the Panel's final report, "[A]lthough evidence of any direct threat from these sightings was wholly lacking, related dangers might well exist resulting from: A. Misidentification of actual enemy artifacts by defense personnel. B. Overloading of emergency reporting channels with 'false' information ('noise to signal ration' analogy—Berkner). C. Subjectivity of public to mass hysteria and greater vulnerability to possible enemy psychological warfare."

They went on, writing, "Although not the concern of the CIA, the first two of these problems may seriously affect the Air Defense intelligence system, and should be studied by experts, possibly under ADC [Air Defense Command]. If UFOs become discredited in a reaction to the 'flying saucer' scare, or if reporting channels are saturated with false and poorly documented reports, our capability of detecting hostile activity will be reduced. Dr. Page noted that more competent screening or filtering of reported sightings at or near the source is required, and that this can best be accomplished by an educational program."

Of all the suggestions in the Panel report, this is the area that has caused the most trouble with interpretation. The Panel was suggesting that if people were more familiar with what was in the sky around them, if they were familiar with natural phenomena that were rare but spectacular, then many sighting reports could be eliminated. How many UFO sightings are explained by Venus, meteors, or bright stars that seemed to hover for hours? In today's environment, with video cameras everywhere, how many times has Venus been taped and offered by witnesses as proof they saw something?

Under the subheading of "Educational Program," the Panel recommended that "the Panel's concept of a broad educational program integrating efforts of all concerned agencies [is] that it should have two major aims: training and 'debunking.' "

The Panel explained, "The training aim would result in proper recognition of unusually illuminated objects (e.g. balloons, aircraft reflections) as well as natural phenomena (meteors, fireballs, mirages, noctilucent clouds). Both visual and radar recognition are concerned. There would be many levels in such education. . . . This training should result in a marked reduction in reports caused by misidentified cases and resultant confusion."

The problem with the next paragraph came from the use of the word "debunking." Many read something nefarious into it, while the use of it, and the tone of the paragraph suggest something that was, at the time, fairly innocuous, at least according to Dr. Edward Condon, who would head another civilian investigation into UFO sightings sixteen years later.

The "debunking" aim would result in reduction in public interest in "flying saucers" which today evokes a strong psychological reaction. This education could be accomplished by mass media such as television, motion pictures, and popular articles. Basis of such education would be actual case histories which had been puzzling at first but later explained. As in the case of conjuring tricks, there is much less stimulation if the "secret" is known. Such a program should tend to reduce the current gullibility of the public and consequently their susceptibility to clever hostile propaganda. The Panel noted that the general absence of Russian propaganda based on a subject with so many obvious possibilities for exploitation might indicate a possible Russian official policy.

They then discussed the planning of the educational program. Some have seen that as a "disinformation" program designed to explain UFOs as mundane. The real reason behind it, however, seems to be to end sighting reports made by those who are unfamiliar with the sky. The educational program was suggested as a teaching tool.

The UFO information presented, according to those who were at some or all of the panel's sessions, was managed. They had limited time and were unable to examine all aspects of the UFO field in the time they had. It can be suggested that a careful management of the data supplied would provide a biased picture and that the conclusions drawn from that specific data would be accurate, but those conclusions would be skewed. It could be argued that the panel was designed specifically so that time would not allow those embarrassing questions to be asked. And, it can be suggested that panel was loaded with scientists who had already made up their minds about the reality of UFOs.

A careful study of the data supplied to the Robertson Panel does suggest that UFOs are little more than anecdotal gossip. The exceptions supplied to them are the two short UFO movies and the data from radar. However, without another piece of data, without some kind of physical evidence that would lead to the extraterrestrial hypothesis, no other conclusions could be drawn. The films were interesting, but there were alternative explanations—while not as satisfactory in the long run—that were certainly no less valid. And radar cases are open to the interpretation of the radar operators. Their training, talent, and expertise are all important factors.

It was at this same time, the beginning of 1953, that the investigative emphasis that had dominated Blue Book for the eighteen months that had preceded the Robertson Panel began to erode. Ruppelt suggests that it was his demands that more investigators be found, but it seems that Blue Book was becoming too visible and too public. Although the project would continue, the investigative responsibility was moved from Blue Book to the 4602d Air Intelligence Service Squadron.

Air Force Regulation 200-2 was in the planning stages with a version approved in August 1953. A year later, August 1954, the regulation went into effect, nearly eliminating Blue Book from the investigative mix. Although the regulation required that ATIC be notified about the UFO investigations, there was nothing in it that required Blue Book be informed. What we have is the classic situation where one agency has the responsibility for the UFO investigations and another has the authority. Blue Book had been effectively eliminated, though it still existed.

Ruppelt left the project and it was handed off to a variety of other officers. At one low point in 1953, it was being run by an airman first class, a rather low enlisted grade. Ruppelt inherited it again for a couple of months, and then he was replaced. In March 1954 Captain Charles Hardin became the director.

In April 1956, Captain George T. Gregory, a man who didn't believe that UFOs were real, led Blue Book into an almost rabid anti-UFO direction. The change in tone is evidenced in the investigations being conducted. During this time, sightings were to be identified, no matter how. The belief was that UFOs were not extraterrestrial spacecraft, and if they weren't, then another, mundane explanation should be available. The list of early sightings explained under this new concept is extraordinary. "Possible" was left off the case files so that it seemed that the explanation was now definite. If they had to reach for the explanation, that was what they did. No explanation was too strange to explain a sighting, as long as it wasn't extraterrestrial.

In December 1958, one of the officers assigned to the UFO project claimed that he found "certain deficiencies" that he felt "must be corrected." Specifically he referred to Air Force Regulation (AFR) 200-2, "dated 5 February 1958 (revised on that date), which essentially stipulates the following . . . to explain or identify all UFO sightings." In other words, the regulation now dictated that explanations be found for sightings.

After December 1958, there was an attempt to transfer Blue Book to some other Air Force agency, specifically, the Secretary of the Air Force, Office of Information (SAFOI). That would move it from the prestigious Foreign Technology Division (FTD) to the less important information office.

On April 1, 1960, in a letter to Major General Dougher at the Pentagon, A. Francis Archer, a scientific advisor to Blue Book commented on a memo written by Colonel Evans, a ranking officer at ATIC. Archer said, "[I] have tried to get Blue Book out of ATIC for ten years . . . and do not agree that the loss of prestige to be a disadvantage."

In 1962, Lieutenant Colonel Robert Friend, who at one time headed Blue Book, wrote to his headquarters that the project should be handed over to a civilian agency that would word its report in such a way as to allow the Air Force to drop the study. At the same time, Edward Trapnell, an assistant to the Secretary of the Air Force, when talking to Dr. Robert Calkins of the Brookings Institute, said pretty much the same thing. Find a civilian committee to study the problem, then have them conclude it the way the Air Force wanted it. One of the stipulations was that this organization, no matter what it was, had to say some positive things about the Air Force's handling of the UFO investigations.

Other government officials suggested closing Blue Book but realized that the public would have to be "educated to accept the closing." By 1966, the Air Force managed to get Blue Book press releases issued by SAFOI. Letters to the public no longer carried the prestigious ATIC or Foreign Technology Division letterhead but only the stamp of the Office of Information.

The major stumbling block was a new wave of sightings that were getting national attention. First, New Mexico police officer Lonnie

Zamora reported an egg-shaped object on the ground near Socorro. He reported seeing two beings near it, and when it took off, it left landing-gear markings and burned vegetation.

The public interest in UFOs began to rise. Network television paid attention and several prestigious magazines began to treat the subject with a little respect. The Air Force's explanations seemed tired, and even the most superficial investigations revealed flaws in their solutions. When Hynek, after hearing about the sightings in Michigan in 1966 suggested they might be swamp gas, all credibility was lost.

Something had to be done because of the growing publicity. The Air Force was in a hole and no one was listening to its threadbare explanations. Someone decided that it was time for another independent study of the phenomenon. The outgrowth of this was the Condon Committee, organized at the University of Colorado and funded by more than half a million dollars of taxpayer money funneled through the Air Force.

Scientific director of the project, the man who received the Air Force grant, was Dr. Edward U. Condon, who was a professor of Physics and Astrophysics, and a fellow of the Joint Institute for Laboratory Astrophysics at the University of Colorado. As a career scientist, Condon had the sort of credentials and prestige the Air Force wanted.

As noted by the documentation that appeared after the declassification of the Project Blue Book files, and as noted here, the formation of the Condon Committee was part of an already existing plan. Find a university to study the problem (flying saucers) and then conclude it the way the Air Force wanted it concluded.

Jacques Vallee, writing about the Condon Committee in *Dimensions*, said, "As early as 1967, members of the Condon Committee were privately approaching their scientific colleagues on other campuses, asking them how they would react if the committee's final report to the Air Force were to recommend closing down Project Blue Book." This tends to confirm the real mission of Condon was not to study the phenomenon but to study ways to end Air Force involvement in it.

Dr. Michael Swords has spent the last several years studying the history of the Condon Committee and confirms the view that the Air Force used Condon. But Condon was a willing participant in the deception. According to a letter discovered by Swords and written by Lieutenant Colonel Robert Hippler to Condon, the plan was laid out in no uncertain terms. Hippler told Condon that no one knew of any extraterrestrial visitation and therefore, there "has been no visitation."

Hippler also pointed out that Condon "must consider" the cost of the investigations of UFOs and to "determine if the taxpayer should support this" for the next ten years. Hippler warned that it would be another decade before another independent study could be mounted that might end the Air Force UFO project.

Condon understood what Hippler was trying to tell him. Three days later in Corning, New York, Condon, in a lecture to scientists including those members of the Corning Section of the American Chemical Society and the Corning Glass Works Chapter of Sigma XI, told them, "It is my inclination right now to recommend that the government get out of this business. My attitude right now is that there is nothing in it. But I am not supposed to reach a conclusion for another year."

Robert Low responded to Hippler's letter a day or so after Condon's Corning talk, telling him that they, the committee, were very happy to now know what they were supposed to do. Low wrote, "[Y]ou indicate what you believe the Air Force wants of us, and I am very glad to have your opinion." Low pointed out that Hippler had answered the questions about the study "quite directly."

In 1969, the Condon Committee released their findings. As had all of those who had passed before them, the Condon Committee found that UFOs posed no threat to the security of the United States. Edward U. Condon in Section I, Recommendations and Conclusions, wrote, "The history of the past twenty-one years has repeatedly led Air Force officers to the conclusion that none of the things seen, or thought to have been seen, which pass by the name 'UFO reports,' constituted any hazard or threat to national security."

After suggesting that such a finding was "out of our province" to study, and if they did find any such evidence, they would pass it on to the Air Force, Condon wrote, "We know of no reason to question the finding of the Air Force that the whole class of UFO reports so far considered does not pose a defense problem."

Included in the Recommendations was the idea that "it is our impression that the defense function could be performed within the framework established for intelligence and surveillance operations without the continuance of a special unit such as Project Blue Book, but this is a question for defense specialists rather than research scientists."

That seems to have taken care of most of the requirements. Condon had confirmed that national security wasn't an issue, had said some positive things about the Air Force's handling of the UFO phenomenon, and had recommended the end of Project Blue Book. He had done his job.

Finally Condon wrote, "It has been contended that the subject has been shrouded in official secrecy. We conclude otherwise. We have no evidence of secrecy concerning UFO reports. What has been miscalled secrecy has been no more than an intelligent policy of delay in releasing data so that the public does not become confused by premature publication of incomplete studies or reports.

It is impossible to understand how Condon could write those words after being handed a stack of Blue Book files stamped SECRET that had been held by the Air Force for more than a decade. It is impossible to understand this, when there was documentation that proves secrecy on the part of the Air Force. It was in 1969, before the official end of the Condon Committee, that Brigadier General C. H. Bolender wrote, [R]eports of unidentified flying objects which could affect national security are made in accordance with JANAP 146 or Air Force Manual 55-11, and are not part of the Blue Book system."

In other words, documentation existed to support the claim there was secrecy. While a case can be made that the regulations and the secrecy are warranted by the circumstances, it can also be argued that the secrecy did exist, contrary to what Condon wrote.

What this does, is demonstrate that the Condon Committee was not an unbiased scientific study of UFOs, but a carefully designed project that had a single objective. To end public Air Force involvement in the UFO phenomenon. After all, according the Hippler, why should the taxpayers fund another ten years of UFO research?

The Condon report suggested there was no evidence of extraterrestrial visitation and that all UFO reports could be explained if sufficient data had been gathered in the beginning. This is exactly what Hippler wrote in his January 1967 letter to Condon. Yet, even when they selected the sightings they would investigate, they failed to explain almost 30 percent of them. In one case (over Labrador, 30 June 1954), they wrote, "This unusual sighting should therefore be assigned to the category of some almost certainly natural phenomenon, which is so rare that it apparently has never been reported before or since."

But even with the holes in the study, even with the contradictory evidence, and even with the proof that something unusual was going on, Condon did what he was paid to do. He ended Project Blue Book. On December 17, 1969, the Air Force announced that it was terminating its study of flying saucers. The twenty-two-year-old study had come to a close.

JUNE 24, 1947:

KENNETH ARNOLD AND FRED JOHNSON

On June 24, 1947, the modern UFO era was ushered in when pilot Kenneth Arnold, a Boise, Idaho, businessman, saw nine objects flash across the sky near Mount Rainier in Washington State. They were flying one behind the other, at about 9,500 feet, at a speed estimated, by Arnold, to be more than 1,500 miles per hour.

Although fascinated by the strange craft, Arnold didn't land immediately to inform the press. Instead, he continued flying, searching for a lost aircraft. When he did land, he talked to reporters and started a mystery that has lasted since that day.

Arnold, in relating the tale later, told military investigators, "The air was so smooth that day that it was a real pleasure flying and, as most pilots do when the air is smooth and they are flying at a higher altitude, I trimmed out my airplane in the direction of Yakima, Washington, which was almost directly east of my position and simply sat in my plane observing the sky and the terrain."

His attention was called to the strange objects when sunlight flashed off the metal surface. "It startled me as I thought I was too close to some other aircraft. I looked everyplace in the sky and couldn't find where the reflection had come from until I looked to the left . . . where I observed a chain of nine peculiar-looking aircraft."

The string of nine objects were flying in a formation that he estimated to be five miles long. They dodged in and out of the mountain peaks in a fluid motion that tilted them up and revealed their bottoms to him. He noted that they were quite far away.

Arnold had also seen a DC-4 that he estimated to be fifteen miles from him. He compared the objects to that aircraft, believing them to be smaller than the four-engine, propeller-driven airplane.

When he landed in Yakima, Washington, he told the assembled reporters that the objects moved with a motion like that of saucers skipping across the water. The shape, however, according to drawings that Arnold completed for the Army, showed objects that were heel-shaped. In later drawings, Arnold elaborated, showing objects that were crescent-shaped with a scalloped, trailing edge.

Hearing Arnold's description of the motion of the objects, reporter Bill Bequette coined the term "flying saucer." The term didn't refer to the shape of the objects, then, but to the style of their movement.

Arnold's sighting didn't gain front-page status immediately. Stories about it appeared in newspapers a day or two later. It was, at that time, the story of an oddity. Arnold claimed later that he thought he had seen some sort of the new or experimental jet aircraft.

Because this was the first of the flying-saucer sightings to gain national attention, it became important for military officers to determine what he had seen. They spent a great deal of time and effort investigating it, and eventually wrote it off as mirages. That is, Arnold, because of the atmospheric conditions that afternoon, had seen a mirage in which the tops of the mountains seemed to be separate from the rest of the ground. It looked as if huge bits of land were hovering above the ground and could, under the proper circumstance appear to be saucer-shaped objects flying near the tops of the mountains.

In a report prepared for the Army Air Forces, Arnold expressed his displeasure at such suggestions. He wrote, "A number of newsmen and experts suggested that I might have been seeing reflections or even a mirage. This I know to be absolutely false, as I observed these objects not only through the glass of my airplane but turned my airplane sideways where I could open my window and observe them with a completely unobstructed view."

That, of course, didn't satisfy those who believed that Arnold had made an error. Dr. J. Allen Hynek, the onetime consultant to Project Blue Book, studied the case for the military. It was Hynek's opinion that if Arnold's estimate of the distance was correct, then he had to have underestimated the size of the objects. If, on the other hand, he had overestimated the distance, then his timing of their flight was wrong. Hynek believed, according to the documents available in the Blue Book files, that the objects were closer than Arnold thought. Hynek wrote, "In all probability, therefore, objects were much closer than thought and moving at definitely 'sub-sonic' speeds."

My comment to that is, So? We still have the sighting of nine objects that are not conventional aircraft. They are flying in a loose formation, and traveling at a fairly high rate of speed. Even if they are subsonic, that doesn't explain what they were, only that the observed speed was within the capability of aircraft being flown in 1947. It doesn't answer the question of what they were.

Others at AMC, apparently impressed with Hynek's analysis, also wrote off the case. In their summary of the flying saucer reports, that is, the Project Sign analysis, someone wrote, "AMC Opinion: The report cannot bear even superficial examination, therefore, must be disregarded. There are strong indications that this report and its attendant publicity is largely responsible for subsequent reports."

It seemed to indicate that those looking at the Arnold report in the late 1940s believed that Arnold had misidentified some kind of known, subsonic aircraft. But the question remains, What were they? The description of them fits nothing in the inventory at the time with the possible exception of the Northrop Flying Wing. It was a large, four-engine, propeller-driven aircraft that was not flying in that area. And, there weren't nine of them available even if they had been flying at the time and in the area.

There is another aspect of the case that needs to be clarified. In the Air Force file on the Arnold sighting, there are "galley-proof" pages from a book written by Donald H. Menzel, the Harvard astronomer who believed that all UFO sightings were misidentifications or outright lies. In the book, Menzel proposes the mirage theory that the Air Force eventually accepted as the answer to the Arnold case.

But Menzel wasn't done with one explanation. He offered many. In his first book about flying saucers, Menzel suggested that Arnold had seen "billowing blasts of snow, ballooning up from the tops of ridges. . . . These rapidly shifting, tilting clouds of snow would reflect the sun like a mirror . . . and the rocking surfaces would make the chain sweep along something like a wave, with only a momentary reflection from crest to crest."

It is an interesting theory and one that makes sense, except longtime residents say that the snow in late June, what there is in the mountains, is wet and heavy and wouldn't be swept around like the powdery stuff that falls in the winter. In other words, Menzel's explanation does not conform to the weather of the time, nor does it account for Arnold's description of the craft.

Menzel, apparently realizing the flaws in his theory, offered the possibility that a high layer of fog, haze, or dust just above or just below Arnold's altitude might account for the sighting. Menzel claimed that these layers could reflect the sun in almost mirrorlike fashion.

Again the explanation fails, if only because Arnold saw movement and that would require some sort of turbulence at altitude. Arnold had remarked about how stable the air was. A perfect day for flying with no real winds, or turbulence, and unlimited visibility.

Menzel, in his book with Lyle G. Boyd, *The World of Flying Saucers*, wrote that Arnold may have seen orographic clouds. These are huge, circular-shaped clouds that can form on the downwind side of mountains. But, as Menzel himself noted, they stand still and are not particularly reflective. In other words, Menzel, after suggesting the clouds, then eliminates them himself.

In the book *The UFO Enigma*, published after his death, and co-authored with Ernest H. Taves, Menzel suggested that Arnold may have been fooled by drops of water on the cockpit windows. He wrote, "I cannot, of course, say definitely that what Arnold saw were merely raindrops on the windows of his plane. He would doubtless insist that there was no rain at the altitude at which he was flying. But many queer things happen at different levels in the earth's atmosphere."

But remember what Arnold said about those who had suggested mirages? ". . . I observed these objects not only through the glass of my airplane but turned my airplane sideways where I could open my window and observe them with a completely unobstructed view." If the object had been water drops on the windows, they would have disappeared when he opened the window for his unobstructed view.

So, the real problem with this report seems to be that Arnold may have underestimated the size of the objects or overestimated the distance to them. These are not fatal flaws. And they are not reason enough to throw out the report. Arnold was, after all, a pilot who had flown in the area before. He was familiar with what the terrain looked like. Instead of nitpicking Arnold's estimates of distance and size of the objects, or inventing multiple explanations that are contradicted by the facts, the military investigators should have been looking for corroboration of the case. Had they looked, they would have found it.

Just about the time that Arnold lost sight of the objects, Fred Johnson, listed as a prospector, reported watching five or six disc-shaped craft as they flew over the Cascade Mountains. He said they were round with a slight tail and about thirty feet in diameter. They were not flying in any sort of formation and as they banked in a turn, the sunlight flashed off them. As they approached, Johnson noticed that his compass began to spin wildly. When the objects finally vanished in the distance, the compass returned to normal.

After learning of the Arnold sighting, Johnson wrote to the Air Force on August 20, 1947, saying,

Saw in the portland [sic] paper a short time ago in regards to an article in regards to the so called flying disc having any basis in fact. I can say [I] am a prospector and was in the Mt Adams district on June 24th the day Kenneth Arnold of Boise Idaho claims he saw a formation of flying disc [sic]. And i saw the same flying objects at about the same time. Having a telescope with me at the time i can assure you there are real and noting like them I ever saw before they did not pass verry high over where I was standing at the time. plolby 1000 ft. they were Round about 30 foot in diameter tapering sharply to a point in the head and in an oval shape. with a bright top surface. I did not hear any noise as you would from a plane. But there was an object in the tail end looked like a big hand of a clock shifting from side to side like a big magnet. There speed was far as i know seemed to be greater than anything I ever saw. Last view I got of the objects they were standing on edge Banking in a cloud.

It is signed, "Yours Respectfully, Fred Johnson."

The Army Air Forces had asked the FBI to interview some of those seeing flying disks. Johnson was one of those interviewed. The FBI report contained essentially the same information as the letter that Johnson had sent to the Army. The FBI report ended saying, "Informant appeared to be a very reliable individual who advised that he had been a prospector in the states of Montana, Washington and Oregon for the past forty years."

Dr. Bruce Maccabee, a physicist with the Navy, wrote in the *International UFO Reporter*, published by the Center for UFO Studies, that the Johnson sighting is important, not because it takes place near where Arnold saw the nine objects, but because it seems to be an extension of the Arnold sighting. It provides independent corroboration for the Arnold sighting, strengthening that case, and reducing to the ridiculous some of the explanations that have been offered to explain it.

Menzel, the Harvard scientist, decided that Johnson was being honest in his report; that is, Johnson was not lying about it. He was merely mistaken in his analysis of the sighting. Menzel wrote that Johnson had probably seen bright reflections from patches of clouds. It didn't seem to matter to Menzel that Johnson saw the objects only about a thousand feet over his head, watched them through a telescope, and had them in sight for almost a minute, before they disappeared by turning toward a cloud.

Johnson's sighting is important for another reason that is noted in the Air Force file. Johnson spoke about his compass behaving oddly as the objects flew overhead. Here is the first example of what would become known as an electromagnetic effect; that is, a type of inter-action with the environment. It would suggest that Johnson was seeing something real, rather than something such as bright reflections from patches of clouds.

The AMC opinion on this case is, "From the limited evidence sub-mitted, it is impossible to reach a definite conclusion. However, two possible psychological factors are readily apparent; one, the observer stated he submitted this report solely because he had read several days following his observation of another sighting. Therefore, he very likely either consciously or inadvertently may have attempted to conform his report to that recounted in the newspaper; and two, he colored his report with interference of huge magnetic fields, as to implications of which he was obviously uninformed."

There is no evidence that Johnson's report was colored by what he read in the newspaper. An equally plausible explanation is that, after seeing the objects, he didn't know where to report it, or even if anyone else would be interested in what he saw. By reading the newspaper, he learned that others had, in fact, seen the objects and there was in-terest in such reports. And, he now knew of a place to report the sighting.

The Air Force investigators also realized that if Johnson's compass was affected by the objects, it was suggestive of a massive magnetic field. They reasoned that such a field does not exist and therefore the reaction of the compass must have had nothing to do with the sighting of the objects. Of course, if the objects did generate a powerful elec-tromagnetic field, then his compass would have been affected just as he suggested.

What we see in these two cases is the classic divide-and-conquer strategy used throughout the UFO investigations. Arnold made his report and had no corroborating witnesses. Johnson made his report because of what he had read about Arnold. What the military officers didn't do was link the cases. If they are not linked, they can be dealt with individually. Neither case, by itself, is particularly impressive. They are single-witness reports, which means they can be interpreted as some sort of individual aberration. But linked, we have not only a multiple-witness case but independent observers that include a pilot in the air, an observer on the ground, and a report of electromagnetic effects.

Why should we link the cases? Because, as noted by Maccabee, it seems that just as Arnold lost sight of the objects in the Mount Rainier area, Johnson spotted them overhead. Arnold said that he lost sight of them in the area where Johnson said he first saw them. It seems to be reasonable to believe that the two reports are related.

If we want to take an objective look, we must be aware that Arnold said there were nine objects but Johnson said he saw only six. The Air Force notes in their file, "There are several major differences, notably as Dr. Hynek points out, that these objects had tails, and that the inferred size, as determined from the estimated distance, is quite different."

But again, we retreat to the evidence in the case file. If Arnold's estimate of distance is correct, then we wouldn't expect him to see fine details on the craft. Even if he badly overestimated the distance, he was still a long way from them. Johnson, on the other hand, was much closer and he looked at them through a telescope. That means, quite simply, that he might have observed details on the craft that were invisible to Arnold because of the distances involved.

We are left with two very interesting cases, which, when linked, provide important corroboration for one another. We are left with two cases that have no good explanation for them. Those explanations tried, are all badly flawed or so outrageous as to be useless. Of course, the fact that the reports are not explained does not mean that either Arnold or Johnson saw extraterrestrial spacecraft. It only means that they saw something unconventional that, at the time, was not explained as aircraft, mirages, blowing snow, or raindrops on the cockpit canopy. That tends to rule out the mundane so that we are left with the extraordinary.

JULY 7, 1947:

THE RHODES PHOTOGRAPHS

Less than two weeks after Kenneth Arnold's sighting hit the newspapers, a self-employed, self-proclaimed scientist living in Phoenix, Arizona, took what might be the first, and the best, photographs of one of the flying saucers.

William A. Rhodes told reporters, FBI agents, and Army investigators basically the same story. He had been on the way to his workshop at the rear of his house when he heard a distinctive *whoosh* that he believed to be from a P-80 "Shooting Star," a jet-powered aircraft. He grabbed a camera from a workshop bench and hurried to a small mound in the backyard. The object was circling in the east at about a thousand feet in the air.

Rhodes sighted along the side of his camera and took a photograph. He advanced the film and then hesitated, thinking that he would wait for it to get closer. Then, worried that it would disappear without coming closer, snapped the second picture. That was all the film he had.

The story, along with the pictures, appeared in the Phoenix newspaper, the *Arizona Republic*. In it, reporter Robert C. Hanika wrote, "Men long experienced in aircraft recognition studied both the print and the negative from which they were made, and declined to make a guess on what the flying object might be." It was also noted that "the marked interest Rhodes has for all aircraft has led most persons who have been in contact with other observers of the 'flying discs' to believe the photographs are the first authentic photographs of the missiles, since Rhodes easily can identify practically any aircraft."

Rhodes said that the object appeared to be elliptical in shape and have a diameter of 20 to 30 feet. It appeared to be at 5,000 feet when first seen and was traveling, according to Rhodes, at 400 to 600 miles per hour. It was gray, which tended to blend with the overcast background of the sky.

The object had, according to Rhodes and a confidential report from the Project Blue Book files, "what appeared to be a cockpit canopy in the center which extended toward the back and beneath the object. The 'cockpit' did not protrude from the surface but was clearly visible with the naked eye." There were no propellers or landing gear, but there did seem to be trails of turbulent air behind the trailing points of the object. Speculation was that there were jet engines of some kind located there. The craft moved silently, although Rhodes had said that a jetlike roar was what called his attention to it.

The news stories apparently alerted the military to Rhodes' sighting. Various investigations were launched. On July 14, 1947, Lynn C. Aldrich, a special agent for the Army's counterintelligence corps (CIC), in a memo for the record available in the Project Blue Book files wrote, "On 8 July 1947, this Agent obtained pictures of unidentifiable objects (Exhibits 1 and 2) from the managing editor of the *Arizona Republic* newspaper. The pictures were taken by Mr. William A. Rhodes [of] Phoenix, Arizona, at sunset, on 7 July 1947."

Then, on August 29, according to a *Memorandum for the Office in Charge*, George Fugate, Jr., a special agent of the CIC and stationed at Fourth Air Force Headquarters, interviewed Rhodes in person. Fugate was accompanied by Special Agent Brower of the Phoenix FBI Office. This interview is important because of some of the confusion about location of the negatives and prints of the photographs that would develop later.

During the interview, Rhodes again told the story, suggesting that he thought, at first, it might have been the Navy's "Flying Flapjack" which had been featured on the May 1947 cover of *Mechanix Illustrated*. He rejected the idea because he saw no propellers or landing gear. Research shows that the Navy built a single "Flapjack" and that it never flew outside the Bridgeport, Connecticut, area.

At the end of Fugate's report, he wrote, "Mr. Rhodes stated that he developed the negatives himself. He still had the negative of the first photograph (Exhibit III), but he could not find the negative for the second photograph."

On February 19, 1948, Lewis C. Gust, the chief technical Project Officer, Intelligence Department (though the Project Blue Book files fail to identify the man or his organization beyond that), wrote what might be considered a preliminary report on the analysis of the photographs. "It is concluded that the image is of true photographic nature, and is not due to imperfections in the emulsion, or lack of development in the section in question. The image exhibits a 'tail' indicating the proper type of distortion due to the type of shutter used, the speed of the object, and the fixed speed of the shutter. This trailing-off conforms to the general information given in the report."

On May 11, 1948, Rhodes was again interviewed, but this time by high-ranking people. Lieutenant Colonel James C. Beam, who worked with the head of intelligence at Wright Field, Colonel Howard McCoy, and Alfred C. Loedding, who was an important civilian at AMC, traveled to Phoenix. In their official report of their trip, they wrote, "Although Mr. Rhodes is currently employed as a piano player in a nightclub, his primary interest is in a small but quite complete laboratory behind his home. According to his business card, this laboratory is called 'Panoramic Research Laboratory' and Mr. Rhodes is referred to as the 'Chief of Staff.' Mr. Rhodes appeared to be completely sincere and apparently is quite interested in scientific experiments."

It would become apparent in later documents, reports, and memos that military investigators were concerned with Rhodes billing himself as a scientist or as the chief of staff of his private laboratory. They seemed to think that there was something about the man's character that could be determined from what seems to be little more than a marketing ploy rather than a willful attempt to misrepresent himself.

In later investigations they would detail his background, noting that Phoenix city directories showed that he had worked at Wayne's Midway Inn and later as a musician. They also interviewed neighbors who all said that Rhodes was a quiet, responsible neighbor, who seemed to be somewhat pompous and egotistical in his public demeanor. But the neighbors also noted that they considered him a genius who had built a telescope to study astronomy and a television with little in the way of outside assistance.

During the interview with Beam and Loedding, Rhodes mentioned that he did not believe that what he had seen was windblown debris. This is an obvious reference to Dr. Irving Langmuir's conclusion published in the Project Grudge report, that the object in the photographs could be "merely paper swept up by the winds."

In fact, that same Grudge report noted, "In subsequent correspondence to the reporter of this incident, the observer refers to himself as Chief of Staff of Panoramic Research Laboratory, the letterhead of which lists photography among its specialities. Yet, the negative was carelessly cut and faultily developed. It is covered with streaks and over a period of six months, has faded very noticeably."

Then, in what must have horrified the Air Force investigators, "An OSI agent discovered that a letter by this observer was published by *Amazing Stories* magazine earlier this year. In this letter he stated that he had been interviewed by two Federal agents, had given them pictures of 'flying discs' and that the pictures had not been returned. He requested the advice of the magazine as to how to sue the Government. This individual is aware of the whereabouts of these pictures, but has never requested their return."

It should be noted that nothing in the report was inaccurate. Rhodes had been interviewed by two federal agents, one from the FBI and one, in civilian clothing, from the counterintelligence corps. Documents in the file reveal that the CIC man had asked the FBI agent not to tell Rhodes about his Army connection. In other words, the CIC agent allowed the FBI agent to show credentials and allowed Rhodes to believe that both were FBI.

It should also be noted that Rhodes did surrender the pictures to the FBI and those were given to the Air Force. There is nothing in the file to suggest that Rhodes attempted to recover his pictures prior to the attempts he would make in 1952.

The AMC opinion in the Project Grudge report, which followed Langmuir's statement about the possibility of windblown debris, was, "In view of the apparent character of the witness, the conclusion of Dr. Langmuir [that the photographs be discounted as paper swept up by the wind] seems entirely probably [sic]."

What we know from the case is that Rhodes did bill himself as the chief of staff of Panoramic Research Laboratory. We also know that he had supplied photographs and negatives to the military investigators. Had he not done so, how would they have known that they were badly cut or had faded over a period of months? More importantly, they acknowledge that he had given them photographs and negatives in correspondence available in the Project Blue Book files.

As we review the file, we learn that there was, in fact, correspondence between Rhodes and various governmental and military officials attempting to recover both his photographs and his negatives. Over two years after he took the pictures, Kenneth W. King wrote to another military organization, "Inclosed [sic] are copies of the photographs now in the custody of the Office of the Assistant Chief of Staff, A-2, Intelligence, Hamilton AFB, California, under the subject of 'Investigation of Flying Discs.'" If we had nothing else, this would prove that Rhodes did surrender the pictures. But there is even more interesting documentation.

On June 5, 1952, now nearly five years after the pictures were taken, and before the massive publicity about UFOs was about to burst on the public consciousness, Colonel Arno H. Luehman, Deputy Director of Public Information wrote about "Declassifying Photographs of Unidentified Flying Objects." In the first paragraph of his letter, he wrote, "This office understands that two photographs were taken by Mr. William A. Rhodes of Phoenix, Arizona, and that these photographs were turned over to Fourth Air Force Intelligence in July of 1947. This office has been contacted by Mr. Rhodes who is requesting return of his original negatives."

The letter continued, "The two photographs were copied by the Photographic Records and Services Division of the Air Adjutant

General's Office at this headquarters and are in a confidential file of Unidentified Missiles as A-34921AC and 34921AC."

Now we return to Rhodes and the summer of 1949. In a long *Report of Investigation*, dated August 17, 1949 (over two years after the sighting), and written by Lynn C. Aldrich of DO #17, Kirtland Air Force Base, we are again treated to a background check of Rhodes. More neighbors are interviewed with the same results. Rhodes is a good neighbor who appears to be somewhat high-strung and full of himself. There are personal details about him including his height and weight in the summer of 1947, though I can't understand why these sorts of statistics are gathered in this sort of an investigation. Maybe it was just routine information that the FBI agents supplied as they investigated all cases, even those related to flying saucers.

But the important part of the document comes at the end. Aldrich wrote, ". . . On the morning of August 30, 1947, when Mr. Rhodes called at the Phoenix office [of the FBI] to deliver the negatives, they were accepted only after he was advised that they were being given to Mr. Fugate, a representative of the Army Air Force Intelligence, United States Army, and that there was little, if any, chance of his getting the negatives back. Mr. Rhodes turned them over to this office with the full understanding that they were being given to the Army and that he would not get them back."

So we learn that Rhodes did surrender his negatives just as he had said. We learn that the Army had this correspondence available to them. We learn that he gave the photographs and negatives to the FBI and was told that the Army would eventually be getting them. Yet the AMC Opinion claims that, in 1949, Rhodes had made no requests for the return of his pictures and negatives.

On July 14, 1952, in still another letter, we learn that the pictures and negatives were turned over to Air Force intelligence representatives at Hamilton Field on August 30, 1947. In that document, they are attempting to trace the course of the pictures from Rhodes to the FBI to Army intelligence. What this suggests is that the Air Force wasn't sure of where the pictures and negatives were. They were attempting to shift the blame to others for the apparent loss of those pictures, including Rhodes himself.

That same July 14 document, written by Gilbert R. Levy, noted, "A background investigation was run on Rhodes, by OSI, for the benefit of AMC, which reflected Rhodes had created the name PANORAMIC RESEARCH LABORATORY, to impress people with his importance. He was reported to be a musician by trade, but had no steady job. Neighbors considered him to be an excellent neighbor, who caused no trouble, but judged him to be emotionally high-strung, egotistical, and a genius in fundamentals of radio. He conducts no business through his 'Laboratory,' but reportedly devotes all his time to research."

What all this means is that Rhodes had surrendered his photographs and negatives to the government. And, although there is a suggestion that he knew where they were, that simply isn't borne out in the documents. Even the Air Force officers didn't know where the photographs were. That was why there were letters written from one office to another.

But, more importantly, there has been no real discussion about why the Air Force investigators labeled the case as a probable hoax. The discussion seemed to center around Rhodes' lifestyle. He didn't have a "real" job and had a letterhead that labeled him as the chief of staff of his laboratory. None of that is a good reason for labeling the case a hoax. If that was all their evidence, then it is fairly weak.

There is, however, one page of analysis of the photographs offered by John A. Clinton. There is no clue, in the files, about Clinton. The analysis is not on a letterhead and there is nothing in the signature block to tell us anything about Clinton, his expertise, or why he was consulted about this particular case.

In the undated analysis of the photographs, Clinton wrote,

Preliminary analysis of the negative and prints leads me to doubt the story told by Mr. William A. Rhodes. Judging from the dimensions, the negative was exposed in a simple camera of the box type, which usually has a fixed focus (about ten feet), fixed shutter speed (about 1⅖ of a second) and a simple lens of the Meniscus type. Because of the above-mentioned facts, it is unreasonable to assume that sharp outlines such as appears on the negative, could be secured from an object at 2,000 feet, traveling 400 to 600 mph. Furthermore, according to the story the object (flying craft) was painted gray to blend in with the clouds. But, even if the object would be painted jet black, under the circumstances described, to obtain a contrast such as appears on the negative is also very doubtful. On all the prints, excepting the print marked "exhibit A," judging from the outlines, the object has a rotating motion (revolves around its center) instead of a forward motion, contradicting the version stated by Mr. Rhodes.

And that's all of the negative analysis of the photograph. Clinton, whoever he is, claims the story told by Rhodes to be in conflict with that shown on the photographs. He assumes that the object is rotating, based on something he sees on the prints, but I confess I don't know what it is. Besides, Rhodes talked of the craft circling east of his house, moving north-to-south when he first saw it. This seems to me to be an explanation for the conclusion drawn by Clinton that might suggest the object is rotating.

More important are the suggestions about the limitations of the camera used and the sharpness of the photographs obtained. Of course, if Rhodes, for whatever reason, overestimated the distance and the speed, then those problems might be resolved.

Finally, I confess that I don't understand the emphasis placed on the letter that Rhodes sent to *Amazing Stories*. There was nothing in the letter that was not true. Rhodes must have forgotten that he had been told that he probably wouldn't receive his negatives and photographs back. Still, that is no reason to dismiss the case as a hoax.

By 1952, when Rhodes was trying to get the pictures back, Air Force investigators, including then captain Dewey Fournet suggested in a telephone conversation with then lieutenant Ed Ruppelt, that "there is no information available as to whether or not Rhodes ever sent his negatives to the Air Force or whether he just sent prints. We do have some rather poor-quality prints of the object. As you know, we have concluded that these photos were probably not authentic. It seems as if Mr. Rhodes attempted to get on the 'picture-selling bandwagon' and if he can prove he sent the negatives to ATIC or to the Air Force and they were never returned, it may lead to a touchy situation."

So now, after all this, Rhodes' photographs are going to be rejected because he wanted to sell them. Five years after the fact, without a single clue that such was the case, we are now told to reject the photographs because Rhodes "may" want to sell them. There is no evidence anywhere that Rhodes ever sold the photographs nor is there any information in the Project Blue Book files to confirm he made a dime from the pictures.

There are a couple of additional complications to this case. The first comes from Kenneth Arnold. Because of his first sighting, he was involved in some of the "official" investigations that were undertaken by military officers in the first days of the modern UFO phenomenon. He was heavily involved in the Maury Island case, working with Army Air Forces officers Captain Davidson and Lieutenant Brown.

Arnold wrote, in his book *The Coming of the Saucers*, about one of the meetings that took place in his hotel room during that investigation. At one point Davidson told Arnold they had found out some interesting things. Arnold wrote,

> He motioned me over to my bed, took a piece of paper from his pocket and drew a picture. It was a disk, almost identical to that one peculiar flying saucer that had been worrying me since my original observation—the one that looked different from the rest and that I had never mentioned to anyone.
>
> As he showed me the drawing, he said, "This is a drawing of one of several photographs we consider authentic. We just received it at Hamilton Field."

Hamilton Field? The Project Blue Book file on the Rhodes case is filled with references to Hamilton Field. Fourth Air Force Headquarters was at Hamilton Field, investigators came from Hamilton Field to interview Rhodes, and inquiries about the distribution of his photographs were sent to Hamilton Field. In other words, the intelligence officers at Hamilton Field are clearly established as having access to the Rhodes photographs and so it is not only possible, but probable, that

Davidson would have drawn for Arnold the craft that Rhodes photographed over Phoenix.

Arnold, in his account, continued, "I turned to Lieutenant Brown for verification. He nodded his head and stated, 'That's right. It came from Phoenix, Arizona, the other day. We have prints of it at Hamilton Field but the original negatives were flown to Washington, D.C.' "

The only problem with Arnold's description of the scene is that it is, quite frankly, hearsay. The two officers were killed not long after in an aircraft accident. They are not able to corroborate the Arnold story.

And, if we're going to be objective, it has to be pointed out that Arnold's book was published in 1952. The Rhodes photographs had been published within hours of the event. There is the possibility that Arnold heard about the photographs through another source or that Ray Palmer, Arnold's publisher, "massaged" the story to make it more exciting.

There is some reason to suspect Palmer. In a story published in the Arizona Republic on November 18, 1958, Don Dedera reported that a recent issue of Ray Palmer's magazine, Flying Saucers, had published most of the front page of the Arizona newspaper about the Rhodes sighting and photographs. Palmer's caption under the pictures said,

A portion of the front page of the Arizona Republic for July 9, 1947, showing two views of a flying saucer photographed by William A. Rhodes . . . Phoenix, Arizona.

All copies of this paper were seized by the Army, in a house-to-house canvass, and all plates of the newspaper, plus the photo negatives and prints.

The only known copy of the paper, plus duplicate negatives, prints from the original negatives, and statements of witnesses outside secret Army files at the time were secured by Flying Saucers editor prior to the arrival of the army on the scene.

Of course, this tale is ridiculous. Copies of the newspaper are easily available to anyone who wants to research the records at the Phoenix Library. While it is certainly true that the military officers and government officials were interested in the Rhodes photographs, as evidenced by the number of interviews they conducted, there is no evidence that anyone confiscated anything at any time.

That is not to mention the logistical impossibility of confiscating every single copy of the newspaper, especially after it has been distributed. No, Palmer was inventing that tale for the excitement it would generate.

But that doesn't mean that those events described by Arnold didn't take place. The meeting probably transpired as Arnold described it, but, to be objective, we must be aware of the other possibilities. We must not reject them, but we should not give them more importance than they deserve.

There is one disturbing thing about the case that is not evident in the Blue Book file. In the mid-1960s, Dr. James E. McDonald corresponded with Rhodes about his case. McDonald wrote to Richard Hall, of NICAP (and later of the Fund for UFO Research), on February 18, 1967,

I did a lot of checking on Rhodes' degrees, because there seemed something odd about an honorary Ph.D. based on the kind of work I could imagine him doing. Columbia said no record of any such degree. Geo. Washington said no record of a B.A. ever given to Rhodes in the period I specified. So I made a trip up there in December and spent an hour or so with him. Devoted most of my querying to the matter of the degree and his associations with inventory [sic], Lee DeForrest. . . . [Rhodes] showed me a photo-miniature in plastic of the alleged Columbia degree, and he said he had the original somewhere in his files but did not show it to me. . . . As I kept going over the thing he finally volunteered the remark that he, himself, had checked with Columbia about a year after DeForrest presented him with the certificate, found no record of it, confronted DeForrest with the information, and was nonplussed by D F putting his arm over his shoulder and saying something to the effect that, "Well, my boy, that's the way those things happen sometimes," and saying no more about it. . . . But the fact that he lists himself in the Phoenix phonebook as Dr.

Wm. Rhodes in the face of that history constitutes [sic] a cloud that would be impossible to overlook. *Everything* else checks out solidly in his story.

There isn't much else to be said about the case. The Air Force eventually removed the possible from in front of hoax and listed it as "Other (Hoax)." They had no other explanation for it and too often, when they could find no plausible explanation, especially in cases of physical evidence such as this, they labeled it as a hoax. As we've seen, there simply is no justification for the label.

It does supply some insights into the workings of the official projects. And it does show that they were very interested in learning the truth but that as time passed, they convinced themselves that the case was a hoax. Rhodes just fit no easy profiles so it was easy to label him an eccentric and his case as a hoax.

But the real fact remains that no one ever showed that Rhodes' tale of seeing the craft was not as he described it. Analysis of the photographs left a great deal to be desired but there was nothing in the photos that suggested hoax.

While such a case does not prove that UFOs are extraterrestrial in nature, it does provide some of the physical evidence demanded by the skeptical community. As I have said, we have photographs that have not been explained. That, in and of itself, is the important fact here.

JANUARY 7, 1948:

THE CASE OF THOMAS MANTELL

Captain Thomas Mantell, of the Kentucky National Guard, has the distinction of being the first man killed during an attempted intercept of a flying saucer. Controversy arose when Air Force explanations failed to explain anything and when they began to contradict one another. The Air Force wanted an explanation for the sighting and, by examining the case, we can see that they didn't care if they were right about their conclusion or not. In the end, the driving factor was being able to slap a label on the case and close the file.

It was just after one o'clock in the afternoon (1:20 P.M.) that the tower crew at Godman Army Air Field at Fort Knox, Kentucky, spotted a bright, disc-shaped object which they failed to easily identify. Others have suggested that the Kentucky Highway Patrol first saw the object and alerted the men in the tower. That doesn't really matter today. What is important is that object was brought to the attention of the base operations officer, the intelligence officer, and finally, the base commander, Colonel Guy F. Hix. None of them were able to identify it.

For about an hour and twenty-five minutes, dozens of people, including Colonel Hix, watched as the UFO seemed to hang motionless in the southwestern sky. In the towns of southern Kentucky, people watched the UFO, some claiming it drifted silently and slowly to the south. Others thought that it hovered for a few minutes and then resumed its slow flight. The witnesses were clearly describing something that was moving very slowly.

At 2:45 P.M., the situation suddenly changed. A flight of F-51 Mustang fighters (it should be noted here that the designation of the Mustang had recently been changed from a P for pursuit, to an F for fighter) flew over Godman Army Air Field. With the UFO still visible, the flight leader, Captain Thomas Mantell, was asked if he would investigate. Mantell replied that he was merely ferrying the aircraft but that he would attempt to intercept. He began a spiraling, climbing turn to 220 degrees and 15,000 feet.

As he reached 15,000 feet, Mantell radioed the tower. Records of that transmission are in dispute. Mantell did say that the object was "above me and appears to be moving about half my speed." Later he would report that it was "metallic and it is tremendous in size." With the UFO still above him, he reported he would continue to climb.

At 22,000 feet, the two wingmen who had stayed with him, Lieutenants A. W. Clements and B. A. Hammond turned back. The oxygen equipment of one of the fighters had failed and military regulations required that oxygen be used above 14,000 feet. Hammond radioed that they were abandoning the intercept, but Mantell, who had no oxygen equipment on his aircraft, continued to climb. He did not acknowledge the message from Hammond.

For thirty minutes, as the flight chased the huge object, each of the wingmen broke off the intercept. Now, at 3:10 P.M., Mantell was the only pilot left chasing the object and he was alone at 23,000 feet. He was still climbing toward the UFO but made no more radio calls to either his wingmen or the control tower at Godman. By 3:15 everyone had lost both radio and visual contact with him.

Fearing the worst, a search was launched and just after 5:00 P.M., on a farm near Franklin, Kentucky, the remains of Mantell's F-51 were found scattered over about a half a mile. Mantell's body was inside the broken cockpit. His watch had stopped at 3:18 P.M. From the evidence it seems that Mantell was killed in the crash of his aircraft.

An investigation was begun immediately. It was a two-pronged attack. One was to determine what happened to Mantell and why he
had crashed. The second was to identify the object, or objects, that he
had chased.

According to the *Army Air Forces Report of Major Accident*, aircraft
number 44–65869, which was built on December 15, 1944, crashed
3.5 miles from Franklin, Kentucky. The narrative section contains a
description of the accident. It stated,

On 7 January 1948 at approximately 1450–1455, Captain Mantell
was leading a flight of four (4) P-51 aircraft on a flight from Marietta Air Base, Marietta, Georgia, to Standiford Field at Louisville,
Kentucky. Nearing Godman Field, Kentucky, the flight was contacted by Godman Field Control Tower and requested to identify
an object in the sky if the mission would permit. Captain Mantell
replied that his mission was ferrying aircraft and that he would
attempt to identify the object in the sky. Captain Mantell began
a maximum climb in left spirals until about 14,000 feet and from
there a straight climb at maximum, on a compass heading of approximately 220 degrees. No conversation between Captain
Mantell and any member of his flight revealed a clue as to his
intentions. One pilot left the flight as the climb began, the remaining two discontinued the climb at approximately 22,000 feet.
When last observed by the wing man, Lieutenant Clements, Captain Mantell was in a maximum climb at 22,500 feet, the aircraft
in perfect control. Captain Mantell was heard to say in ship-to-
ship conversation that he would go to 25,000 feet for about ten
minutes and then come down. Transmission was garbled and attempts to contact Captain Mantell by his flight were unanswered.
Lieutenant Clements was the only pilot equipped with an oxygen
mask. This flight had been planned and scheduled as a ferry and
navigational trip at low level.

It continued, "Consensus is that Captain Mantell lost consciousness
at approximately 25,000 feet, the P-51 being trimmed for a maximum
climb continued to climb, gradually levelling out as increasing altitude

caused decrease in power. The aircraft began to fly in reasonably level attitude at about 30,000 feet. It then began a gradual turn to the left because of torque, slowly increasing degree of bank as the nose depressed, finally began a spiraling dive which resulted in excessive speeds causing gradual disintegration of aircraft which probably began between 10,000 and 20,000 feet."

The report pointed out, "Since canopy lock was in place after the crash, bright enough to be seen in the daylight, it would have blended easily into the surrounding sky. If there was even the lightest of haze, Venus probably wouldn't have been visible to those on the ground." Or, in other words, Venus was not an acceptable explanation, and the cause of the sighting would have to be found elsewhere.

Later, official investigations suggested a huge balloon, or two balloons, and finally two balloons and Venus had caused the sighting. The investigating officers believed that someone in the tower sighted Venus, lost sight of it, but then as they searched the sky for the unknown object, spotted one of the two balloons. They suggested that Mantell had chased a weather balloon.

There were those inside the military who weren't happy with that answer. They spent a great deal of time on the Mantell case, probably because of the sensational aspects of it. Here was a World War II ace killed while chasing a flying saucer. There was a closed-casket funeral and a secret investigation. It certainly had all the elements of a great mystery, a great story and a grand conspiracy.

At one point Air Force investigators settled on Venus as the final answer. In the official files, one of the reports goes into depth about Venus. "[U]nder exceptionally good atmospheric conditions and the eye shielded from the direct rays of the sun, Venus might be seen as an exceeding tiny bright point of light. It can be shown that it was definitely brighter than the surrounding sky, for on the date in question, Venus has a semidiameter of six seconds of arc. . . . While it is thus physically possible to see Venus at such times, usually its pinpoint character and large expanse of sky makes its casual detection very unlikely." They were, in effect, saying that Venus was visible but they didn't think it was the answer.

The Air Force investigator was not finished with the Venus

double-talk, however. He wrote, "The chances, of course, of looking at just the right spot are very few. Once done, however, it is usually fairly easy to relocate the object and call the attention of others to it. However, atmospheric conditions must be exceptionally good."

What all this does, is suggest that after saying the object might have been Venus was that it couldn't have been Venus. Although Venus was in the right spot at the right time, it probably does not account for the object seen by those in the tower.

Venus was no longer the preferred answer. The official report said, "It had been unofficially reported that the object was a Navy cosmic-ray balloon. If this can be established, it is to be the preferred explanation."

But this report was anything but consistent. Having said that it was Venus, that it wasn't Venus, and that it was a balloon, the investigator now explained why it wasn't a balloon. "If one accepts the assumption that reports from various locations in the state refer to the same object, any such device must have been a good many miles up . . . 25 to 50 . . . in order to have been seen clearly, almost simultaneously, from places 175 miles apart."

Now, having run through all sorts of explanations, the investigator wrote, "It is entirely possible, of course, that the first sightings were of some sort of balloon or aircraft and that when the reports came to Godman Field, a careful scrutiny of the sky revealed Venus, and it could be that Lieutenant [sic] Mantell did actually give chase to Venus."

Having gone through all that, the investigator now explained why he believed that Mantell had chased Venus. It did not appear to move away from him. Of course, if the object was, in fact, an extraterrestrial spacecraft, it might be that it was maneuvering to avoid the close approach of Mantell's fighter. That idea didn't seem to cross the mind of the Air Force investigator, and that says something about the mind-set of the military as they were writing their reports.

The final conclusions of the report are a masterpiece of double-talk. Now the investigator wrote, again, that it was Venus, but for that explanation to work properly, he needed a balloon and one other object as well. Given these three items, though there is no evidence that all three existed, he believed he could explain the case. He wrote,

"Such a hypothesis [that is, Mantell chasing Venus] does still necessitate the inclusion of at least two other objects."

All of this suggests something about the investigations as they were being carried out in that era. It was a search for labels, but not necessarily a search for solutions. They were willing to accept nearly anything as an answer as long as they could remove a mysterious case from the files. And Mantell's case—because of the sensational aspects, as well as the public interest—was certainly one of those to be solved at all costs.

By late 1948, the Air Force became disgusted with the idea of UFOs. In the reports Air Force officers created, they explained as many of the cases as they could and suggested the remainder could be explained if there was sufficient information. They found nothing to suggest that UFOs were real. The problem, if ignored, would go away.

In 1952, a major magazine wanted to print an article about how spectacular UFO sightings had been explained through proper research and investigation. Because the spin of the article was that flying saucers did not exist, the Pentagon cooperated with the writer and the magazine. High-ranking Air Force officers assured the magazine editors that Mantell had chased Venus. In a move that was sure to anger the reporter and the magazine editor, the week after the magazine was published, the Air Force released a new answer. Mantell had chased a balloon.

In the early 1950s, the UFO project was reorganized, and cases that had been "solved" were again examined. Ed Ruppelt, seeing that the Mantell case was one of the thickest, asked for a microfilm copy of it. Unfortunately, something had been spilled on part of it, so that it was difficult, if not impossible, to read.

Ruppelt had one advantage that those who had made the original investigations didn't. He knew of the Navy's high-altitude research using huge balloons that were called "Skyhooks." He tried to find records that would prove that Skyhook was responsible, but could find nothing that would put one of the balloons over Godman Field at the right time. Because he had no conclusive evidence, he left the case listed as a "probable balloon."

Ruppelt did try to find the evidence. He gathered wind charts that showed if a balloon had been released from Clinton Air Force Base, Ohio, on January 7, 1948, it might have been in the right position to cause the sighting over Godman Army Air Field on that date. But Ruppelt could not confirm it.

In 1956, Ruppelt published a book about his experiences as the chief of Project Blue Book. Because he was seen as an insider, when he drew conclusions, they carried some weight. When he said that he could find no records that proved a Skyhook balloon, or that any other balloon was responsible, people listened.

Later, the controversy continued to rage. Dr. J. Allen Hynek, who was the scientific consultant for Project Blue Book, said that he didn't believe that Mantell was chasing Venus. He did say, however, "It is possible that Venus was also a cause to this sighting, and was observed by some of the witnesses on the ground. However, the prime culprit is believed to have been the Skyhook balloon released by the Navy. Captain Mantell was attempting to close in one this balloon which was still more than 40,000 feet above him."

When the Air Force ended the barrage of answers, the civilian UFO community was only too ready to pick up. Many of those writing about the Mantell case have suggested that the object was first spotted on radar. There are no accounts of radar sightings in the official records. Ruppelt makes no mention of it. In fact, the earliest reference to radar that I can find is in a book published in 1956. After that book appeared, others have picked up the idea that radar confirmed the UFO.

Others have claimed that Mantell was a World War II ace. Military records show that Mantell was a transport pilot during the war and therefore couldn't have shot down the five enemy aircraft necessary to become an ace. This doesn't mean that Mantell wasn't a good pilot or that he was a careless pilot. It merely proves that he wasn't a fighter pilot and didn't shoot down enemy planes.

In fact, he seemed to have been a very brave man. According to a letter sent to me by Mantell's sister, Bettye Mantell Risley, "Tommy was awarded the Distinguished Flying Cross for his calm and courageous action on D-Day [that is, the Normandy Invasion on June 6, 1944]. On that day he was ferrying a glider plane to a designated point behind German lines. His instructions were to cut the glider loose and return to base if attacked. Tommy was attacked but proceeded to [his] destination where men in the glider would be with others for mutual safety. He was then able to get his badly damaged plane back to his base in England."

Others have created rumors apparently to make the story more exciting. There are claims that Mantell's last words, suppressed by the Air Force, were about seeing men inside the craft. Others have claimed that Mantell's body was never found. Others have said that Mantell's F-51 had been disintegrated by a ray from the object. None of these claims are supported by fact or documentation or even witness testimony.

So what did happen to Mantell? Can we, after fifty years, make any determination about the case? I think the answer is yes, and now that we have access to all the information, we can supply the answer to the mystery.

In a statement given on January 15, 1948, Technical Sergeant Quinton Blackwell provided clues about the Mantell mystery. Mantell and his plane did attempt to find the object, and "at about 1445 or 1450 National Guard 869 [Mantell's plane number] notified Godman Tower he was [at] approximately 15,000 feet."

Mantell is then quoted as saying, "I have an object in sight above and ahead of me and it appears to be moving at about half my speed or approximately 180 miles an hour." That, of course, is Mantell's estimate and should not be considered a hard fact.

He was asked for a description, and again, according to Blackwell's statement, said, "It appears to be a metallic object or possibly a reflection of the sun from a metallic object, and it is of tremendous size."

The last communication from Mantell came at about 1515 or 1520, that is, about a quarter after three in the afternoon. He told the men in the tower, "[The object] is directly ahead of me and slightly above, and is now moving at about my speed or better. I am trying to close for a better look."

Other statements of the witnesses, taken at the time of the event or shortly after it, provided additional clues. One of the witnesses said of the object, "It was huge, fluid. It had a metallic sheen and looked like an upside-down ice cream cone."

There are also a number of drawings in the official file. These were made by the men who were in the tower during the incident. The drawings look like an upside-down ice cream cone. Or, to put a different face on it, they look like a Skyhook balloon seen from a long ways away.

The solution to this case would have come much sooner had the Air Force not been interested in disproving UFOs but interested in finding answers. Clearly Venus has nothing to do with this sighting. The fact that it was in the sky near the right location at the time is irrelevant and has confused people for much too long. Venus, as a culprit, has been eliminated from the case.

Second, there is no need to create a number of balloons or other unidentified and unreported aircraft in the area to find a solution. All the talk of another balloon or object is also irrelevant.

Given the descriptions provided, the fact that Skyhook balloons were being launched, and given the size and shape of those balloons, it seems reasonable to believe that Mantell chased a Skyhook. Neither he, nor anyone else at Godman Army Air Field, would have been familiar with the Skyhooks. They were classified in 1948. They certainly would have been huge, fluid, and would have looked metallic because they were made of polyethylene.

When the file is carefully studied, when the descriptions are considered, and when the nonsense is removed from the case, there is but a single conclusion. This was a Skyhook balloon.

By studying this case, we do see the mind-set of the military officials. Because of that mind-set, they did more damage to their investigations than they did to anything else. Had they been honest and candid as they began their search they would have been believed. Clearly, in 1948, without the knowledge of the existence of the Skyhook project, they should have declared the case to be unidentified.

But rather than that, they kept manipulating the data to provide multiple answers to the case. Even if the evidence didn't fit the facts as they knew them, they chopped and cut until they did fit, and by doing that, created an air of suspicion about their investigation.

The Mantell case is a tragic accident. Mantell tried to fly higher than his aircraft was equipped to fly. Lack of oxygen at high altitudes is a very real problem. It affects judgment and it can kill. Air Force pilots are routinely exposed to the altitude chamber in which they learn the effects of oxygen deprivation. Even the simple task of separating playing cards into black and red becomes impossible. Judgment is clearly impaired and irrational decisions are made.

Mantell was killed in an aircraft accident. He was chasing a Skyhook balloon. This case should now be eliminated from the UFO case files.

JULY 24, 1948:

THE CHILES AND WHITTED CASE

In the Project Blue Book files are some cases that are extremely puzzling. If we look only at the master index for every case in the files, we see lots of explanations that, on the surface, seem plausible. Only after studying the reports do we see that the explanation often explains nothing but does fill one square. Such is the report made by Eastern Airlines pilots Clarence S. Chiles and John B. Whitted.

According to the files, Chiles and Whitted were flying a DC-3 at about 5,000 feet, on a bright, cloudless, and star-filled night. Twenty miles southwest of Montgomery, Alabama, they spotted, slightly above them and to the right, what they thought was a jet aircraft of some type. Within seconds it was close enough that they could see a torpedo-shaped object that had a double row of square windows.

Chiles called the attention of his copilot to the object, saying, "Look, here comes a new Army jet job." The object approached in a slight dive, deflected a little to the left and passed the plane on the right, almost level to the flight path. After passing, it pulled up sharply and disappeared into a cloud.

Questioned within hours of the event by investigators, both men said that they believed the object was about a hundred feet long. Whitted said, "The fuselage appeared to be about three times the circumference of a B-29 fuselage. The windows were very large and seemed square. They were white with light which seemed to be caused by some type of combustion. I estimate we watched the object for at least five seconds and not more than ten seconds. We heard no noise nor did we feel any turbulence from the object. It seemed to be at about 5,500 feet."

Chiles, in a statement dated August 3, 1948, wrote, "It was clear there were no wings present, that it was powered by some jet or other type of power shooting flame from the rear some fifty feet . . . Underneath the ship there was a blue glow of light."

Apparently all the passengers were asleep with the exception of Clarence L. McKelvie. Chiles wrote, "After talking to the only passenger awake at the time, he saw only the trail of fire as it passed and pulled into the clouds."

Within hours of the sighting, Chiles and Whitted were on radio station WCON in Atlanta, Georgia. They were also interviewed by William Key, a newspaper reporter. At some point during the interviews, someone suggested they had been startled by a meteor, but both men rejected the idea. They had seen many meteors during their night flights and were aware of what they looked like and how they performed.

There are some other points to be made. In a newspaper article written by Albert Riley, he quotes the pilots as saying, "Its prop-wash or jet-wash rocked our DC-3."

In another article that is part of the Blue Book files, Chiles is again quoted as having said there was a prop wash. "[B]oth reported they could feel the UFO's backwash rock their DC-3."

This was, of course, one of the first cases that Project Sign could review. The study had been in existence for only about seven months, but it was on the scene of the report quickly. A review of the files, shows that they did search for an answer and went to extraordinary lengths to find evidence. They gathered information from every airline which could possibly have had aircraft in a position to see the object. They also queried all branches of the military, searching for any other pilots who might have glimpsed the object but who had failed to report it.

What they found in the search was that other pilots had "strange" encounters that night. About fifteen minutes before Chiles and Whitted had their sighting, there was another report from the Blackstone, Virginia, area. According to the Blue Book files, "Object number 2 was observed by Feldary, Mansfield and Kingsley at 0230 hours 24 July 1948, while airborne, between Blackstone, Virginia, and Greensboro, North Carolina. This sighting is considered separately [from the Chiles-Whitted sighting] since the descriptions of speed as 'meteoric' or 'terrific,' the manner of travel described as an arc or horizontal, and the fact that it 'faded like a meteor' seem to indicate that the object seen was not the one observed in Incident 1 [that is, the Chiles-Whitted report]."

Other sightings in the Chiles-Whitted folder are from events that took place two nights later. They are included because the descriptions of the objects seem to match some of those made by Chiles and Whitted. Again, those sightings seem to be of a meteor.

The search for additional information turned up a report from Robins Air Force Base, Georgia. Walter Massey, a twenty-three-year-old ground maintenance crewman, said that he saw an cigar-shaped object fly over. Massey was interviewed on August 10, 1948, by Lieutenant Colonel Cropper, the Acting District Commander, Sixth District Office of Special Investigations (that is, AFOSI).

He learned that Massey was "standing fire guard on a C-47 [the military version of a DC-3], directly across from Operations, and I had to take down the take-off time which was between 0140 and 0150." Because of that, we have a good idea of the exact time of his sighting.

He told Cropper, "It was coming out of the north. I was facing the north and actually didn't see it until it was overhead, but it came out of the north and was in my view for about twenty seconds. The last I saw of it the object was taking a southwest course."

He continued, saying, "The first thing I saw was a stream of fire and I was undecided as to what it could be, but as it got overhead, it was a fairly clear outline and appeared to be a cylindrical-shaped object with a long stream of fire coming out of the tail end. I am sure it would not be a jet since I have observed P-84s in flight at night on two occasions."

Massey thought the object was about 3,000 feet high, but said that at night he couldn't be sure. He also said that he thought, at first, it was a "shooting star or meteor, but a shooting star falls perpendicular. This object was on a straight and level plane."

Of course, we know that meteors can seem to fly at all sorts of angles, and given the location of the observer and the meteor, it can seem that the flight is, more or less, straight and level. Massey was asked how the object differed from a meteor and pointed out that what he saw was long and cylindrical in shape. In other words, he was describing an object that trailed a glow.

Interestingly, Cropper asked, "Did it give you the impression that there were windows or holes and did the decks appear to be divided into sections?"

Massey answered, "I am not sure. It would be hard to tell if there were windows and a divided deck could not be recognized from the ground."

That was a good answer on Massey's part. Clearly he wasn't taking his cues from Cropper who then asked, "Did you read the newspaper account of the two civilian pilots who saw this strange object about the same time, and did the paper's description seem to refer to the object you saw?"

Massey responded, "I read the write-up about the rate of speed. I don't see how they could tell if it had square windows or round windows but the description seemed to fit my impression."

When asked specific questions about the object, Massey said, "It looked like it was about the size of a B-29. . . . It was too large for a jet. It seemed to be a dark color and constructed of an unknown metallic type."

Under the questioning about seeing anything like this at any other time, Massey said, "During the Battle of the Bulge, a sergeant and myself were on guard duty and saw something that resembled this object in question. We later found that we had witnessed the launching of a German V-2 rocket. It carried a stream of fire that more or less resembled this object. This object looked like rocket propulsion rather than jet propulsion, but the speed and size was much greater."

Because of the similarities in the description of the craft, the locations, and the timing, Air Force investigators linked the two cases. They wondered, rightly, if the various witnesses could have seen the same object. They also wondered why it had taken the craft an hour to fly the 200 miles between the two locations. If it was moving at the 700 miles an hour estimated by Chiles, then it should have gotten to the Montgomery area faster than it did.

J. Allen Hynek was asked for his assessment of the case. He could find no "astronomical explanation" if the case was accepted at face value. In other words, Hynek was saying that if the testimony of Chiles and Whitted was accurate, then it couldn't be explained. He also wrote, "[The] sheer improbability of the facts as stated . . . makes it necessary to see whether any other explanation, even though far-fetched, can be considered." He was saying that there could be no flying saucers and we should therefore accept any other answer no matter how ridiculous it might seem because it was preferable to a flying saucer.

Let's fall back, for a moment, to the timing of the event. This was July 1948. It was about the time that those at Project Sign who believed that flying saucers represented extraterrestrial visitation had put together their estimate of the situation. General Vandenberg rejected it and almost everyone who had been involved was replaced at Project Sign.

What this does is provide us with a couple of conclusions for this case. First, Captain Robert R. Sneider, one of those who lost his job in the great Sign cleaning, wrote on November 12, 1948, "A preponderance of evidence is available to establish that in almost all cases an unidentified object was seen within stated times and dates over an extended area, pursuing a general southerly course. Descriptions as to size, shape, color and movements are fairly consistent."

Sneider also wrote, "The flying anomaly observed, remains unidentified as to origin, construction and power source."

But eventually there was another solution offered. Hynek, in his attempts to explain the case, suggested that Massey might have been mistaken. Maybe he saw the object at the same time as Chiles and

Whitted. If that was the case, then, according to Hynek, "the object must have been an extraordinary meteor." The glowing ion trail might have produced the "subjective impression of a ship with lighted windows." Hynek thought that psychological research would be needed to answer the question of whether such an impression would result from the stimuli of a bright meteor seen close.

Philip J. Klass—who believes that all flying-saucer reports can be explained in the mundane—in *UFOs Explained* wrote about a series of sightings that took place on March 3, 1968, over parts of Tennessee, Indiana, and Ohio. In Tennessee, three people, including the mayor of a large city, were talking when one of them saw something in the distance and pointed it out to the others. As the object approached, they saw an orange-colored flame firing from the rear. All thought the object was a fat cigar, "the size of one of our largest airplane fuselages. . . ."

The woman sent a letter to the Air Force in which she described square-shaped windows that appeared to be brightly lighted. And she thought the fuselage had been constructed of flat metal riveted together. She provided a drawing for the Air Force investigators.

At about the same time, a group of six near Shoals, Indiana, saw a huge, cigar-shaped craft with a flaming tail and many brightly lighted windows flash overhead. The people thought the object was at treetop level. One of those who reported the sighting to the Air Force even suggested that it wasn't a meteor because "meteors don't have windows and don't turn corners."

There were other sightings in Ohio on that same night at about that same time. A schoolteacher with four academic degrees including a Ph.D. was out walking her dog when she saw three objects fly overhead. These craft looked like inverted saucers and she thought they were about 1,500 feet above the ground.

But hers wasn't the only sighting in Ohio. An industrial executive who lived in Dayton was returning from Cincinnati when he saw three bright objects in what he thought of as a triangular formation. As they flew, they seemed to make a "distinct curve" in their flight path. Because of their speed, and a lack of noise, the executive believed that the three objects were under intelligent control.

If we assume that the observers in Tennessee and Indiana saw the same objects that were sighted in Ohio, and we check the time carefully, we learn that the reentry of a Soviet booster of the *Zond IV* occurred about the same time. Is it possible that the *Zond IV* is responsible for the series of sightings, including those of a cigar-shaped craft that is quite similar to that reported by Chiles and Whitted almost twenty years earlier?

There is a problem with that assumption, however. The witnesses in Tennessee and Indiana saw a single object. Their descriptions do mirror those of Chiles and Whitted. But the witnesses in Ohio saw *three* objects. If we separate the sightings, then we have two events, not a single case. And, if there are two events, then the *Zond IV* reentry is inadequate to explain everything. In fact, the witnesses in Tennessee and Indiana might have seen exactly what they reported, and if that is the case, then a link to explaining Chiles and Whitted as a natural phenomenon is broken. There is no reason to assume that Chiles and Whitted saw a meteor, nor is there sufficient reason to believe that the witnesses in Tennessee and Indiana saw *Zond IV*.

The connection was the similarity of the drawings made by Chiles and Whitted and one of the observers in Tennessee. If she saw *Zond IV*, then that would be suggestive of a psychological aberration that would induce the hallucination of windows on bright streaks of light. But once again, we have the same problem that Hynek had two decades before. There is no solid scientific evidence to support the conclusion.

During the interviews with newspaper reporters, Chiles and Whitted supposedly said that they had felt turbulence that they believed was the result of the passage of the object. If true, that single fact would rule out a meteor as the culprit.

A search of the Blue Book files reveals that Chiles said in a statement he signed on August 3, 1948, "There was no prop wash or rough air felt as it passed."

In a statement taken by military officers in the days that followed the sighting, Whitted said, "We heard no noise nor did we feel any turbulence from the object."

It would seem, then, that neither man reported any turbulence or disturbance of the air as the object passed them. The quotes from the newspapers would, therefore, be in error.

On July 13, 1961, Dr. Donald H. Menzel, wrote to Major William T. Coleman at the Pentagon, discussing UFO sightings and a book that Menzel was writing. Menzel noted, "One further question that we have. Our study of the famous Chiles case indicates that the UFO was merely a meteor. Apparently this was a considered solution in the early days. We wonder why it was abandoned."

Of course, he is referring to Hynek's suggestion that had not gained much support at Sign in 1948. By way of contrast to Menzel's argument for the meteor theory is Dr. James McDonald's counterargument which was based on his review of the newspaper files and his own, personal interviews with Chiles and Whitted. McDonald wrote, "Both pilots reiterated to me, quite recently, that each saw square ports or windows along the side of the fuselage-shaped object from the rear of which a cherry-red wake emerged, extending back 50–100 feet aft of the object. To term this a 'meteor' is not even *qualitatively* reasonable. One can reject testimony; but reason forbids calling the object a meteor."

And, we can take this one step further. As mentioned, it is well known that meteors can appear to fly parallel to the ground. They can fall straight. They come in a variety of colors that can fool people. But they never trail upward. Remember, Chiles, in his statement, explained that they lost sight of the object as it "pulled up sharply" and disappeared into a cloud. That description alone should be sufficient to eliminate a meteor from consideration for the explanation.

So we're back to where we started. Two airline pilots see something flash through the sky at them. Both talk of a double row of square windows, a cigar shape, and a red flame from the rear. A passenger on the plane sees a streak of light, but no details.

An hour earlier a man at Robins Air Force Base sees a cigar-shaped craft flash overhead. He sees no windows, but his position on the ground, and his viewing angle of the craft, might have precluded those details. His general description matches those given by the pilots. If the cases are linked, then the meteor answer is lost.

If the cases are separated, then it might be conceivable that Chiles and Whitted saw a meteor. But there seems to be no indication that someone confronted with a bright light that streaks past them would "manufacture" a double row of windows and a cigar shape. No one has conducted the experimentation to learn if this is something the mind does when confronted with the sudden appearance of a "streak of light."

And, an examination of the case file reveals no persuasive evidence to suggest that a meteor is, in fact, responsible for the sighting. If, as Sneider, one of the Air Force investigators on the case suggested, we take the sighting at face value, then contrary to the Air Force opinion, there is no solution for the sighting. It should have stayed as "unknown" or "unidentified."

In this case we see clear-cut evidence that the Air Force was interested in solving cases regardless of the circumstances. Hynek said that if you reject the evidence and consider even the most far-fetched explanations, then this could be a meteor. But that idea is predicated on the assumption that there were no flying saucers and therefore anything seen must be explainable as a common object.

If we do not separate the cases, and we accept Massey's timing of his sighting, then the meteor explanation fails completely. And, we must remember that Massey was standing fire guard for an aircraft that took off shortly after the sighting. In other words, there was a written record to corroborate his timing of the event. We are therefore left with two sightings of a single object that has no solid explanation.

We come back to the original point. There is no solution for this case. That does not mean that Chiles and Whitted saw a craft built on another planet. Witness testimony, by itself, is never going to be sufficient to prove that theory. However, given their description of the object, their credibility, and that both men had been pilots during the Second World War, and had hundred if not thousands of flying hours, it is reasonable to believe they reported accurately what they saw. Those are the facts. Everything else is speculation.

AUGUST 19, 1952:

THE BEST HOAX
IN UFO HISTORY?

Captain Edward Ruppelt wrote in his book *The Report on Unidentified Flying Objects* about his UFO investigations into this case for the Air Force, "We wrote off the incident as a hoax. The best hoax in UFO history."

It all started about 9:30 P.M. on August 19, 1952. Scoutmaster D. S. "Sonny" Desvergers of West Palm Beach, Florida, was taking three Boy Scouts home after the regular meeting. They were traveling south, on Military Trail, when, according to Desvergers, he "caught a flash of light out of the corner of my eye. I looked around and saw a series of fuzzy lights like the cabin windows of an airliner."

He stopped the car momentarily, but started on again and then thought about it. If it was an airliner that was crashing, or in some other kind of trouble, he wanted to help. He turned around and headed back. He stopped at the side of the road and told the boys to wait about ten minutes. If he wasn't back by the time a radio program ended, he wanted them to go for help.

Desvergers believed the lights were about two miles into the palmettos off to the side of the road. He kept his path straight by reference to the stars and was shining his light across the ground, searching for an easy path through the thicket. He glanced at his watch, found that he had been walking for only four minutes, and then noticed an open area in front of him.

He stopped, thinking he might have reached a lake or a marsh, but realized that it was just a clearing. Later, he told Air Force investigators, "I carefully stepped forward with the light pointing toward the ground. I had a second two-cell flashlight in my back pocket."

As he entered the clearing, he noticed a peculiar odor. He also had the feeling that someone or something was watching him. And, he began to feel heat, as if he were approaching a hot oven or fireplace. He glanced up but could no longer see the stars. The sky above him was black. Something was hovering just overhead, blocking a portion of the sky.

Now, according to the statement he provided to Air Force officers, "I stood frozen in my tracks. I wanted to throw something or hit it with my machete."

At that point, he had not told the investigators that he was looking up at some kind of object, only that a portion of the sky had been blocked. He finally described it for them, saying, "The bottom of the object was dull black with no seams, joints, or rivet lines. It had dirty streaks running straight across as if oil or dust had blown back. I tried to run but froze, I was so scared. The object was six inches to eight inches above the pine trees."

Still feeling the heat, Desvergers backed out from under the edge of the ship which he could see silhouetted against the black night sky. He said that the ship was "round, with a dome-shape top and with holes and fins running around the edge. The bottom edge seemed to glow with a spot of phosphorescent glow. . . ."

Desvergers heard a metal-against-metal noise that reminded him of a hatch opening. He told the Air Force investigators that he said a million prayers and kept emphasizing how scared he was by the craft and his feelings of being watched by something. He finally saw "a red flare which appeared slowly to move toward me. It came out of the side, I couldn't yell I was so scared."

As the red glow came toward him, Desvergers put his hands up, over his face with his fists closed. He could see that the red glow that he now described as mist had engulfed him. That was the last thing that he remembered for a moment.

When he woke up, he was standing next to a tree. He couldn't see at first and his eyes burned. As his sight returned, he could see lights in the distance and began to run toward them. According to his statement, "I thought I might be dead. Next I met the deputies and we went back to get my light." The deputies had apparently been summoned by the boys after their scoutmaster had been engulfed by the red mist.

There were three Boy Scouts who had been involved in the sighting. The boys, Charles Stevens, David Rowan, and the unofficial leader, Robert Ruffing, were interviewed by Air Force officers including Ruppelt on September 9, 1952, at the regular meeting of the Boy Scout troop in West Palm Beach.

In the official report it was noted that, "in general, the Boy Scouts were rather difficult to talk to. They were rather excited and nervous about the whole thing and in many cases their answers did not make a lot of sense. It is not believed that this was because they weren't telling the truth, but they were just youngsters and were a little bit nervous."

According to the boys, after the regular meeting, Desvergers took four Boy Scouts out to his car to give them a ride home. They first drove to the Wagon Wheel, a drive-in restaurant. They had a cold drink and then headed out toward a drive-in theater, but something happened and they decided not to go. Air Force investigators noted that none of the boys would explain what had happened and that they didn't answer questions about that.

Instead, they drove toward a stock-car speedway to see how much water was on the track from recent rains. Although the track was closed and dark, they stayed there for several minutes before driving down Military Trail. One of the boys was taken home so that only three remained in the car.

Now driving south on Military Trail, Desvergers saw something out of the corner of his eye, but the boys didn't see it. Desvergers told them, at the time, he thought it might be an aircraft in trouble or a flying saucer. He then got out of the car, giving the boys his instructions, and then walked into the palmettos.

Ruffing, interviewed separately from the others, told the Air Force officers that he saw Desvergers walk into the woods and that the next thing he saw was a series of red lights in the clearing. Ruffing said that as soon as he saw the red lights, he saw Desvergers stiffen and fall.

The other two boys, Stevens and Rowan, were interviewed together. They reinforced the story about the ride out to the spot where Desvergers claimed to have seen the lights going down into the trees. They watched their scoutmaster moving through the woods, his progress obvious by motion of his flashlight. The light disappeared and a few seconds later they saw the red lights. They described it as a "lot like flares or skyrockets."

Frightened, they got out of the car and ran down the road for help. They found a lighted farmhouse and told the people that their scoutmaster was in trouble. The people called the Sheriff's Department.

The Air Force investigators noted, "All in all, the boys' stories were rather conflicting and it was very difficult to obtain the facts. The only fact that seemed to stand out in all of their minds was the fact that they did see red lights out in the palmetto grove after Desvergers had gone in."

Sheriff's Deputy Mott Partin was one of those who responded to the call. As he reached the scene, Desvergers staggered from the woods. Partin told Air Force investigators and reporters who spoke to him later that he didn't believe that Desvergers was faking. He said, "In nineteen years of law enforcement, I've never seen anyone as upset as he was."

With the law enforcement officers, Desvergers returned to the palmetto to search for his dropped equipment. They found a place in the grass that looked as if someone had fallen there. They located his machete and one of his flashlights. It was still burning. They marked the spots.

One of the deputies took the Boy Scouts home. But the scoutmaster followed the deputies back into town. He complained about burns and when they arrived at the sheriff's office, they noticed that he had been burned on the arms and face. His cap had also been scorched. At that point one of the deputies called the Air Force.

It seemed that almost everyone was impressed with the story told by Desvergers. There were corroborating witnesses, there was some physical evidence in the form of burns, and an examination of his cap revealed additional burns that had been overlooked, further validating his tale.

Testing of the items carried by Desvergers revealed nothing unusual. The machete had not been magnetized, or subjected to heat or radiation. The same could be said about the flashlight. No radiation was found in the palmetto groves, either. Nothing out of the ordinary.

The day after Ruppelt—along with Second Lieutenant Robert M. Olsson, a couple of Air Force pilots, and the local intelligence officer and his sergeant—interviewed Desvergers, his story appeared in the newspaper. Although Desvergers had asked Ruppelt if he could talk about the sighting and was told that the Air Force had no policy of restricting civilians, Desvergers told reporters he had been silenced. The newspaper reported that Desvergers had conferred with "high" brass from Washington, D.C., who had confirmed his sighting by telling him exactly what he had seen, but who didn't want him talking about it.

That irritated the Air Force officers. There had been no high brass, just several captains and a second lieutenant. They had not suggested to Desvergers that they knew what he had seen, though he had asked them repeatedly for an explanation. And they hadn't muzzled him.

Before Ruppelt left Florida, one of the deputies had suggested they look into the background of Desvergers. The deputy had said that Desvergers was a former Marine, and that aspect was played up in the newspapers. He also told some stories of secret missions into the Pacific during the Second World War. He told of a horrible accident when a car had fallen on him and he'd spent months in the hospital recuperating from his injuries. All these were facts that could be checked and while they had nothing to do directly with the UFO story, they did speak to the character of the witness.

In his book, Ruppelt pointed out that Desvergers had a reputation for telling tall tales. In the official Project Blue Book file I read it was noted,

Once during a birthday party, Desvergers stated that during the war he was a Marine and had been on sea duty on a battleship. He stated that one day he was contacted by an Officer of Naval Intelligence who asked him to go on a secret mission. He was taken to Washington and given a briefing by a group of Colonels then taken to California to go to school with some more Colonels from Washington. He was flown to the Pacific to map Jap-held islands that were unchartered [sic]. He stated that he was taken to the island under cover of darkness in a PBY aircraft along with his surveying cryptography equipment and that as they approached the island a life raft was inflated and thrown out the waist window of the PBY. The PBY landed in the dark in unchartered waters next to the raft and put Desvergers and his equipment into the raft. With the cover of darkness he paddled up to the beach and buried all his equipment. Desvergers stated that at the beginning of the story the island was 7 × 3 miles long and at the end, it was 25 × 50. After about two weeks of hiding from the Japs all day and digging up his equipment and surveying at night, he had mapped the island. In many cases he had brushes with Japanese Officers and once during his two weeks he was lying in some bushes hiding during the day when the Japs walked by so close to him they could touch him. When the job was finished he had set up a rendezvous with the PBY and it landed at night. However, the Japs saw the airplane land and knew that he was on the island. He inflated his rubber raft and started paddling toward the aircraft but the Japanese started to fire at him and sunk his life raft; however, in the raft he had a Gibson Girl radio with a balloon for an antenna. He quickly inflated the balloon, crawled on it and floated out to the PBY. As he was being picked up by the aircraft, people were reaching out of the hatch helping him. During this time the Japs were shooting at them and several of the sailors who were helping him were badly wounded.

The problems with this "war story" are many. First, it smacks of being just that, a war story. Secret missions are not developed in that fashion and they don't select the soldiers, or in this case, Marine, in such a haphazard fashion. They are given to highly trained personnel who have expertise that is critical to the mission.

But more importantly is the service record of Desvergers. Here is a man who was in the Marines during the Second World War. It was a time when the expansion of the various services including the Marines demanded huge numbers of recruits. The fighting in Europe, Africa, and the Pacific was grinding up men in terrible numbers. Yet, according to the record, Desvergers had been tossed out of the Marines with a less-than-honorable discharge in 1944. Ruppelt noted, "He had been booted out of the Marines after a few months for being AWOL and stealing an automobile." He apparently went from lone hero to disgraced Marine in a very short time.

To me, this spoke volumes about the reliability of the man. That is not to mention the other factors on his record. He had told various people at various times that he had been a PFC test pilot in the Marines and had flown every type of naval and Marine fighting aircraft. Of course, prior to the war, the Marines did have "flying sergeants," that is, enlisted men who were pilots. They had no PFC test pilots, however.

He told high-school friends about his automobile accident. He said that he had finished work late, after everyone else had gone home for the day when, somehow, a car had fallen on him. For hours he was pinned under the car, screaming for help. But, when Air Force investigators checked, they learned that others had been there to help at the time of the accident. He had been taken to the hospital and released quickly. He had taken the real event and embellished the account into a truly horrifying tale.

Had a single person suggested that Desvergers spun tall tales, it might be suggested that some sort of a vendetta existed. But many people related that Desvergers had told them similar things. One man even said that if Desvergers had told him the sun was shining, he would go out to look.

Other details of his personal life were equally revealing when reported. Many of the people who knew him had heard the stories and dismissed them as fantasy. Ruppelt, among others, "pointed out that this fact alone meant nothing. . . ." The UFO sighting could have been the one time that Desvergers was telling the truth.

Then the Air Force investigators made another discovery. The clearing where Desvergers had been attacked by the UFO was invisible from the road. Olsson and the local intelligence officer tried to see the clearing under about the same lighting conditions as the night of the event. Only by standing *on* the car could they see down into the thicket where the Boy Scouts had thought their leader had been attacked.

Suddenly, the tale of a brave ex-Marine and Boy Scout leader, who had the corroboration of three Boy Scouts, didn't look so good. It wasn't that anyone believed the Boy Scouts were lying. They thought the kids had gotten caught up in the excitement and had imagined some of the things they thought they saw, especially under the careful guidance of their scoutmaster. In the final analysis, they hadn't seen all that much anyway.

So the tale hung on Desvergers and his reputation. His reputation had fallen apart. He wasn't the upstanding and honest ex-Marine hero of a secret Pacific campaign that he had seemed to be. His background was less than sterling and involved, among other things, petty theft. The case began to look like a hoax after all.

The day after Ruppelt and the others had interviewed Desvergers, he hired publicity agent Art Weil. Rather than providing Desvergers' story to newspapers and magazines, Weil was going to sell the tale to the highest bidder. Desvergers had already been approached by a number of people including a couple of college professors, newspaper reporters, and at least one writer from a large-circulation news magazine. Or rather, that was what Desvergers had said.

Not long after that, Weil quit. He had learned about the problems with Desvergers' background and realized that no reputable magazine would pay for such a story. The only thing going for the story was the reputation of the man telling it. If his reputation wouldn't stand up to the background checks, which it wouldn't, then no one from a reputable magazine would take a chance on the tale.

So it seems that this was just a hoax. Desvergers, to add weight to it, had singed the hair from his arms with his own cigarette lighter, or so the investigators believed. The slight reddening observed by some was gone within a day or two. The tale of lights, or a mystery craft, in the palmetto was not corroborated by anyone.

But Ruppelt had called this the best hoax in UFO history. There was nothing in the official Blue Book record to explain that. It seemed to be more of a routine, and not very clever, hoax. Except for one thing. According to Ruppelt in his book, they had forgotten about the soil and grass samples gathered in the clearing. They had taken the machete, the flashlight, and the cap for testing, but in the rush to get out of Florida, they'd left the soil samples behind. Ruppelt asked the local intelligence officer to forward them to Blue Book, which he did.

When the lab, which we now know to be the Battelle Memorial Institute, reported back to Ruppelt, they asked, "How did the roots [of the grass] get charred?"

What they had discovered is that the roots of the grass had been heated to about 300 degrees. They had no way to explain it and the only way they could duplicate it was to put the grass in a pan and heat it. Of course, that was not what had been done in the field. The samples had been taken from the undisturbed ground.

Ruppelt and the others checked the area carefully and found nothing that would account for the charring. He did learn that induction heating could duplicate the effect in the field but there was no evidence such was the case. Ruppelt quoted from an engineering text that suggested a method for induction heating. A metal rod, when subjected to an alternating magnetic field, would create "eddy currents" that caused a rise in temperature. Ruppelt suggested that by replacing the metal bar with wet sand such as that in the clearing for the electrical conductor and an assumption of a strong, alternating magnetic field created by the proper equipment, the charred roots could be explained. Of course, it required heavy equipment to do it and there was no evidence of that equipment in the palmetto grove that night or at any other time.

Suddenly there was a bit of physical evidence that couldn't be explained easily. Ruppelt and the others were still convinced that the story was a hoax, even if they couldn't explain how the roots of the grass had been charred.

And Olsson, in a "memo for the record" found in the Project Blue Book files, had talked to the people at the "Flare and Signal Branch." They suggested that the burns in the hat were consistent with those from a flare, but that didn't mean the burns had occurred in that way or that Desvergers had used a flare.

But more importantly, Olsson learned that had a flare been used to hoax part of the sighting, the grass should have burned. He was told, "It seems likely that if a flare was used in the incident at West Palm, a fire would have started in the dry grass. No evidence of a fire was present down there as far as we could see."

These facts were what made the case the best hoax in UFO history. That, and the fact that no one had proven that Desvergers was lying in this instance. As the deputy said, "It could have been the one time in his life that he told the truth."

What is interesting about the Project Blue Book file is there is nothing about these grass samples in it. There are "memos for the record" that cover the testing done on the machete, the flashlight, and the cap. There are reports that suggest there was nothing unusual about the machete or the flashlight, and detail the holes burned in the cap. The scorching on the hat, along with some tiny holes burned in it, were puzzling but not solid evidence that the tale told by Desvergers was the truth.

All these documents are in the file. There are even longer, detailed statements about Desvergers' background that suggest his character wasn't sterling. There are many tales that he had spun that had no basis in fact. These are particularly persuasive. It provides the profile of a man who enjoys the spotlight, who has spun more than one tale to put himself in that spotlight, and who seems to have invented the story of a flying-saucer attack to grab the spotlight once again. In today's environment, he would claim to have been abducted and would appear on a dozen or so of the television talk shows to explain what had happened to him.

But there is nothing in the file about the grass and soil samples.

Without Ruppelt's candid description of the case in his book, we would know nothing about this aspect of it.

To me, the evidence in the file is persuasive. I have no doubt that Desvergers invented the tale of the flying-saucer attack. There are just too many instances where Desvergers made up stories to impress his friends and coworkers. With what I found by reading the file, I would be willing—in fact, I would be enthusiastic—to label this case a hoax if not for one thing.

Where are those reports about the charred grass roots?

MAY 5, 1955:

PROJECT BLUE BOOK
SPECIAL REPORT #14

During a short part of its existence, the officers involved with Project Blue Book issued a series of reports. They were numbered one through twelve and began while Blue Book was still operating under the old code name of Grudge. *Special Report #14* was issued some two years after the last of the regular reports. There is no credible evidence that a report numbered thirteen ever existed. It has been suggested that number thirteen was incorporated into *Special Report #14*.

The actual story of these reports begins on December 26 and 27, 1951, when Ed Ruppelt and Colonel S. H. Kirkland of the Air Technical Intelligence Center met with members of Battelle Memorial Institute, a think tank located in Columbus, Ohio. The idea was to analyze the UFO data "scientifically" and see if any sort of patterns could be found and to provide information so that better data could be gathered. Ruppelt had also complained that he needed experts to assist in the evaluation of UFO reports if any sort of meaningful conclusions were to be drawn.

Ruppelt, who used the fictional code name of Project Bear for Battelle, later wrote, "[S]everal hundred engineers and scientists who make up the run from experts on soils to nuclear physicists . . . they would make these people available to me. . . . They would do two studies for us; a study of how much a person can be expected to see and remember from a UFO sighting, and a statistical study of UFO reports."

According to a document dated January 8, 1952, the Battelle representatives agreed that there was enough material available to make the scientific study. The document said, "It is very reasonable to believe that some type of unusual object or phenomenon is being observed as many of the sightings have been made by highly qualified sources."

There were five areas of study, or five requirements, made of the Battelle Corporation, officially code-named Project Stork, and supervised by William Reid. They were to "provide a panel of consultants . . . Assist in improving the interrogation forms . . . Analyze existing sighting reports . . . Subscribe to a clipping service . . . Apprise the sponsor monthly of all work done."

The project began on March 31, 1952. They couldn't have picked a better time, or a worse one, depending on one's point of view. The 1952 wave was just beginning, and by the end of 1952, the Air Force had collected an additional 1,500 reports, of which, 303 remained as unidentified. In *Status Report #7*, dated November 10, 1952, it was noted that sighting reports had improved in both numbers and quality.

In the second of the reports under the auspices of Stork, dated June 6, 1952, it was noted that the preliminary analysis of the existing reports had been completed. They had also developed a preliminary new questionnaire. They had developed a list of about thirty different characteristics of a report that could be keyed onto IBM punch cards for the statistical analysis. These included geographic location, duration of the sighting, color, speed, number, shape, and brightness of the craft and even the evaluation of both the sighting report and the observer.

Although the contracts called for the completion of the study by October 1, 1953, it is apparent that reports were gathered until the spring of 1955. The findings of Project Stork were then, apparently, incorporated into *Blue Book Special Report #14*.

They began with 4,000 UFO sightings but eliminated nearly 800 for a variety of reasons including those too poorly documented to be useful for the study. This left 3,201 UFO sightings, the majority of which were from the Project Blue Book files dating back to the original Project Sign, with a few coming from other, outside sources.

First they wanted to gather the essential facts from the reports. They also worked to establish the credibility of the witnesses. They looked at the internal consistency of the report and the quality of it. Finally they attempted to make an identification of it. They tried to fit it into some category of natural or conventional identification.

The first run at identification was done by the individual who transcribed the report onto a worksheet they had developed. That would be passed to a member of the identification panel who would also evaluate the report without knowing what the first pass had revealed. If two of the evaluators arrived at the same conclusion, then that was accepted as a final identification. If there was a disagreement, then the report was passed on to the other panel members for more analysis.

If either or both suggested the case was unidentified, the whole panel studied it. The unidentified cases, or "unknowns" as they were labeled by the Stork scientists and researchers, were defined as "those reports of sightings wherein the description of the objects and its [sic] maneuvers could not be fitted to the pattern of any known object or phenomenon."

Once all analysis of the data was completed, the cases were reduced to statistical fields so that some sort of conclusions could be drawn. When all those aspects of the report were completed, then the final draft was put together which included a summary of the data and conclusions drawn by the Battelle scientists.

When *Special Report #14* was finally released to the public and the news media, it was the summary that was examined first. It suggested that better reporting, undoubtedly because of the improved questionnaires, and better investigative techniques developed by the Battelle scientists, had reduced the percentage of "unknowns." For the final two years of the study, that is, 1953 and 1954, the number of unknowns was only 9 percent, and for the first few months of 1955, that had been reduced even further, to 3 percent. Those figures, of course, overlooked 1952 when the number of unknowns was about 20 percent.

It was being suggested by the Battelle scientists and the Air Force investigators that the improved techniques were demonstrating that with enough information and with proper investigation, all sightings could eventually be explained. Again, as usual, the media seized on this idea, included in the summary, and reported that the Air Force study had proven that flying saucers were just another myth.

Dr. Bruce Maccabee, who studied *Special Report #14*, related in a document published by CUFOS, that "despite the use of information contained in the summary as part of the press release, it is clear that it was not written as a press release. Rather, it was written to supplement the information given in the main text. In other words, it was assumed that whoever read the summary would also read the main text."

I disagree with Dr. Maccabee on one point. I believe that those writing the summary assumed that those outside of the relatively few members of the military who were interested would ever read the main text. All had been around Washington long enough to know that journalists, congressmen, and government officials never read whole documents. It was the reason that executive summaries had been created. Pack them with information and that would be all that would be examined. Those who only read the conclusions would not be aware that the information in the main body of the text did not support the conclusions drawn in the summary. I'm convinced that those who wrote the summary counted on it being all that was read.

Ruppelt, who had with Kirkland originated the idea of the report, criticized it on its release for what he called "weasel wording." For example, there is nowhere in the report where it is stated, positively, that UFOs *don't* exist. Instead, as Maccabee points out, they suggest in "probability arguments" that UFOs don't exist. They can't prove it, so it is reduced to "UFOs probably don't exist," which by 1955 was the conclusion the Air Force wanted drawn. The original rationale for the report had long been lost.

Again, for example, one of these probability arguments was their attempt to "create" a "flying-saucer model." Maccabee wrote, "Here they imply that because none of the sightings matched each other identically, the probability that any sighting was valid 'is concluded to be extremely small.'" Of course, this overlooks the fact that only one UFO sighting has to be valid for the whole argument to be eliminated.

The Battelle researchers had selected twelve cases that were un-knowns and used them as a basis for constructing their "flying-saucer model." They looked at the overall descriptions, the flight dynamics, and other observed data, as well as the reliability of the witnesses and the duration of the sighting.

With all that in mind, they then attempted to bring it together into a single type of craft, or flying saucer. Maccabee wrote about this:

Thus we must assume that even the Battelle investigators believed that each of the other sightings was valid. This would explain why they did not attempt to explain each one, but rather to explain them away by "conglomeration": in combination, the cases do not point to a single model "flying saucer"; therefore, avoids the sticky problem of explaining how a Reserve Air Force captain and an airline captain could be fooled into thinking that they saw a circular craft with a flashing light on top and steady lights on the bottom pass in front of the airliner they were flying. [This is a reference to Case XI in the Battelle report from March 20, 1950, in which the pilots watched a circular object.] The object was in view for about half a minute.

Maccabee also notes,

Still another case they avoided explaining may be one of the most credible on record. The summary in SR 14 [*Special Report #14*] does not do the case justice. . . . Case X [which took place on May 24, 1949] describes a sighting by two aeronautical engineers who worked at the Ames Research Laboratory and three other people. Each engineer had the opportunity to observe a "flying saucer" through binoculars for a period exceeding 60 seconds. The drawings produced by these witnesses were extremely de-tailed. The intelligence information on this case is missing from the Project Blue Book section of the microfilm record at the National Archives. However, Maccabee has found the original interviews, etc., in the Office of Special Investigations section of the microfilm record and has published the information along with some supplementary weather data.

Air Force writers had suggested, "It can never be absolutely proven that 'flying saucers' do not exist. This would be true if the data obtained were to include complete scientific measurements of the attributes of each sighting, as well as complete and detailed descriptions of the objects sighted. It might be possible to demonstrate the existence of 'flying saucers' with data of this type, *IF* they were to exist."

So now we see the problem they had—explain the sightings with "incomplete" data or so they would have us believe. But, as Maccabee pointed out, Case X had the very attributes the Air Force suggested didn't exist. There were qualified witnesses, that is, two aeronautical engineers, who had ample opportunity to observe the craft through binoculars. This wasn't a case such as the Chiles-Whitted sighting, in which the object flashed by. This was a case where minutes passed as the observation continued, enabling the witnesses to take notes.

In fact, what we see from this report is that there is *too* much information to allow investigators to find a plausible explanation. They have all the information they could desire, from the location and exact time, to the descriptions of the craft including detailed drawings. No natural phenomenon is going to explain it. Nor will it be eliminated as a misidentification of military or civilian aircraft. It will remain unknown.

To eliminate it, then, it is combined with other cases in which there is no good, plausible explanation. All the information is correlated and an attempt is made to produce a single type of flying saucer. The assumption seems to be that if flying saucers were real, then we would be able to take the cases and combine them to produce a composite "model" of a flying saucer in much the same way that police artists can produce a composite of a single criminal.

The assumption being made here, and one that should be obvious to everyone, is that more than one type of craft could be involved. Take, for example, an aircraft carrier from our modern Navy. It's floating in the Mediterranean Sea and launching a variety of aircraft to survey the surrounding territory. We know that such ships carry two or three different types of jet fighters, as well as a variety of reconnaissance aircraft, tankers, and even helicopters.

Now, let's say that we have a number of people who have seen those various aircraft over a period of a couple of months. We interview them, study the weather, length of sighting, and location of each of them. From that we attempt to build a model of the aircraft on the carrier, assuming there to be a single type.

Given that we have a craft with swept wings and a narrow fuselage, a huge craft with two engines, another with no wings but a rotor overhead, with different configurations for the lighting, we would be unable to manufacture a single model. Should we then conclude that no sightings were made? Should we conclude that, with better information, we would have been able to answer the questions? No. We have more than one type and by combining information that shouldn't be combined, we have destroyed our database.

Of course, by combining that information we can suggest that there is no commonality among the sightings. We can deduce that each of the witnesses is mistaken in some critical observation. We can suggest that this proves there is nothing to the sightings of these very common, to us, aircraft. And each of these conclusions would be wrong, though, to a hurried and noncritical reader of our work, we have demonstrated a "flaw" in the sighting reports. We can now reject them.

There were many other critics of *Special Report #14*. Leon Davidson, who had been a scientist at Los Alamos Scientific Laboratory, and who had been a member of the group who had studied the Green Fireballs in the late 1940s and early 1950s, printed and sold copies of the report along with his analysis. He believed that flying saucers did exist and saw the report as a clever attempt to hide the fact. Davidson pointed out the discrepancy between the information contained in the report's summary and the contents of the press release that "announced" it.

He noted that in the report, "unknown sightings constitute 33.3 percent of all the object sightings for which the reliability of the sighting is considered 'excellent.'" In other words, contrary to what the report's authors had suggested, the better the report, the more likely it was going to be an "unknown." It wasn't the reports from unqualified observers who saw an object for seconds that caused the most trouble. It was reports from trained and qualified witnesses that were more likely to be inexplicable.

The National Investigations Committee on Aerial Phenomena, a civilian organization based in Washington, D.C., also disputed the idea that a model couldn't be created. They cited a 1949 Project Grudge analysis, which reported, "The most numerous reports indicate day-time observations of metallic disclike objects roughly in diameter ten times their thickness. . . . From this official description a working model of a UFO or flying saucer can be built without the slightest trouble."

In other words, there was one "official" report that refuted another official report. The argument about creating the model was actually an argument over the cosmetics of the situation. Looked at in that way, then a model can be created, and one of the major conclusions of the Battelle report has been eliminated.

Hynek, as Blue Book's chief scientific consultant, was in a unique position. He had been on the inside as many of the cases were investigated. He had participated in many of those investigations, and knew the people involved. Even with his close working relationship with Blue Book, he was surprised at the allegation in *Special Report #14* that there was no difference between the knowns and the unknowns. What the reported suggest was that the characteristics of the known cases matched those of the unknowns. Scientists had assumed that there would be a difference between the knowns and unknowns. A lack of difference suggested that the UFO phenomenon was little more that misidentifications of natural phenomena and conventional aircraft. That was a point, this lack of difference, that had been seized upon to suggest that UFO sightings were simple misidentifications.

The Battelle researchers had applied the chi-square test to the two groups of data, that is, the known and unknown categories. The chi-square test for independence is used for comparing two or more groups to determine if different patterns of frequencies exist in the groups. The theory behind the use of the chi-square test by Battelle was that the known cases should differ from the unknown cases if there were UFOs.

Textbooks argue that chi-square is a frequently misused statistical procedure. It often looks good, but the analysis can be of little real value when misapplied as it was here.

To make the point in an even more dramatic fashion, *Yale Scientific Magazine* in April 1963 reported, "Based upon unreliable and unscientific surmises as data, the Air Force develops elaborate statistical findings which seem impressive to the uninitiated public unschooled in the fallacies of the statistical method. One must conclude that the highly publicized Air Force pronouncements based upon unsound statistics serve merely to misrepresent the true character of the UFO phenomena."

According to the analysis by Leon Davidson, the chi-square test has shown, as even the Battelle researchers had to admit, that "there was very little probability that the Unknowns were the same as the Knowns. But they refused to admit that this meant that 'saucers' could be a real type of novel object." What Davidson had discovered was that the Battelle scientists had misrepresented their data to reach the conclusion the Air Force desired them to reach.

Following that same notion, Hynek wrote about the conclusions in *Special Report #14,* "[The report] completely disregards the results of these [chi-square] tests most brazenly, as if they did not exist."

And Maccabee reported that the data indicated that the "best-qualified observers make the best reports and are most likely to be reporting true Unknowns, while the poorest observers make the poorest reports (most Insuf. Info. [insufficient data]) and are the least likely to be reporting true Unknowns."

This finding alone suggested there was something to the UFO phenomenon, but it was unacceptable to the Project Stork scientists. Instead they "could only guess" that the "psychological makeup" of witnesses in the unknown cases, plus a single unrecognized source, such as a balloon, airplane, or whatever, was responsible for many of the sightings, and had skewed the results "so as to create an artificial distinction between knowns and unknowns."

Of course, it is necessary to point out that in the summary, the Battelle analysts suggested there was no significant difference between the witnesses who reported objects that were later identified and those who reported objects that remained unidentified. Then, later, when it suited their purposes, they suggested there was a difference. In other words, they were contradicting their own findings when it suited their purposes. This is not good science.

What we see as we read *Special Report #14* is the history of the belief structures of those writing the reports. In the very beginning, as Ruppelt proposed the idea, Project Grudge, and later Blue Book, was conducting unbiased investigations into the phenomenon. They wanted answers, but they wanted answers that were accurate. Solving a case just to put a label on it had no appeal to Ruppelt and his staff.

In the first of the status reports, the information supplied discusses what is going to happen in the near future. These reports were about what was happening with the UFO investigations. The third report, for example, dated July 7, 1952, mentioned that Hynek had been hired as an astronomical consultant and that he would interview other astronomers regarding their opinions about UFOs and UFO reports.

The sixth report, dated October 10, 1952, again reports on the status of the Battelle investigation. But, there is a comment that should be singled out. It mentions the analysis of a 35mm spectroscopic film and a section of gun-camera spectrographic film. Maccabee in his report noted, "Apparently these films were supplied to Battelle without enough data on how the films were obtained for the analysts to be able to make any positive conclusions."

Or maybe, these films were too explosive for the results to be reviewed in documents that were classified, at the highest, as secret. Hynek wrote that he believed the involvement of Battelle was "top secret" but the reports don't reflect this.

But that is a digression. The point is that someone had provided the technical equipment to fighter units to allow for gun-camera spectroscopic filming of UFOs, but in all case files I have examined, and in all the work done by so many others, I know of no one who has ever located those films. Spectroscopic analysis of the UFOs could provide some interesting clues about the propulsion systems used by them, to the sources of the light that seem to surround them and other technical aspects of those sightings.

It would also seem that the use of spectroscopic film implies planning by someone. It would suggest a controlled experiment which, if successful, would go a long way to answering the questions about the nature of the UFOs. We can assume, that since the data have not been released, that they provided evidence of the extraterrestrial nature of the flying saucers. Otherwise, as we have seen, we would have possession of that data.

In arguing about the evidence held by the military, or the government, concerning UFOs, researchers have often claimed secret documents and studies that have not seen the light of day. This seems to be corroboration of that claim because gun-camera footage that can provide for a spectroscopic analysis has not been released.

Returning to the other aspects of the Battelle study, we learn that the reports from them ended with number seven. In December 1952, and in January and February 1953, there were single-page letters that updated the ongoing analysis. These were composed by Reid, the project supervisor.

But what is interesting is the timing. If we go back to the history of the UFO project, we see that the pendulum has swung the other way, that is, away from an extraterrestrial hypothesis. UFO sightings were again in the realm of science fiction. It was at this time, January 1953, that Blue Book was beginning to lose its special status. The staff, which had been so busy in the summer and fall of 1952, was reduced, and by the spring of 1953 it was a single officer and a single enlisted man. At one point that spring, there were no officers, and an airman first class, a low-ranking man, had control of Project Blue Book.

And, it was at this time that the investigative responsibility was taken away from Blue Book and passed to the 4602d Air Intelligence Service Squadron. Although there would still be some investigations carried out by Blue Book personnel, the real investigation rested with the 4602d. That is evidenced by the implementation of Air Force Regulation 200-2, which placed the investigative responsibility directly on the shoulders of the 4602d.

An examination of the documentation available about the 4602d's involvement suggests that they saw the UFO investigation as an opportunity to practice their interrogation techniques. They were also hostile to the addition of the mission to investigate UFOs. In

Volume II of the Unit History, there is a "UFOB Summery" in which the author wrote,

> First recorded instances of genuine UFOs occurred in 1948 [sic] with the appearance of the "Flying Saucers" in different parts of the United States. Rapid diffusion to all parts of the world, including the Soviet Union and its satellites. . . . Birth of a new literary genre "Science Fiction" which in most cases is entirely fictitious and unscientific. [This whole point is irrelevant and wrong. Science fiction had existed for decades and had been introduced to Americans in the 1920s.] . . . Emotional stimulus of speculation on the fantastic. . . . General Public not qualified to evaluate material propounded in science fiction. Absurd and fantastic theories given credence solely on the basis of ignorance. . . . UFOB reports even though patently ridiculous receive undue attention through latent fear, etc.

This, then, was the attitude of the people doing the investigations of UFOs after the various regulations, both those written by the Air Defense Command and by the Air Force including AFR 200-2, went into effect. By the time *Blue Book Special Report #14* was publicly available, those inside the military establishment had the attitude of those at the 4602d. Is it little wonder that the conclusions drawn in the report are that UFOs don't exist, there is no evidence they exist, and that it is impossible to prove they don't exist? In other words, the conclusions were not based on the data presented, but on the beliefs and attitudes being expressed by those who were now controlling the purse, and the course of the investigation.

There is one other factor that must be addressed. In the original contract, it called for a timely conclusion of Project Stork. The sudden surge of cases during the summer of 1952 certainly would have caused some delays because no one had anticipated what would happen. But even after that, with the final status reports becoming single-page letters, it took two years for the final report to be written. A legitimate question about the delay can be asked.

For my part, I think the delay was caused by the change in official policy and attitudes reflected in the Project Blue Book files. The CIA's Robertson Panel had looked at the data and decided there was nothing to it. They recommended that the investigations continue, but that the emphasis be on "education." Teach people that UFOs didn't exist. It wouldn't be wise for a private company under contract to the federal government to issue a report that suggested that UFOs did exist, which was in conflict with what the CIA had just done.

The delay, then, made it possible to rewrite and reevaluate some of the report and draw conclusions that were not supported by evidence in the body of the text. The thinking had to be that no one would wade through the pages and pages of statistics, and those who did, probably wouldn't understand them anyway. The few people who did examine the report, including Ruppelt, acknowledged the weaknesses, but their voices were not heard.

Instead, there was the two-or three-page summary that gave the conclusion that UFOs don't exist. Rather than presenting scientific evidence for their conclusions, they were now spouting the party line. An idea that originally had merit was reduced to just one more example of how the information was manipulated so that we could be told there was nothing to the UFO phenomenon.

The only problem is that the investigations continued.

AUGUST 13, 1956:

THE FIRST BENTWATERS CASE

If there is a case that proves that the officers and investigators for Project Blue Book were not interested in finding any answers except those they wanted, this is the report. It involves radar sightings on more than one set at more than one location, it involves jet fighters and attempted intercepts, and it involves visual sightings from the ground. It contains the physical evidence required of the skeptics in the form of radar returns, and it contains the corroborative visual confirmation of something unusual in the sky. But, in the end, the Air Force investigators fumbled the case away suggesting a combination of events that rivals the first of those multiple excuses provided for the Mantell incident of eight years earlier.

It began, according to the Blue Book files at 213Z, or 9:30 P.M. local time, when Tech Sergeant Elmer L. Whenry, a GCA (Ground Controlled Approach) radar operator for the USAF's 1264th AACS Squadron at the RAF Station Bentwaters, England, spotted twelve to fifteen blips on his radarscope. These were not correlated to any of the aircraft known to be in the area at the time.

According to the official Blue Book files, "This group was picked up approximately eight miles southwest of RAF Station Bentwaters and were tracked on the radarscope clearly until the objects were approximately fourteen miles northeast of Bentwaters. At the latter point on the course of these objects, they faded considerably on the radar scope."

The Blue Book report continued, "At the approximate forty-mile range individual objects . . . appeared to converge into one very large object which appeared to be several times larger than a B-36 aircraft due to the size of the blip on the radarscope. At the time that the individual objects seemed to converge into one large object, the large object appeared to remain stationary for ten to fifteen minutes. The large object then moved NE approximately five or six miles then stopped its movement for three to five minutes then moved north disappearing off the radarscope."

At about the same time, Airman Second Class John Vaccare, Jr., another radar operator, spotted a single blip twenty-five to thirty miles southeast. As he watched, the blip seemed to be moving on a 295-degree heading at a very high rate of speed. After about thirty seconds, the blip was fifteen to twenty miles from the radar site, where it disappeared. According to the conservative figures, the object was moving at 5,000 miles an hour.

At about 10:00 P.M., about five minutes after Whenry's first sighting had ended, he saw another blip located about thirty miles east of the station. Although the blip was on screen for only sixteen seconds, it moved to a point where it was west of the station and then faded. Calculations suggested that it moved at about 12,000 miles an hour.

From the Bentwaters control tower, others including Staff Sergeant Lawrence S. Wright, reported a bright light, according to the Air Force file. It was the size of a pinhead held at arm's length and rose slowly from a point about 10 degrees above the horizon. It remained in sight for about an hour, appearing and disappearing. Nearly everyone who has looked at the file and checked the various star charts and maps have concluded that this object was Mars.

As Whenry was tracking the objects on his scope, a flight of two T-33 jets from the 512th Fighter Interceptor Squadron, returned to Bentwaters after a routine mission. The two pilots, identified in the Blue Book files only as Metz and Rowe (other data revealed their full names as First Lieutenant Charles V. Metz and First Lieutenant Andrew

C. Rowe), were asked to try to find the objects. Although they searched the area for forty-five minutes, vectored by the radar operators, they failed to find anything. They broke off and landed about 10: 15 P.M.

At 10:55 P.M., another target was spotted, about thirty miles to the east and heading west at only 2,000 to 4,000 miles an hour. It passed directly overhead and disappeared from the radar screen, about thirty miles from the base. This time, however, there was an airborne observation. A C-47 pilot saw the object flash beneath his plane. To him it looked like little more than a blur of light.

The pilot wasn't the only person to see the light. On the ground, a number of people, looking up, saw the same bright blur. They provided little in the way of useful description of the object.

There were those who believed that this one segment of the case could be identified, just as Mars seems to have explained the Bentwaters control tower sighting. Analysis by UFO debunker Philip Klass led him to speculate that the pilot only saw a meteor, one of the many that can be seen during the Perseid meteor showers. Atmospheric physicist James McDonald, who also reviewed the case, disagreed, using the ground observations and the pilot's sighting to suggest the object was between ground level and 4,000 feet. Klass failed to mention that there were ground observations of that object as he writes it off. But even if Klass was right (thought I doubt it) about this one sighting, there were others that were not so easily explained.

The sighting by the pilot and the people on the ground was the last of the events at the Bentwaters base. The action shifted to the west-northwest as Lakenheath Air Force Base radars began to pick up the objects. Ground personnel saw a luminous object approach from a southwesterly direction, stop, then shoot off toward the east. Not much later, two white lights appeared, "joined up with another and both disappeared in formation together." Before they vanished, the objects had performed a number of high-speed maneuvers. Most importantly, all of this was seen on two separate radar screens at Lakenheath.

The Blue Book files noted, "Thus two radar sets [that is, Lakenheath GCA and the RATCC radars] and three ground observers report substantially the same thing . . . the fact that radar and ground visual observations were made on its rapid acceleration and abrupt stops certainly lend credulance [sic] to the report."

But Klass, in his analysis of the case, finds what he believes to the be fatal flaw here too. He seizes on the point that the blip stopped to hover. He wrote,

> With the radar operating in the moving-target indicator (MTI) mode, *only moving targets* should appear on the scope—IF the MTI is functioning properly. In radars of that early vintage, MTI was a relatively new feature and one that often caused problems. For example, the instruction book for the MPN-11A [the designation of that particular radar set design] radar, which also had MTI, specifically warned radar operators and maintenance personnel of the possibility of *spurious signals* being caused by an MTI malfunction. In chapter 5, on page 12, the Technical Order (as the instruction book is called) warned that MTI "circuits are complex; the stability requirements are severe; the tolerances are close." And on page 18 of chapter 4, the same manual warns operators of still another potential source of spurious signals that can result from what is called "extra-time-around signals." [Emphasis in original.]

What Klass is suggesting, without going into a complex and detailed discussion of the workings of radars that are now more than forty years old, is that "this condition can arise during anomalous-propagation weather conditions when echoes from distant fixed targets on the ground far beyond the selected maximum radar operating range defeat the MTI function. Under this condition, the Tech Order warned, 'the signal from this distant fixed target may appear *as a false moving target* . . .'" (Klass's added emphasis.)

Klass is arguing, based on the technical specifications of the radars in use, that the blips during this first sighting are anomalous propagation. In other words, the returns were not of real craft but a "phantom" created by the weather conditions outside and the electronic characteristics of the radars being used.

About midnight one of the operators at Lakenheath called the chief fighter controller at the RAF Station at Neatishead, Norfolk, in England, and reported a strange object buzzing the base. F. H. C. Wimbledon would later say, "I scrambled a Venom night fighter from the Battle Flight through Sector, and my controller in the Interception Control team would consist of one Fighter Controller, a Corporal, a tracker and a height reader. That is, four highly trained personnel in addition to myself could now see the object on our radarscopes."

Blue Book files, which are often confusing, suggest that it took the two-man fighter between 30 and 45 minutes to arrive at Lakenheath. As the aircraft approached, according to the reports, "Pilot advised he had a bright light in sight and would investigate. At thirteen miles west, he reported loss of target and white light."

Immediately afterward the interceptor was directed to another target over Bedford, and the navigator locked on it with his radar. He said it was the "clearest target I have ever seen on radar."

The radar contact was broken, and the Lakenheath controllers reported that the object had passed the Venom fighter and was now behind it, that is, at the six o'clock position, in the lingo of fighter pilots. The pilot acknowledged the message and tried various maneuvers to reverse the situation, that is, to get behind the object. Unable to shake the object, the pilot asked for assistance.

But the Venom was now low on fuel and the pilot decided to return to base. According to the Blue Book documents, "Second Venom was vectored to other radar targets but was unable to make contact." The second aircraft returned to the base and no other fighters were sent. By 3:30 A.M., all targets were gone.

When the Condon Committee—also known as the University of Colorado study, an Air Force-sponsored investigation into UFOs—began, one of the controllers who had been on duty that night at Bentwaters, sent a letter describing the events. Although it had been about a dozen years, the memory seemed to be well etched. Naturally there were some discrepancies in the letter but nothing of a significant nature.

The man pointed out that he had not told anyone of the events because he was "pretty sure it is considered (or was) classified, and the only reason I feel free to give you details is because you are an official government agency."

His long letter then described most of the events of that night. He provided a detailed look at the attempted intercept. He made a number of interesting observations in the letter, including the information about the intercept. He wrote,

> The first movement of the UFO was so swift (circling behind the interceptor), I missed it entirely, but it was seen by other controllers. However, the fact that this had occurred was confirmed by the pilot of the interceptor. The pilot of the interceptor told us he would try to shake the UFO and would try it again. He tried everything—he climbed, dived, circled, etc., but the UFO acted like it was glued right behind him, always the same distance, very close, but we always had two distinct targets. Note: Target resolution on our radar at the range they were from the antenna (about 10 to 30 miles, all in the southerly sectors from Lakenheath) would be between 200 and 600 feet probably. Closer than that we would have got one target from both aircraft and UFO. Most specifications say 500 feet is the minimum but I believe it varies and 200 to 600 feet is closer to the truth. . . .

What all this boils down to are a series of radar observations of objects that displayed characteristics that were outside the capabilities of aircraft of the day. In at least one of the reports from Bentwaters, the radar sightings coincided with visual observations on the ground and by a pilot in the C-47 (the sighting that Klass had "identified" as a meteor). This should not be confused with the observation of Mars made by tower personnel. That aspect of the case has been resolved to the satisfaction of everyone whether a believer or a skeptic or an Air Force investigator.

On the ground at Lakenheath were witnesses who saw two luminous objects in fast flight. They witnessed the course reversals and the dead stops. The maneuvers rule out meteors which some have suggested were responsible for the sightings.

Dr. James McDonald in his paper, "Science in Default," published in *UFOs—A Scientific Debate*, wrote, "The file does, however, include a lengthy dispatch that proposes a series of what I must term wholly irrelevant hypotheses about Perseid meteors with 'ionized gases in their wake which may be traced on radarscopes,' and inversions that 'may cause interference between two radar stations some distance apart.' Such basically irrelevant remarks are all too typical of Blue Book critique over the years."

He also pointed out that "not only are the radar frequencies here about two orders of magnitude too high to afford even marginal likelihood of meteor-wake returns, but there is absolutely no kinematic similarity between the reported UFO movements and the essentially straight-line hypersonic movement of a meteor, to cite just a few of the objections to meteor hypotheses."

Two separate radars at Lakenheath, having different radar parameters, were concurrently observing movements of one or more unknown targets over an extended period of time. One of the ways that the reliability of a return on one radar is checked is to compare it to another. If they are operating at different frequencies, then an inversion layer, if affecting the returns, will be different on the two sets. Or one will show it and the second will not. It eliminates the possibility of a spurious target.

That is not to mention the fact that the Blue Book files suggest that some of the two-radar sightings were coincident with the visual observations on the ground. In other words, not only were the objects seen on multiple radars, but there were people outside who saw the lights in the sky.

Klass, in his report, attempting to dismiss the case as anomalous propagation, wrote, "If it were not for the incident involving the first Venom pilot's reported radar-visual encounter with the UFO, this case would deserve scant attention because of the erratic behavior of the radar-UFOs is so characteristic of spurious targets. . . ."

Klass then goes on to explain the cockpit configuration of the Venom fighter, reporting, accurately, that it is set up so that the pilot sits on the left and the radar operator sits on the right. Controls for the radar, and the screen, are situated so that it would be difficult for the pilot to both fly the plane and work the radar. He suggests, based on the reported communications between the pilot and the ground, that there was no radar operator in the cockpit. This, Klass believes, explains why there seems to be a radar-visual sighting. The pilot, doing double duty, was "overwhelmed" by the workload and made a simple mistake.

But this is speculation by Klass. He pointed out, "Never once did the words 'we' or 'radar operator' appear in the reports; only the words 'I' and 'pilot.' "

This was a "scrambled" intercept mission. It is unlikely that the aircraft took off without a full cockpit crew. In other words, regardless of the speculations by Klass, there would have been a man sitting in the right seat to work the radar. And, if that is the case, then his whole theory is in error and should be rejected.

And even if he was correct about there being a single occupant of the Venom aircraft, that does not explain the other visual sightings at the scene. The case is made of more than a single misidentified blip on the radars. It is a complex case that should have been carefully researched by those who claimed to be interested in finding answers.

The Condon Committee, which did investigate the case in a very limited fashion, suggested that they were hampered by receiving the case late. It wasn't until the letter from the controller arrived that they even began to look at it. Only then did they request the Air Force file.

One interesting point is that Klass, of course, criticizes some researchers for relying on the twelve-year-old memories of the controller, preferring to rely on the reports written within days of the sighting. The Condon Committee, however, noted, "One of the interesting aspects of this case is the remarkable accuracy of the account of the witness as given in the letter . . . which was apparently written from memory twelve years after the incident. There are a number of minor discrepancies, mostly a matter of figures (the C-47 at 5,000 feet was evidently actually at 4,000 feet), and he seems to have confused the identity of location C with B [as noted in his letter]; however all of the major details of his account seem to be well confirmed by the Blue Book account."

After their review of the case, the Condon Committee, which was financed by the Air Force, reported, "In conclusion, although conventional or natural explanations certainly cannot be ruled out, the probability of such seems low in this case and the probability that at least *one genuine UFO was involved* seems high."

Let's look at that conclusion again, remembering that Ed Condon, in authoring his report to the Air Force, claimed they found no evidence for UFOs. But the conclusion reached by the scientists of the Condon Committee was, ". . . the probability that at least *one genuine UFO was involved* seems high."

Hynek, in a "memorandum for record" found in the Project Blue Book files, wrote about the case, "The Lakenheath case could constitute a source of embarrassment to the Air Force, and should the facts, as so far reported, get into the public domain, it is not necessary to point out what excellent use the several dozen UFO societies and other 'publicity artists' would make of such an incident. It is, therefore, of great importance that further information on the technical aspects of the original observations be obtained, without loss of time from the original observers."

There is no evidence that anyone did any follow-up work, at least in the Blue Book files. Here is a case that, if properly researched, could have given us a great deal of information about UFOs. It contains the elements that the scientific community demands. Not only do we have the reports of the radar operators about what they were seeing on the scopes, but we have visual confirmation by other personnel including two pilots. Clearly something other than weather-related phenomena was present.

Even the Condon Committee scientists, who by the time this case arrived, were predisposed to believe that UFOs were nothing more than imagination, misidentification and illusion, wrote that there was a genuine UFO involved. I should point out here that a genuine UFO does not translate directly into extraterrestrial spacecraft.

Klass, at the end of his report about the case, wrote, "UFOlogical principal number 10: Many UFO cases seem puzzling and unexplainable simply because case investigators have failed to devote a sufficiently rigorous effort to the investigation." He added, "This is not really surprising because the vast majority of UFO investigators are persons who want to believe in extraterrestrial spaceships, either consciously or unconsciously. The larger the number of seemingly unexplainable cases, the stronger the apparent support for the extra-terrestrial hypothesis."

Except, in this case, some of the most persuasive of the arguments came from the Condon Committee scientists. They didn't want to believe at all, and in fact, had hung ridiculous explanations on some of the reports simply to have them labeled as "identified." But here, with this case, they reported it was a genuine UFO.

But the point is that Blue Book and the Air Force had this case in their hands. They were alerted as required by Air Force Regulation 200-2 demanded, and they had access to all the witnesses. At worst, some of them would have been civilians assigned to one of the bases involved. Yet there is no evidence in the Blue Book files that they followed up on the reports. There is no evidence that they cared what the facts were. Instead, someone said meteors might be in the area, and meteors became a source of the visual sightings. Someone suggested that anomalous propagation might be responsible and anomalous prop-agation became the source of the radar returns.

In fact, one writer suggested that as the objects approached the radar sites, they seemed to fade, and then came back stronger. To him, this meant anomalous propagation because this was a classic symptom of it. The targets often faded and became stronger under those circum-stances.

There is, of course, another, equally plausible explanation. Radar sites are designed so that there is little in the way of signal strength directly overhead. The radars are set up to find targets approaching and to display those targets. If the object flies directly overhead, then the signal fades and the target fades, only to come back strong on the other side, once it is out of this "cone of silence."

In other words, if a real, solid object flew over the top of the radar site, the operator could expect it to fade out and then come back. The returns on the scopes did exactly what they should have, not because they were anomalous propagation but because the target had flown over the top of the site.

What this case demonstrates, however, is that the Air Force, by the mid-1950s, had started to stick explanations on sighting reports. It made little or no difference if those sightings were explained or not. If they could sell the explanation to one another, and no one worked hard to slap them down, then that became the explanation.

This case should have been investigated with the intensity that was applied to the Florida scoutmaster case. The contrast in the investigations is staggering. In Florida, the Air Force investigators tried to find all the witnesses, they knocked on doors, checked the background of the man involved, interviewed the Boy Scouts, and took samples for testing.

At Bentwaters-Lakenheath, they took their teletype messages, checked the star charts, and let it go. There are some statements from some of the witnesses, but they take up only a few pages. No other investigation was completed. Nothing else was done. At least that is the evidence available in the Blue Book files.

McDonald, after reviewing the case, wrote, "Doesn't a UFO case like Lakenheath warrant more than a mere shrug of the shoulders from scientists?"

And to that I add, Didn't it warrant more of an investigation than that given to what is essentially a single-witness case in Florida? Here was just another of the missed opportunities in the Air Force files.

SEPTEMBER 19, 1961:

THE STRANGE CASE OF
BARNEY AND BETTY HILL

This is not going to be an argument about the legitimacy of the Hill abduction case. It is going to be a look at the Air Force attitude to the subject they were supposed to be investigating. The case file reveals some very interesting attitudes and suggests what was happening in the UFO project in 1961.

For those who are unfamiliar with the case, it began late at night as Barney and Betty Hill were heading home after a vacation. As they drove through the mountains, Betty Hill noticed a bright star near the moon. She was sure that it hadn't been there before, and she was sure that it was getting brighter. Finally, she pointed it out to Barney and he told her he thought it was nothing more than an artificial satellite.

The bright "star" intrigued them both. Several times during the next hour, they stopped. Once or twice they got out a pair of binoculars to try to see any detail behind the light. Betty was now convinced they were looking at something out of the ordinary, but Barney kept insisting that it was nothing more unusual than an airplane or a satellite, or maybe just a very bright star.

During one of the stops, Barney used the binoculars to study the light. He saw red, amber, green, and blue lights rotating around it. To

Barney it looked like an aircraft fuselage with no wings. He could hear no sound from engines. When he returned to the car, he realized that he was frightened. He didn't want Betty to know that and tried to tell her again the object was nothing more exciting than an airplane flying along the terrain.

The object swooped down and began to pace the car. Betty watched through the binoculars. She demanded that Barney stop the car but he refused for several minutes. Finally he stopped in the middle of the road and when Betty handed him the binoculars, he got out, leaving the engine running. Now he took a good look at the object, seeing for the first time that it was a large disc. Again he told Betty, "It must be a plane or something."

Although he was afraid, he stepped away from the car and began to walk across the road, toward the object. He kept walking until he was deep in the field where he could see the craft which was hovering just above the trees. Through the binoculars he could clearly see a double row of windows, and behind them were six beings. One, who Barney thought of as "the leader," wore a black leather jacket.

As he watched, five of the six turned their backs and seemed to manipulate controls. The saucer began a slow descent. Fins holding red lights spread along the craft, and something, possibly landing gear, lowered from the belly of the object.

Barney now focused on the remaining face behind the windows of the object and was overwhelmed with the feeling that he was going to be captured. He jerked the binoculars from his eyes, spun, and ran back toward Betty and the car. Shouting that they were going to be kidnapped, he threw the binoculars on the backseat and slid beneath the wheel. He slammed the car into gear and roared off as fast as possible. He ordered Betty to watch for the thing, but it had apparently disappeared.

As Barney began to calm and slow, they heard a series of strange electronic beeps. Both seemed to feel drowsy. The beeps came again and they saw a sign that told them Concord was seventeen miles. They continued home, arriving about five in the morning.

Once they reached home, they unpacked before going to bed. Betty took a bath and, according to Coral Lorenzen of APRO, who spoke to Betty many times, "for no reason whatsoever, bundled up the dress and shoes she had been wearing and shoved them into the deep recesses of her closet."

Six days after the event, Betty Hill wrote Major Donald E. Keyhoe, a writer and director of the National Investigations Committee on Aerial Phenomena (NICAP), describing what had happened to her and her husband. She also suggested that she was thinking of finding a reputable psychiatrist to perform hypnotic regression to recover memories because Barney was having trouble remembering parts of the story.

In December 1963, more than two years after they had seen the strange light, after Barney began to have stomach trouble, and after he had consulted with two different doctors, he was sent on to Dr. Benjamin Simons, a well-known and highly qualified neurosurgeon who eventually used hypnosis on both the Hills.

Under hypnosis, conducted as part of the therapy session to find a reason for the stomach trouble, Barney Hill told of what happened after they heard the first set of beeping sounds. For some reason, Barney turned down a dirt road and drove up to a roadblock where the engine quit. Several men appeared around the car who guided both the Hills through a wooded area to the craft which was sitting on the ground.

Betty Hill later described the beings as having a Mongoloid appearance with broad, flat faces, large slanting eyes, and small, flattened noses. Barney added to the description, saying that the "leader" had very large, almond-shaped eyes that seemed to wrap around to the side of his head. The mouth was a slit with a vertical line on each side. The skin, according to Betty, had a bluish gray cast to it.

According to the Betty, Barney kept his eyes closed during most of the time they were on the craft. Some researchers have suggested that this is why his tale was never as rich in detail as that told by his wife. He did, however, mention a medical examination and that he was put on a table that was too short for him.

Betty described her examination, saying that unusual instruments touched her body in various places, that samples of skin and fingernails were taken and hair was pulled from her head. A long needle was pushed into her navel. She screamed at the "examiner" and the "leader" passed a hand over her eyes, stopping the pain.

Betty communicated with the "leader" though there is no real indication that they spoke out loud. She had the impression that the "leader" was keeping the rest of the crew away from her. She was also told that she didn't have to worry about Barney, he would be all right. During the discussion, she asked where they came from, and the "leader" showed her a map but asked Betty where the sun was. When Betty failed to identify it, he told her that the map would do her no good.

Betty was then escorted from the ship and joined Barney in the car. There was the second series of beeps, and they "awakened" traveling down the road, nearing Concord.

The hypnotherapy by Dr. Benjamin Simons took several months. When it was over, Simons said that he thought the Hills were recounting a fantasy. He believed that Betty had originated the tale and shared it with Barney by telling him of her dreams. Simons believed this because Barney's account was less detailed than Betty's.

There is one additional fact. The letter that Betty wrote detailed much of the story. Later, investigators reported that Barney often sat in listening as Betty told of the experiences with them. While it may be said that Barney and Betty didn't discuss the case between themselves, Barney was always there when Betty was talking about the sighting. He certainly had plenty of opportunity to learn the details of Betty's dreams if that was, in fact, the source of the abduction portion of the sighting.

The star map that Betty saw on the craft became one point of corroboration. Marjorie Fish, an Ohio schoolteacher, spent years trying to find a pattern in the stars that matched that drawn by Betty under hypnosis. She created a three-dimensional model of our section of the galaxy and then examined it from all angles, searching for a match to that particular pattern. Her first attempts failed, but in 1972 after six years of intensive work, she finally discovered a pattern that matched what Betty Hill had drawn.

Fish discovered that the main stars in the map were Zeti I and

Zeti II Reticuli, star systems about 37.5 light-years from Earth. The map showed what might be interpreted as lines of communication. Heavy lines between the closest stars and lighter lines between those farther away. A single line connected the sun into the mix, suggesting that the sun was a relatively unimportant star.

Walter Webb, a onetime APRO consultant in Astronomy, wrote an analysis of Marjorie Fish's work. He was impressed by the fact the lines on the map, as developed by Fish, connected stars that were exclusively the type defined as suited for life. A random pattern of stars would not generate that sort of subtle, yet corroborative evidence. Webb also wrote that "the pattern happens to contain a phenomenally high percentage of all the known stars suitable for life in our solar neighborhood."

What was interesting, according to Webb, was that Fish had believed that dozens of patterns would emerge. Instead, after six years of work, she found only a single pattern that met all the criteria she had arbitrarily established. If the map was accurate, if Betty Hill remembered the map correctly, and if the details of the abduction weren't just vivid and frightening dreams, then a good clue had been found about the location of one group of alien visitors.

The Air Force never really investigated the case, according to the Project Blue Book files. Although there is a file, it is clear that the material is from magazine articles and letters. Little of it suggests any sort of Air Force investigation. But what is more important is the tone of those documents concerning the Hill case.

One of them began with, "The Hill case is closed, and has *zero* priority." But after that opening statement, it is clear the beliefs of the writer had taken over. In fact, there is a tone of hostility in the document that comes through even in its written form.

According to the document, an obvious response to the magazine article that was based on *The Interrupted Journey* by John Fuller,

1. Foreign does NOT mean foreign to Earth, it means foreign to the United States.
2. FTD is directed by AFSC at Andrews AFB, NOT the CIA. The CIA does not investigate UNIDENTIFIEDS.

3. Name ONE scientist or "astrophysicist" studying this case.

4. NICAP is not a "scientific" group.

5. Walter Webb Astronomer? Yes, No?

6. Is Hill emotionally mature?

7. Note that they withheld [sic] information and waited two days. They reported only that there was a bright star moving toward them in a northerly direction.

8. "Two Years later?" . . . Evaluated in 1961. (Info supplied to Herbert S. Taylor in 1963.)

9. Records? indicate a [sic] intensive [investigation?] Come on. We did not even bother to contact the Hills personally. Need I point out that this is exactly the problem. American citizens reported to the Air Force their UFO sighting and the Air Force attitude was to ignore it.

10. No one else saw the same object the Hills did, Who are the others???

11. Sought psychiatric help. Does this indicate emotional maturity? Actually, that is exactly what it does indicate. Barney Hill saw the psychiatrist after consulting doctors for an unrelated medical problem.

12. What are the conclusions of the Psychiatrist?

13. Who was the accredited scientific investigator who heard the tapes?

14. Final evaluations made at Wright-Patterson on the data submitted from Pease [Air Force Base] and other information from their own investigation into the matter. I thought that, according to this same letter, Records? indicate a [sic] intensive [investigation?] Come on. We did not even bother to contact the Hills personally."

15. The time motion sequence is missing in all reports. Such directions as "to the right" "up" ect (sic) have no validity. Only directions reported in azimuth and elevation have value.

16. The files are maintained at Wright-Patterson, not Pease AFB.

The obvious anger of the writer comes through on the written page. He is doing little more than attempting to assassinate the character of

Barney Hill by suggesting emotional immaturity. There is nothing in the case to suggest that either of the Hills are emotionally immature. Believing that they had seen a flying saucer does not make them immature. It might suggest that they were unable to identify a natural object, one of the planets, for example, but that is all it suggests. At the end of the statement collected by Major Paul Henderson at Pease in the days that followed the incident, he wrote in apparent contradiction of the above, "Information contained herein was collected by means of telephone conversation between the observers and the preparing individual. The reliability of the observer cannot be judged and while his apparent honesty and seriousness appears to be valid it cannot be judged at this time."

This is, in itself quite revealing. It suggests that the Hills, or in this particular case, Barney, was a sincere and honest man who was reporting what he believed to be a flying saucer. The officer listened, collected the data, and did nothing else. Please note, the Air Force investigators did nothing else.

At no point in this case am I going to argue either for a conclusion of extraterrestrial intervention or of a solution of a natural occurrence simply because it is not relevant to my point. The Air Force in September 1961 was charged with the investigation of UFO sightings. The Hills reported just such a sighting but it wasn't investigated. Instead, like so many other sightings, it was swept away once the "possible" or "probable" explanation was discovered.

On September 27, 1961, Project Blue Book officers reported,

The Barney Hill sighting was investigated by officials from Pease AFB. The case is carried as insufficient data in the Air Force files. No direction (azimuth) was reported and there are inconsistencies in the report. The sighting occurred about midnight and the object was observed for at least one hour. No specific details on maneuverability were given. The planet Jupiter was in the South West, at about 20 degrees elevation and would have set at the approximate time that the object disappeared. Without positional data the case could not be evaluated as Jupiter. There was a strong inversion in the area. The actual light source is not known. As no lateral or vertical movement was noted, the object was in all probability Jupiter. No evidence was presented to indicate that the object was due to other than natural causes.

This paragraph speaks volumes about the investigation. Before we look at that, however, we must remember one fact. Project Blue Book had a single mission. It was to investigate sightings of UFOs. Officers at other bases, as one of their additional duties, were tasked with collecting data about UFOs and forwarding those reports, in accordance with Air Force regulations, to Project Blue Book.

I point this out only to stop the argument that the Air Force had better things to do that listen to the tales told by Barney and Betty Hill. In this circumstance, that is exactly what they were tasked to do. Listen to Barney and Betty Hill.

That said, let's look at the Air Force's statement. They complain because no azimuth was given. Whose fault is that? Certainly not Barney Hill. Had the Air Force desired that information, they could have determined it. Maybe someone would have had to drive to the Hill residence, or, maybe they could have asked the Hills to come in for additional interrogation. After all, Barney Hill had already demonstrated that he would cooperate with the Air Force authorities because he had called with his sighting report.

Instead, the officer, in this case Major Henderson, forwarded incomplete data to Project Blue Book. There, they decided they didn't have enough data to solve the puzzle, so they stamped it with insufficient data, said they thought it was Jupiter, and closed the case. Apparently no one thought to pick up the telephone and see if the missing data could be recovered so that they would be able to solve the case.

Now, more than thirty-five years later, we have had books written about the Hill case. It is considered one of the best and is responsible for bringing the whole of the abduction phenomenon into the mainstream. Both Barney and Betty Hill were seen as honest individuals who were telling, frankly, an incredible story. It is clear that they had not invented the tale consciously. They were not involved in some elaborate hoax to push themselves into the spotlight. They believed what they said.

But let's think about what the Air Force could have done, especially since it was their job to do it. They could have taken the Hills back to the road and had them point out where they had seen the object. An officer could have used a compass to determine the direction to the object from the road, and he could have determined the elevation, two facts that the Air Force didn't have.

Had that been done, wouldn't the Air Force be able to say the UFO sighting was the result of Jupiter, if Jupiter was in the right position to cause the sighting? Had the Air Force done that, wouldn't a number of questions about the case have been resolved? Instead of having more than thirty-five years of speculation, wouldn't we have been able to suggest a plausible explanation for the sighting rather than slapping the "insufficient data" label on it? And, wasn't it the job of the Air Force to find solutions rather than just label cases?

In 1955, a sixty-one-year-old elementary schoolteacher reported much the same thing as the Hills. She watched an object for about an hour and a half as it seemed to pace her car. She believed that the object was tracking her and was afraid that she would be captured.

The official Blue Book file showed that "One pear shaped obj [ect], similar to [a] lightbulb, seemed to be intense blue light. Light appeared in front of observer's car. Observer stated obj [ect] was seen on all sides of her car, and believed obj [ect] was interested in capturing her and her car. Obj [ect] left with approach of dawn, disappearing behind mountain range to east."

Under comments it was noted, "Ascribe report to psychological causes of witness."

It was also noted that the witness was "apparently sincere. No publicity was given [sic] in local papers. Observers believe that object was interested in capturing her and auto and was persistent enough to stay for one and one-half to two hours, leaving only with approaching dawn. Observer is apparently intelligent but possibility of paranoiac symptoms."

This case is important because it foreshadows the Hill sighting by six years. It suggests that something other than a "viewing" of a particularly bright planet or star had happened. But the Air Force didn't bother to investigate further. They had an answer. The woman was paranoid. We all know that UFOs don't pace cars or capture people. Those who believe such things are obviously paranoid.

Had the Air Force searched their own files, as I did, they would have found this case which suggests something might be happening. Suddenly the Hills' believing they were being followed by a UFO isn't so strange. In fact, if we examine the history of UFO sightings, we find that it is a pattern that is repeated a number of times. Military and airline pilots had reported that strange craft paced their aircraft and people driving the highways had suggested UFOs had followed them. What this demonstrates is not a psychological problem, but a reported occurrence that seemed to have been missed by the Air Force investigators.

But we do see a pattern in the Air Force investigation. The schoolteacher was paranoid and therefore additional investigation was not required. The Hills were crazy, had even sought psychiatric help, and therefore additional investigation was not required. We see in the Hill file the one officer's notes about emotional maturity. He hammered that point home believing that Barney Hill was not emotionally mature.

Even if we reject the idea of alien abduction, here was a case that deserved to be reviewed. The Air Force paid lip service to the regulations, interviewed Barney Hill on the telephone, and then used the lack of investigation as proof that there was nothing to the case. After all, if it was an important case, there would have been more of an investigation by the Air Force.

What we also see in this case is the anger with which some officers approached their mission. They didn't want to be chasing flying saucers because everyone knows those things aren't real. Rather than answer the questions about the case, rather than take the time and put in the effort to learn the facts, they rejected the story as told because, to them, it was incredible. This is one of those cases that can't be true and therefore it is not true.

Again, the case itself, in this one instance, isn't important. It is the attitude of the officers who investigated it. They couldn't be troubled with doing the job they were required to do by Air Force regulation. In the end, they were able to label the case, and that is all that they really cared about. It didn't count against them because it didn't land in the "unidentified" category. All we have to do is ignore the fact that with a little effort, they might have been able to put the right label on the case. That, it seems, was too much trouble for them.

OCTOBER 2, 1961:

A DAYLIGHT DISC

At night there are many things that can fool those not familiar with the sky. Bright stars, artificial satellites, radio towers, and even the pattern of lights on an aircraft can conspire to fool even the most careful observer. During the day, the number of atmospheric phenomena that exist is reduced, and it is easier for people to identify even the unusual when the sun is out to provide additional clues.

Waldo J. Harris, a private pilot and real-estate broker from the Salt Lake City area, encountered, according to the Project Blue Book files, a natural phenomenon on October 2, 1961. Others have suggested that it was the classic daylight disc.

Harris, himself, provided a long account of the sighting. He wrote,

About noon . . . I was preparing to take off in a Mooney Mark 20A from North-South runway at Utah Central Airport when I noticed a bright spot in the sky over the southern end of the Salt Lake Valley. I began my takeoff run without paying much attention to the bright spot as I assumed that it was some aircraft reflecting the sun as it turned. After I was airborne and trimed [sic] for my climb-out I noticed that the bright spot was still about in the same position as before. I still thought it must be the sun reflecting from an airplane, so I made my turn onto my crosswind leg of the traffic pattern, and was about to turn downwind when I noticed that the spot was in the same spot still. I turned out of the pattern and proceeded toward the spot to get a better look.

As I drew nearer I could see that the object had no wings nor tail nor any other exterior control surfaces protruding from what appeared to be the fusilage [sic]. It seemed to be hovering with a little rocking motion. As it rocked up away from me I could see that it was a disc-shaped object. I would guess the diameter about 50 to 55 feet, the thickness in the middle at about 8 to 10 feet. It had the appearance of sandblasted aluminum. I could see no windows or doors or any other openings, nor could I see any landing gear doors, etc., protruding nor showing.

I believe at the closest point I was about 2 miles from the object at the same altitude, or a little above, the object. It rose abruptly about 1,000 feet above me as I closed in giving me an excellent view of the underneath side, which was exactly like the upper side as far as I could tell. Then it went off on a course of about 170 degrees for about 10 miles where it again hovered with that little rocking motion.

I again approached the object but not so closely this time when it departed on a course of about 245 degrees climbing at about 18 to 20 degrees above the horizon. It went completely out of sight in about 2 or 3 seconds. . . . I can keep our fastest jets in sight for several minutes, so you can see that this object was moving rather rapidly.

All of the time I was observing the object, after getting visual confirmation from the ground, I was describing what I had seen on radio unicom frequency. I was answering questions from the ground both from Utah Central and Provo. The voice at Provo said that they could not see the object, but at least 8 or 10 people did see it from the ground at Utah Central Airport. . . .

I was returning to the field after it had departed when I was asked over the radio if I still could see the object, and I reported that I could not. They said they had it in sight again. I turned back and saw it at much greater distance only for about a second or two when it completely vanished. The guys on the ground said it went straight up as it finally left, but I didn't see that departure.

Harris wasn't, of course, the only witness to the sighting. Air Force Project Blue Book files show that Douglas M. Crouch at Hill Air Force Base, who a year later would investigate the first part of the case of an object that flashed over central Utah to explode east of Las Vegas, reported, in accordance with AFR 200-2, what he learned. On October 9, he wrote,

At 1916Z [Greenwich Mean Time] on 2 October 1961 a report of a[n] UFO sighting was received from civilian sources at Utah Valley Airport, Salt Lake City, Utah, via Flight Operations Division, Hill AFB, Utah, and the Salt Lake City Utah Air National Guard Control Tower. Six of the eight persons [identified as Mr. and Mrs. Jay Galbraith, Clyde Card, Duane Sinclair, Robert Butler, and Russ Woods] who reported seeing the object were available and interviewed at the Central Valley Airport and tape-recorded statements obtained. All six of the persons agreed that the object had no similarity to manned aircraft, either in configuration, speed, or maneuverability. The sixth person attempted to make an interception of the object and stated he flew within three to five miles of the object before it rose rapidly, started off in an upward southerly direction, paused and then disappeared to the west at a speed believed in excess of 1,000 miles per hour. Federal Aeronautics and Utah National Guard personnel at the Salt Lake Municipal Airport were contacted and reported no radar contacts had been made with the object. Wind velocities at various altitudes in the area discounted the possibility that the object could have been a weather balloon moved rapidly at times by the wind, and no balloons released during the period locally had assumed such a direction or path. No unusual meteorological or astronomical conditions were present which might account for the sighting.

By examining all of the report made by Crouch, we can find some interesting facts. On page three of his report, in an interview with Russ Woods, it was reported that the object "had an oval shape when sun was shining on the object. When it disappeared to those watching it without binoculars, it looked to him like it was dark and more or less cigar-shaped. That the oval shape was like a football."

Although Harris reported the object moving, it seems some of those on the ground did not see it move. Instead, they observed it in different positions. Typical of that are the responses to Crouch's questions about flight path and maneuvers. One observer said, "I saw it in one position low on the horizon, and a second time it was to the right and higher, maybe eight to ten thousand feet variation. It was approximately five minutes between the two sightings."

But another of the ground observers, Jay Galbraith, told Crouch, "It was climbing and changing altitude. It seemed to go to the east for some time and hover in one position," then the last he remembered it was going west, "climbing and going west. Some of the maneuvers were at rapid speed, and some were slow. At one time it climbed quite fast, with abrupt changes of direction."

In his assessment of that witness, Crouch wrote, "[He] appears to be a logical, mature person in his early fifties, and has been a private pilot for approximately twenty years, with approximately 2,000 hours flying time. His report of the sighting was very coherent."

Still another of the observers, Robert Butler, reported that he "noticed a flight path of straight up and also to the west. Flight upward was at a rapid speed, the flight to the west was fairly slow. No abrupt change in flight."

This man, Crouch wrote, "appears to be a mature, reliable person in his early thirties, and has been working around airports for some time. He has a student pilot's license, with fifty-five flying hours, and appeared very proficient in the identification of conventional-type aircraft."

Another witness told Crouch about additional maneuvers. "It was climbing and changing altitude. It seemed to go to the east for some time and hover in one position, then the last he remembered it was going west, climbing and going west," Crouch wrote. "Some of the maneuvers were at rapid speed, and some were slow. At one time it climbed quite fast, with abrupt changes of directions."

Of Harris, the private pilot who had attempted the airborne intercept, Crouch wrote, "Harris appears to be an emotionally stable person in his late forties, and gave a consistent and coherent account of his sightings. He holds a private pilot's license and has approximately six hundred hours flying time. Fellow pilots at the airport described Harris as reliable and very truthful."

Crouch completed his investigation and submitted his final report to Project Blue Book. He wrote,

> Preliminary analysis indicates that each of the six observers interviewed were logical, mature persons, five of whom had some connection with aviation, and that each person was convinced that he had observed some tangible object not identifiable as a balloon or conventional-type aircraft. The observer who attempted interception [Harris] and reported closing within three to five miles of the object and within one thousand feet of its altitude gave a definite and coherent description of the size and shape of the reported object, and emphatically and consistently described the maneuvers and flight path of the object. No leads or clues were developed which would lead to the identity of the object or explain the sighting. . . . With the completion of this initial investigation, it is believed that all local efforts to explain the sighting and identify the object have been exhausted.

Crouch, a security specialist and a GS-9, signed the report. Charles W. Brion, an Air Force major, and the Chief, Security and Law Enforcement Division, approved it before it was sent on to Blue Book headquarters.

Within two days of Crouch's report arriving at Blue Book, unnamed "Air Force officers at the Pentagon" found a solution for the sighting. According to them, Harris and the others had seen Venus . . . or a research balloon.

Harris responded, telling reporters, "If the Pentagon thinks I have eyes good enough to see Venus at high noon, they are really off the beam. The object I saw was saucer-shaped, had a gray color, and moved under intelligent control. I got within three miles of it, and that is a lot closer than Venus is. I have seen a lot of balloons too, and this was no balloon. It just doesn't make sense for the Pentagon to make such statements."

What is interesting here is that Crouch, during his investigation, checked into the possibility of balloons being responsible for the sighting. He found no evidence of balloon launches that would place one in a location to be seen. The Air Force spokesman seemed to have overlooked the fact that the object was observed by witnesses on the ground who used binoculars. All of these facts rule out the conventional balloons and the old standby of Venus. This is just another example of the Air Force reaching into the grab bag and pulling out an answer. That it didn't fit the facts, as discovered by their own investigators, seems to be irrelevant to them. They can announce a solution and get back to their "real" work.

Venus, of course, would have been a physical impossibility. Harris, while attempting to intercept, saw the object against the backdrop of the mountains. Venus might be visible near the horizon during the day, but certainly not below it at any time. Venus, as a culprit, was eliminated if we accept the testimony provided by Harris.

The Air Force gave up on Venus and the weather balloons, probably because such explanations had already been overworked by 1961. But they did come up with an explanation that satisfied them. The witnesses had seen a sun dog.

In the final summary of the case, the Air Force officers wrote,

Sun at time and date of this sighting was in a direction coincident with that reported for UFO. UFO was reported to be at elevation of approx. 22 degrees above horizon while absolute elev. of sun f [rom] Salt Lake area was 46 degrees 59' 42" at time of sighting. This would put obj[ec]t at approx. 24 degrees below sun. It is noted that weather conditions at time of sighting indicate high cirrus clouds. Cirrus clouds are associated with ice crystals at 22 a half degrees and sometimes 45 degrees from sun. All indications in this case are directed toward obj[ec]t being a sun dog.

It is significant that witnesses on the ground observed obj[ec]t to be stationary while airborne witnesses indicate motion—probably his own. There is no available evidence which would indicate the objt of sighting was not a sun dog.

No available evidence which would indicate the object of the sighting was not a sun dog? Did I miss something in the case file, which I have read? There is nothing in the file to suggest high cirrus clouds. Nothing. Instead we are told that "visibility was forty miles with ceiling unlimited. . . ." In another part of the report, Crouch wrote, "Woods stated the weather was clear with no cloud cover, and there was very little surface wind."

In still another part of the report, Crouch wrote that one witness said "The weather was bright and clear with no clouds, and that there was very little wind."

And another of the witnesses said, "Clear in every quadrant, with little surface wind."

What this tells me is that there were no clouds, not even the high cirrus clouds that can indicate ice in the air. There is absolutely no evidence of clouds, based on the witnesses' statements who were on the field at the time of the sighting.

This overlooks the fact that none of the descriptions of the object resembles a sun dog. Harris, in his initial statement had suggested that the craft he saw was between thirty-five and fifty feet in diameter and about four feet thick, possibly thicker in the center. Later he would amend the dimensions, suggesting it was fifty to fifty-five feet in diameter and eight to ten feet thick.

Skeptics would seize on this change in the dimensions and suggest that some sort of hoax was being perpetuated. Of course that theory breaks down when the testimony of the other witnesses is brought in. They were respectable citizens who had no reason to lie about this. Therefore, it is reasonable to conclude that an object was seen in the sky. The sighting was of something real and the change in Harris's dimensions of the craft are irrelevant trivia.

The point is that Harris, and the others, are not describing something that is a glow of light that is related by the sun reflecting from, or through, ice crystals in the air. And, there were those on the ground who looked at the object through binoculars. A sun dog seen through binoculars would remain a sun dog. It would not be resolved into something that looked like a metallic craft.

And, I had selected from the various interviews that Crouch submitted to Blue Book, those in which the witnesses on the ground reported movement. In other words, the Air Force claim that "it is significant that witnesses on the ground observed the object to be stationary . . ." is simply not true. They did see it move.

Finally, the witnesses both on the ground and in the air were pilots or associated with aviation. If one or more of them were unfamiliar with sun dogs, surely one of them would have recognized it as such. The Air Force, however, ignored all this information and invented ice crystals and cirrus clouds so that they could invent an answer.

There is one final, disturbing aspect to this case. In many of the files I have found "galley proofs" from one or more debunking books all authored by Dr. Donald H. Menzel. In this case it is Donald Menzel's *World of Flying Saucers*. Although I'm not sure why the Air Force went out of its way to get the galley proofs from Menzel's books, it might be that it validated their own ridiculous conclusions.

Menzel and coauthor Lyle G. Boyd wrote, "Since the ground observers remained in one place, their position relative to the sun dog did not change and it seemed to remain stationary. The pilot, however, was in a moving plane and changing his position relative to the UFO; hence it seemed to move rapidly away from him. . . . The angular distance between the sun and the UFO was exactly that to be expected between the sun and mock sun, at that time and place."

But again, that analysis is not based on the witnesses' testimony. To reject what the witnesses say, there must be some persuasive evidence presented for that rejection. Neither the Air Force nor Menzel and Boyd presented any such evidence. They just rejected the testimony, drew the conclusions they wanted based on their opinions, and continued to suggest an answer.

Dr. James E. McDonald, the atmospheric physicist with the University of Arizona, didn't believe the sun dog solution. He wrote,

The altitude of the noon sun at Salt Lake City that day was about 40 degrees, and sun dogs, if there had been any, would have occurred to the right and left at essentially the same annular altitude, far above the position in the sky where Harris and others saw the objects hovering. Furthermore, the skies were almost cloudless [or completely cloudless according to the witnesses], the observers emphasized. This case is just one more of hundreds of glaring examples of casually erroneous Bluebook [sic] explanations put out by untrained men and passed on to the press and public by PIOs who are equally untrained and cannot recognize elementary scientific absurdities when they see them. Yet this kind of balderdash has left the bulk of the public with the impression that UFOs can't exist because the Air Force has disproved virtually all the reports they've ever received.

What McDonald is pointing out is that Project Blue Book was not in the business of investigating UFO sightings. They were to resolve them, slapping a label on them regardless of the facts. The campaign was successful because of the localized nature of the reports. When the answer was offered, it was published in Salt Lake City. Those involved, the witnesses, knew that the answer was ridiculous, but to others, who didn't know the facts and who didn't know the witnesses, such an explanation sounded plausible. It was accepted.

When I begin to examine the case files, I find that same thing over and over. An explanation is offered, it is ridiculous when the facts are examined, but it is accepted. The image is of an Air Force doing the job it is paid to do. In reality, that simply was not the case.

SEPTEMBER 4, 1964:

IS A BENT ARROW PHYSICAL EVIDENCE?

The Air Force received some very strange cases while Project Blue Book was in operation. They investigated some of them, offering explanations that were less than accurate. Others they avoided by suggesting psychological problems had manifested themselves. In nearly every case involving the sighting of occupants, or aliens, or creatures from the interior of the craft, the preferred answer was a suggestion of psychological aberration.

The witness in this case, who wishes that his name not be used (though I have been able to find it by searching the files carefully), said that he, with two friends, headed into the mountains in the Cisco Grove area of California to do some hunting with bow and arrow. They set up their camp, and then, late in the evening, split up. The witness lost his way, and realizing that he would not be able to find the camp that night, decided that he would have to remain where he was overnight.

Like many hunters who have found themselves alone in the wilderness at night, he decided that he would sleep in a tree. It raised him off the ground where the animals of the night scurried. Sitting in the tree, he noticed a white light in the distance. Believing it to be a searchlight from a helicopter, possibly flown by rescuers, the witness climbed from his perch, and started three fires on the large rocks near him. He hoped to draw the attention of whomever was piloting the aircraft and apparently he was successful. The light turned and began flying toward him. Only after it neared did he realize there was no sound from it. That was when he began to get scared, according to the story he told later.

The light hovered between two trees, some fifty or sixty yards away. He could see three glowing, rectangular panels, set on the vertical in a stepping-down pattern. The lights seemed to circle around until they were no more than fifty feet away. There was a flash from the middle panel, and something came out of it. It fell down the hill, landing on a bush. The witness believed that whatever had fallen was now on the ground, down the hill a short distance from him.

There was a scrambling around, a crashing, that came from the bushes, and a humanoid figure emerged from the darkness. It wore a light-colored, silver, or whitish uniform with bellows at the elbows and knees. The eyes were large and dark and looked like welder's goggles. It seemed to be doing something on the ground, and before long was joined by a second, similar-appearing creature. The two entities worked their way toward the tree and were soon standing at the base, looking up at the witness.

While the first object, or rather the lights, continued to hover, the thrashing noise began in another part of the forest. Along the ridge he could see big glowing spots that reminded him of two flashlights hooked together. Finally he could see it was another being of some kind because those lights were bright enough for him to see the face. He described it as square and metallic with a hinged mouth that hung open. This alien was about five feet tall, just slightly taller than the humanoids that the witness had seen earlier at the base of his tree.

The metallic being, a robot of some kind, joined the two humanoids at the base of the tree and stood staring up at him. Eventually the robot walked over to one of the fires, swept an arm through it and then walked back to the humanoids. It put its hand to its mouth and a white vapor came out, drifting upward, toward the witness. He gasped for breath, and then lost consciousness, falling across his bow, which kept him in the tree.

When he regained consciousness, he believed just minutes later, he was sick to his stomach. Convinced that the beings wanted to capture him, he decided he was going to fight. First he lighted a book of matches and tossed it down. When the entities backed up, he set his hat on fire and threw it down. This forced them back farther, but when the fires began to die, the beings came forward again.

Now he started lighting everything he could and throwing it down, hoping to set the ground cover on fire. He eventually burned everything in his pockets and the camouflage clothes he wore until he was left in a T-shirt, jeans, and his shoes. But the fires kept the beings away from him for a few minutes.

With nothing left to do, the witness resorted to his bow. He pulled it back as far as he could and let an arrow fly at the metallic creature. The tip hit with a flash like an arc of electricity. The witness fired all three of the arrows he had with him. Each time he hit the robot, it was pushed back, with a flash of bluish light.

But he had quickly run out of arrows. He climbed higher in the tree, and tied himself to the trunk with his belt. The robot let loose with another cloud of vapor and the witness passed out again. When he came to, the two humanoids were trying to climb the tree. When one of them began to make any progress, the witness would shake the tree as violently as he could. They would scramble down, apparently unaware of what had happened.

This pattern went on for a period of time. The robotic creature would emit a mist, the witness would lose consciousness and then awaken to find the humanoids trying to climb to him. He'd then shake the tree, and they'd get down.

Finally he began breaking branches from the tree to throw at them. He tossed the change in his pocket, his canteen, and anything else he could find, trying to distract them. The pattern kept up through the night with the witness once howling like the coyotes, hoping the creatures would think there was more of him around.

A second robot had joined the group during the night, and just before dawn, stood face-to-face with the other robot. "Arc flashes" passed between them, lighting up the area. A fog was generated by the "conversation," which rose slowly. The witness blacked out again and when he awakened, he was hanging by his belt and all the creatures, both metallic and humanoid, had disappeared.

With the creatures gone, and no sign of the lights that seemed to have brought them, the witness climbed down from the tree. He recovered the things he'd thrown in the night and found the arrows he'd shot at the robot. Only the coins from his pockets were missing. (Though I confess I don't know what kind of hunter travels into the bush with coins in his pocket.)

One of the witness's friends eventually wrote—to NICAP investigator Paul Cerny who did the best work on this case—that,

> I was the one that found [the witness] as he was heading towards camp. The nights have been very cold, and all he had on at the time . . . was a thin cotton tee shirt and his pants. He was weak and exhausted. . . . I helped him to camp, fixed some soup for him and put him to sleep. He kept on saying that he would have been all right if they had left him alone. I didn't know what he meant so we let him sleep. He slept for about six hours. When he awoke, we asked him how he felt. He said fine. Then he said, "Turn on the radio . . . there may be something on the news about the spaceship I saw." The news did say something about a light in the sky. I also saw the light as I was working my way thru the canyon to camp. (I got lost too that night.) We asked him what had happened to his clothes and then he told us his experiences . . .

There were a number of investigations of the case by both official organizations and private groups. APRO researchers were among the first to interview the witness. According to Coral Lorenzen, writing in *Flying Saucer Occupants*, "We learned about this particular incident quite by chance through rumors in the Sacramento area, and notified Dr. James Harder, one of APRO's advisors."

The first account of the witness's tale appeared in the July-August

1966 issue of the *APRO Bulletin*. The witness received a copy of that report and noted many inaccuracies in it.

The day after the events, the witness's mother-in-law phoned Victor W. Killick, an astronomer, and told him the extraordinary tale. The story didn't seem all that interesting to Killick, but he asked for additional details. At that point the witness was put on the phone and outlined what had happened. Killick decided that the story was interesting enough that he wanted to meet the man and arranged an interview for September 8.

Impressed with the story, and the sincerity of the witness, Killick wrote to Mather Air Force Base, telling officers there, "As far as my contact with them goes, these people all appear to be in good health and rational. The family believes the man's story. They told me that when he got home he was 'as pale as a sheet,' and badly shaken up. I did a little probing to try to find an ulterior motive without success."

On September 25, according to the tale, a colonel and a master sergeant from the intelligence office at McClellan Air Force Base interviewed the witness. In reality, it seems, according to the Blue Book file, that it was a captain named McCloud and a Senior Master Sergeant R. Barnes, who conducted the interview. The real point is not the ranks of the individuals, but that someone with an official standing from the Air Force did, in fact, interview the witness.

In their report, they wrote, "Mr. [name blanked in original] is a local resident and . . . married and recently employed at a local missile production plant. He appears stable and consistent in telling his story and believes that the [events] occurred as described."

Before the Air Force personnel left, the witness provided them with a map of the area and one of the arrowheads, which they promised to return. It should be noted that he never received the arrowhead back, and it should also be noted that the Air Force had forwarded it to the University of Colorado UFO project, that is, the Condon Committee, for analysis.

The Air Force eventually solved this case, at least to their satisfaction. According to them, after abandoning their attempts to convince the witness he had seen either Japanese tourists or teenage pranksters, the witness had seen "owls and/or other mundane creatures of the woods" and let his imagination supply the rest of the details. It was, in effect, a retreat to the "psychological" category.

Yet there seems to be evidence that the Air Force took a more active interest in the case than they let on. According to the witness, about a month after the sighting, he, along with his brother and his two hunting companions returned to the scene of the standoff. It appeared to them that someone had "raked over" the area. They found cigarette butts from many different brands, along with cigar butts scattered. Other than that, the area appeared to have been cleared, although the site was remote and inaccessible.

Paul Cerny, the NICAP field investigator, was brought in when the witness's wife wrote to the organization's national headquarters. Cerny interviewed the witness in July 1965 and was given the remaining two arrowheads. Analysis, however, revealed nothing. It had been hoped that metal from the robot might have become embedded on the arrowhead, but nothing was found. Cerny said that there had been a platinum-colored smear on one of the blades, but it was possible that it had been worn off or dislodged during transit.

Cerny, who stayed in contact with the witness and his family long after the event was over, was impressed with his sincerity and sanity. In fact, in November 1995, Cerny added an "epilogue" to the case. In a boxed addition to an article in the *International UFO Reporter,* Cerny wrote,

Having just reviewed the case files on this fascinating and unusual encounter, there is absolutely no doubt in my mind that this incident is factual and authentic. I have spent considerable time and many visits with the main witness, and along with the testimony of the other witnesses, I can rule out any possibility of a hoax. This also includes the involvement of the USAF investigation team.

The psychological effects on [the witness] were extremely convincing and traumatic due to the aftereffects of his experience. Also noteworthy were the unusual detail, proximity, and reactions of the Alien Crew.

What is most surprising in this case is the fact that the Air Force actually investigated. For the most part, they managed to stay away from reports involving the occupants from the crafts. In the Barney and Betty Hill case, Blue Book almost refused to acknowledge its existence. Then, in the file, noted that officers at Pease Air Force Base conducted the investigation which was a telephone call to Barney Hill, or rather, the results of a call from Hill. The entire file is made up of little other than magazine articles and newspaper clippings.

In August 1955, the Sutton family in the Kelly-Hopkinsville area of southern Kentucky, reported that their farmhouse had been assaulted by small alien creatures. The siege lasted through the night with the men shooting at the small beings with shotguns. Eventually the family deserted the farmhouse and drove to the sheriff's office to tell the tale. Because a UFO had been seen, and because the creatures were apparently alien, there were those who believed that Project Blue Book would be involved in the investigation.

But, according to the case file, Project Blue Book did not investigate. They had no real interest in the sighting, although the Blue Book files do contain documents that suggest one active-duty officer, and possibly more, did some sort of investigation. This one was "unofficial."

Without any sort of physical evidence, or proof that the Kelly-Hopkinsville tale was true, most people were quite skeptical. The media reflected that attitude. The Air Force, though still claiming there was no investigation, issued two statements. The Air Force told all that they were not investigating the case and that there was no basis for investigating it. In other words, the case was so unimportant that the Air Force wasn't going to waste its time or limited resources on a family of "hicks" who thought that alien beings had landed near their farmhouse and attacked them through the night.

Although it seems that military personnel, from Fort Campbell, Kentucky did visit the house, and interviews with the Sutton family were conducted in 1955, an investigation by the Air Force didn't take place until two years later. According to Project Blue Book files, apparently, in August 1957, prior to the publication of a magazine article that would review the case, someone decided they should "investigate."

In a letter from the ATIC at Wright-Patterson, to the commander of Campbell Air Force Base, Wallace W. Elwood wrote, "1. This Center requests any factual data, together with pertinent comments regarding an unusual incident reported to have taken place six miles north of Hopkinsville, Kentucky, on subject date [21 August 1955]. Briefly, the incident involved an all-night attack on a family named Sutton by goblin-like creatures reported to have emerged from a so-called 'flying saucer.' "

Later in the letter, Elwood wrote, "3. Lacking factual, confirming data, no credence can be given this almost fantastic report. As the incident has never been officially reported to the Air Force, it has not taken official cognizance of the matter."

The matter was assigned to First Lieutenant Charles N. Kirk, an Air Force officer at Campbell Air Force Base. He apparently spent about six weeks investigating the case before sending the material on to ATIC on October 1, 1957. He researched the story using the Hopkinsville newspaper from August 22, 1955, and September 11, 1955. He also had a letter from Captain Robert J. Hertell, a statement from Glennie Lankford [the matriarch of the Sutton family] and a statement given to Kirk by Major John E. Albert [who unofficially investigated the case in 1955] and a copy of an article written by Glennie Lankford.

Albert's statement provides some interesting information. Remember, the Air Force was claiming that the case had not been officially reported and therefore the Air Force had not investigated. It seems that here we get lost in the semantics of the situation and the question that begs to be asked is, What the hell does all that mean?

It sounds suspiciously like a police officer who, seeing a robbery in progress, then ignores it because it hasn't been reported to the station and he wasn't dispatched by headquarters. A police officer can't ignore the crime and it seems reasonable to assume that the Air Force shouldn't have ignored this case. The sighting was reported in the media including the radio. Newspapers from various locations around the country were reporting what had happened on that hot August night. Although the Air Force officers at Blue Book or ATIC must have known that the sighting had been made, they chose to ignore it. If the sighting wasn't reported through official channels, then it didn't exist. Since no one reported this case through official channels, the sighting never happened.

Or is that the case? Lieutenant Kirk, in his report in 1957, sent a copy of the statement made by Major John E. Albert on September 26, 1957, on to ATIC. The very first paragraph seems to suggest that notification was made to Campbell Air Force Base which should have, according to regulations in effect at that time (1955), reported it in official channels. The regulation is quite clear on the point and it doesn't matter if everyone in the military believed the sighting to be a hoax, a hallucination, or the real thing, it should have been investigated.

That investigation would not have been conducted by ATIC and Project Blue Book but by the 4602d Air Intelligence Service Squadron. The version of AFR 200-2 in effect at the time, tells us exactly what should have happened to the report. It should have been passed on to the 4602d. If that was the case, it apparently disappeared there.

In the statement, Albert said,

On about August 22, 1955, about 8 A.M., I heard a news broadcast concerning an incident at Kelly Station, approximately six miles north of Hopkinsville. At the time I heard this news broadcast, I was at Gracey, Kentucky, on my way to Campbell Air Force Base, where I am assigned for reserve training. I called the Air Base and asked them if they had heard anything about an alleged flying saucer report. They stated that they had not and it was suggested that as long as I was close to the area, that I should determine if there was anything to this report. I immediately drove to the scene at [Kelly] [for some reason the word was blacked out, but it seems reasonable to assume the word is Kelly] Station and located the home belonging to a [Mrs. Glennie Lankford] [again the name is blacked out], who is the one who first reported the incident. (A copy of Mrs. Lankford's statement is attached to this report).

Albert's statement continued,

Deputy Sheriff Batts was at the scene where this supposedly flying saucer had landed and he could not show any evidence that any object had landed in the vicinity. There was nothing to show that there was anything to prove this incident.

Mrs. Lankford was an impoverished widow woman who had grown up in this small community just outside of Hopkinsville, with very little education. She belonged to the Holy Roller Church and the night and evening of this occurrence, had gone to a religious meeting and she indicated that the members of the congregation and her two sons and their wives and some friends of her son, were also at this religious meeting and were worked up into a frenzy, becoming emotionally unbalanced and that after the religious meeting, they had discussed this article which she had heard about over the radio and had sent for them from the Kingdom Publishers, Fort Worth 1, Texas, and they had sent her this article with a picture which appeared to be a little man when it actually was a monkey, painted silver. This article had to be returned to Mrs. Lankford as she stated it was her property. However, a copy of the writing is attached to this statement and if it is necessary, a photograph can be obtained from the above-mentioned publishers.

There are a number of problems with the first couple of paragraphs of Albert's statement, but those are trivial. As an example, it wasn't Glennie Lankford who first reported the incident, but the whole family who had traveled into town to alert the police.

The third paragraph, however, is filled with things that bear no resemblance to reality. Lankford was not a member of the Holy Rollers, but was, in fact a member of the Trinity Pentecostal Church. Neither she, nor any of the family, had been to any religious service the night of the "attack." She couldn't have heard about any article on the radio because there was no radio in the farmhouse. And there was no evidence that Lankford ever sent anywhere for any kind of article about flying saucers and little creatures. In other words, Albert had written the case off, almost before his "investigation" began because of his false impressions. Apparently he was only interested in facts that would allow him to debunk the case and not in learning what had happened during the night.

Further evidence of this is provided in the next paragraph of his statement. "It is my opinion that the report [by] Mrs. Lankford or her son, Elmer Sutton, was caused by one of two reasons. Either they actually did see what they thought was a little man and at the time, there was a circus in the area and a monkey might have escaped, giving the appearance of a small man. Two, being emotionally upset, and discussing the article and showing pictures of this little monkey, that appeared like a man, their imaginations ran away with them and they really did believe what they saw, which they thought was a little man."

It is interesting to note that Albert is not suggesting that the witnesses were engaged in inventing a hoax. Instead, with absolutely no evidence, Albert invented the tale of a monkey that fooled the people. That does not explain how the monkey was able to survive the shots fired at it by the terrified people in the house, especially if it was as close to the house as the witnesses suggested. In other words, with shotguns and rifles being fired at the little man, someone should have hit it and there should have been broken bits of monkey all over the farmland.

But Albert wasn't through with the little-monkey theory. "The home that Mrs. Lankford lived in was in a very run-down condition and there were about eight people sleeping in two rooms. The window that was pointed out to be the one that she saw the small silver shining object about two and a half feet tall, that had its hands on the screen looking in, was a very low window and a small monkey could put his hands on the top of it while standing on the ground."

The final sentence of Albert's account said, "It is felt that the report cannot be substantiated as far as any actual object appearing in the vicinity at that time." It was then signed by Kirk, who was reviewing everything for the Air Force.

What is interesting is that Albert, and then Kirk, were willing to ignore the report of the object because there was nothing to substantiate it. But, they were willing to buy the monkey theory, though there was nothing to substantiate it, either. They needed "a little man" for the family to see and they created one because a "monkey might have escaped."

Glennie Lankford might have inspired the little-monkey story with her own statement. In a handwritten statement signed on August 22, 1955, she wrote,

> My name is Glennie Lankford age 50 and I live at Kelly Station, Hopkinsville Route 6, Kentucky.
>
> On Sunday night Aug 21, '55, about 10:30 P.M. I was walking through the hallway which is located in the middle of my house and I looked ou[t] the back door (south) and saw a bright silver object about two and a half feet tall appearing round. I became excited and did not look at it long enough to see if it had any eyes or move. I was about 15 or 20 feet from it. I fell backward, and then was carried into the bedroom.
>
> My two sons, Elmer Sutton aged 25 and his wife Vera age 29, J. C. Sutton age 21 and his wife Aline age 27 and their friends Billy Taylor age 21 and his wife June, 18 were all in the house and saw this little man that looked like a monkey.

So the Air Force seized on her description and turned it into a possible solution, suggesting, with no justification, that the Suttons had been attacked by a horde of monkeys which were immune to shotguns. They overlooked the evidence of the case, dispatched someone to look into it unofficially, and then denied that they had investigated.

That was the pattern they would follow with almost every case in which alien beings were reported. If you saw the creatures, then clearly you had psychological problems. The exception that proves the rule is, of course, the Lonnie Zamora landing case from Socorro, New Mexico, in 1964.

Keeping with their tradition of labeling cases but not solving them, the Air Force officers, as they had done in the Kelly-Hopkinsville case, decided that the Cisco Grove witness had psychological problems.

There is no need to investigate if the witness is unreliable. Can we say that we are surprised with the cavalier way they treated the evidence, that is, the arrowhead, passing it along and then losing it? Can we say that we're surprised with the way they handled the investigation considering the track record they had already established? Can we say that we're surprised with their conclusion, considering their belief that UFOs don't exist and if you see the creatures from one, then you must be psychologically disturbed?

The Cisco Grove occupant report is just one more example of an opportunity that was missed. Or rather, one that seems to have been missed. What we don't know is who had been out in the forest cleaning the area in which the witness claimed to have seen the alien beings. Just who could have done that?

APRIL 17, 1966:

THE *CLOSE ENCOUNTERS* CHASE

At the beginning of the film, *Close Encounters of the Third Kind*, a number of police officers, in their cruisers, chase lights across Indiana. It is a funny variation on the cops and robbers movies that always require a car chase. And what is more interesting is that it is based on fact. The chase happened on the early morning hours of Sunday, April 17, 1966, in eastern Ohio and western Pennsylvania.

The Air Force would investigate and, of course, find a mundane explanation for the sightings. They would claim that the photographs submitted of the objects were nothing more than processing flaws on the negatives. They would attribute part of the sighting to an artificial satellite. And, they would attribute the rest to that old standby, Venus. On the Project Record Card, there is a handwritten note initialed by J. Allen Hynek. He wrote simply, "Do not agree."

As you read the account, remember how the Air Force explained the sightings. Remember that their investigation consisted of a couple of telephone calls to talk to the deputies involved, Dale Spaur and Wilbur Neff, and that no one from Wright-Patterson Air Force Base bothered to visit in person until forced to do so by congressional interest. And, remember that this all took place in Ohio. Yes, Wright-

Patterson is at one end of the state and Portage County at the other, almost as far away as possible and still remain in Ohio. But it is in Ohio and at the time the Air Force, by regulation, was supposed to investigate UFO sightings, especially those of a multiple-witness nature when the witnesses were police officers.

Portage County Deputy Sheriff Dale F. Spaur was teamed with Wilbur "Barney" Neff, an auxiliary deputy, on the early morning of April 17. They were at the scene of an accident just east of Cleveland where a driver had slammed into a utility pole. They were there at 4:45 A.M., talking to the repairman, and listening as radio traffic between Portage and Summit counties described some strange events. A woman in Akron had called to say that a bright object "as big as a house" had flown over the neighborhood at an amazingly low altitude. No one in any of the police or sheriff's departments took the call seriously, including Spaur and Neff.

Not long after that, having left the accident scene, about three miles from Randolph, they passed an old truck on the side of the road. They pulled in behind it and walked toward it. Spaur glanced over his right shoulder and saw a moving light visible through the trees at the top of a small hill. He pointed it out to Neff, thinking, "That must be the UFO that's been talked about."

The object continued moving toward them, coming from the west, climbed, turned to the right, and flew over the road. It stopped, hovering only fifty to a hundred feet in the air. The object was oval-shaped and gave off a brilliant blue-white light that caused Spaur's eyes to water. He told Air Force investigators, "The only shape was the roundness of it, unperfect circle, egg-shaped, almost oblong, but not real oblong." Whenever it moved, it tipped toward the direction it was going.

Spaur told the Air Force, "[It] didn't have a red light. No wind. When it came over us it lighted the whole area. The ground was lighted by this object. Like looking at an arc welder, blue-white light. The only sound heard was humming sound like a power transformer, no thrust like a jet. No sudden surge of power."

Without saying a word to one another, both deputies broke for the car. Spaur, according to the Air Force file: "We ran back and had a camera. Kept under surveillance till it could be possibly photographed. Those were our instructions after we had called in."

Spaur cautiously drove toward the object. He had a better view of it and thought the craft was about twenty feet thick and about thirty-five to forty-five feet in diameter. The UFO began to drift away from them, climbing to five hundred feet and speeding up. Soon the chase was reaching speeds over eighty miles an hour. Spaur, apparently using his speedometer as a guide told the Air Force officers, "Object was first going eighty to eight-three miles an hour."

Remember, as we discuss, the descriptions that have been given by Spaur. At no point has he suggested a light in the night sky. He is not speaking of a tiny source, but a large one that is lighting the ground as it flies over. Keep that in mind as we find out what the Air Force officers concluded at the end of their telephonic investigation.

They chased the object, using the roads available to them. At one point it crossed the road in front of the patrol car, the light so bright that Spaur told his fellow deputies that he didn't need his headlights. It passed over a construction site near Atwater Center, and illuminated the heavy equipment parked there.

At the Berlin Reservoir in Mahoning County, the object climbed to a thousand feet and crossed the highway once again. Spaur was still on Highway 224, chasing the object at speeds now approaching a hundred miles an hour. Still the object maintained the same distance between the police car and itself.

The chase continued, heading toward Pennsylvania. The UFO, now on the left side of the road, was beginning to pull away. It swung around, to the south, and flew over the road once again.

With the sun rising, Spaur got a better look at the object's structure. He said it had a domelike top surface, an antenna or "finlike" device that was about eighteen feet long and about a foot wide at the base, jutting up from the rear-center. He was describing what he'd seen on the craft that was clearly more substantial than a point of light.

Patrolman H. Wayne Huston, listening to the radio traffic, realized that the chase was coming toward him. Using the radio, he conferred with Spaur, and said that he would join him when he got close to East Palestine, Ohio. In a statement made eight days later, he said, "I saw the thing when Dale was about five miles away from me . . . It was running down Route 14, about eight to nine hundred feet up when it came by. That was the lowest I ever saw it."

Huston told investigators, "As it flew by, I was standing by my cruiser. I watched it go right overhead. It was shaped something like an ice cream cone, with a sort of partly melted-down top. I don't know whether the bottom was solid or not. It might have been like a search-light beam, coming to a point, but it was so bright I would say it was brighter than the sun when it came up. . . ."

He continued, "Spaur and Neff came down the road right after it. I fell in behind them. We were going eighty to eighty-five miles an hour, a couple of times to around a hundred and five miles an hour. At one point at least, I was almost on Spaur's bumper, and we checked with each other what we saw. It was right straight ahead of us, a half to three-fourths of a mile ahead."

He finished his statement. "I am familiar enough with Rochester [Pennsylvania] and I guided him [Spaur] because I couldn't pass him in Bridgewater to lead him. At Brady's Run Park, a car started to come out, hit the traffic light treadle, and some trucks were there. We had to slow down and lost sight of it. We came on down Route 51. Just after we came out of the railroad underpass in Bridgewater, coming out of Fallston, we spotted it again, and then in front of them again we turned to Rochester."

Another police officer, Frank Panzanella, who had just finished his morning coffee, was driving up a hill. To his right, he saw a shiny object that he thought was a reflection from an aircraft. He told Air Force investigators, "I got to Mickey's Lounge on the top of the hill and I looked back and it wasn't moving so I turned the police car around and came back down Eleventh Street and went to Adamoski Service Station on Tenth Street and Route Sixty-five. I then got out of the police car and looked at the object again. I rubbed my eyes three or four times but didn't say anything to anyone for the time being. I saw two other patrol cars pull up and the officers got out and asked me if I saw it. I replied, 'SAW WHAT!' They pointed to the object and I told them I had been watching it for the last ten minutes. The object was the shape of a half of football, was very bright and about twenty-five to thirty-five feet in diameter. The object then moved out towards Harmony Township approximately [at] one thousand feet high, then it stopped, then went straight up real fast to about thirty-five hundred feet."

At this point there were four police officers directly involved. Each described the object in a similar fashion and if the estimates of the size don't match exactly, it's not that important. What is important is that the police officers could see the moon with Venus to its right. The UFO was to the left. And, once again, they were not describing a point of light, but a solid object.

At some point during the sighting, the chief of the Mantua, Ohio, police, Gerald Buchert, headed out in search of the object. He found it, or believed that he had. He watched it for fifteen or twenty minutes as it seemed to move erratically in the sky. Using a small camera with black-and-white film, he took a number of pictures of the object he was seeing.

It seems obvious, from the description provided in his statement, that Chief Buchert was looking at, and attempting to photograph, Venus. When someone stares at a point source of bright light in the darkened sky, normal movement of the eyeball, called autokinesis, gives the impression of rapid, erratic movement. The fact that the object was a point source of light and remaining stationary suggests it was not the object being chased by the police and deputies in other locations.

Analysis of the photographs, submitted to Project Blue Book, produced little of value. Major Hector Quintanilla, Jr., then chief of Blue Book, wrote to Buchert on April 25, 1966. In the letter, he said, "The most probable cause of the object which you were trying to photograph was the planet Venus and this was the reason that you were unable to photograph it with your camera. In order to photograph Venus, you would have to photograph it with a time exposure. This cannot be done with the type of camera you were using. Thank you for your cooperation and your interest in this matter."

Overlooking the condescending attitude shown in the letter, complete with a lecture on the proper way to photograph Venus with a small handheld camera, it seems reasonable to accept that analysis. The Chief saw Venus. Had he had a better camera and better film, he might have gotten a good picture. I took one of Venus near Sierra Vista, Arizona that is beautiful because of the colors of the rising sun. And no, I held the camera in my hand and didn't make a time exposure. I just used a faster, color film.

There is another aspect of the case that is puzzling as well. There are police officers who suggest that the Air Force attempted to intercept the object. Panzanella called the Rochester Police and spoke to radio operator John Beighey. He suggested Beighey alert the Greater Pittsburgh Airport about the sightings, apparently believing that the Reserve unit or National Guard unit there would be able to intercept the unknown. A short time after he made the suggestion, Panzanella saw what he thought was a vapor trail in the west. Someone came over the radio and said that the interception was in progress. At that point, the UFO shot high into the sky and disappeared.

Although Panzanella had decided to wait where he was while the Ohio police officers headed home, he was told by Beighey that someone at the Air Force office in Pittsburgh wanted to interview the witnesses. There was also some discussion about an overheard remark, that someone at the airport had said the object was on the screen, meaning that it was being tracked by the airport's radar.

Panzanella, headed out, red light flashing, and caught up with the other officers, that is, Spaur, Neff, and Huston. He told them that the Air Force wanted to interview them.

Another police officer, Henry Kwaitanowski, who had been listening to the discussion between Panzanella and Beighey, was standing near his patrol car when he spotted jets flying away from him. He thought they looked more like commercial aircraft than fighters, but behind them he saw a shiny, football-shaped object that he thought was about the same size and altitude as the jets.

There are other hints that an interception might have taken place. According to a statement made by police officer Lonny Johnson (who was teamed with Ray Esterly),

> We went to Prospect Street partway down the hill, when we saw the object in the distance at an elevation of approximately 25 degrees, estimated altitude 10,000–20,000 feet. . . . Actually, first

we saw one jet, then the object in front of it. We could see the jet, the exhaust space, and the contrail. The jet seemed at the same altitude of the object, going southeast. The jet seemed to be pursuing the object. While we watched, for an estimated time of no more than two minutes, we saw two more jets coming from behind, in the same direction. These two had arcing contrails, either down or curved horizontally. The object was ([according to] Esterly) less than three or even ([according to] Johnson) 1 mile(s) away, in front of the first jet. The other two were about ten miles back.

The statement continued, "The object was a bright ball, about five times the size of the jet behind it. Its color was reddish orange, perhaps from sky reflection. Brighter than the planes. We could hear no noise from the object, nor from the jets. The object's brightness did not vary."

A few moments later, according to the statement, "We returned to the Salem Police station when the four objects flew out of view. . . . The UFO appeared to be in level flight all the time while we watched it. When we came in, the pursuit vehicle reported its location as near (the object was above) Firestone Farms, east of Columbiana."

To add to the strangeness of this end of the sightings, radio operator Jack Cramer and Police Lieutenant Richard Whinnery were startled to hear, over the police radio, an unfamiliar voice, say loud and clear, "I'm going down to take a look at it. . . . I'm right above it. . . . It's about forty-five feet across, and it's trailing something."

The Air Force would later deny that any intercept had been attempted, but the evidence suggesting otherwise continued to grow. While the original officers to see the craft, Spaur and Neff, said nothing about a jet intercept, Panzanella suggested that he, and Johnson and Esterly, had seen two streaks that were reminiscent of jet fighters.

William B. Weitzel, a field investigator for NICAP, interviewed a number of the principals in the case. He found more evidence of an attempted intercept of the UFO. Columbiana County Sheriff's Deputy Dave Brothers told Weitzel, "But about all I saw in the sky was, I did see three airplanes, which was denied in the newspaper, that there was no airplane. I saw three planes, and they were going in the same direction, east, into Pennsylvania. And the planes left a little vapor trail, but they weren't jets . . . they were running too slow for jets, because I was keeping up to them. . . . I could make out the image of what they were, airplanes. And I only saw one jet, but that was farther east, and it looked like he was . . . coming west, and he just turned around and went back east, because you could see this vapor trail when he turned around and went east. But other than that, I never spotted the object they were chasing."

An Associated Press report suggested confirmation of the intercept attempts. "Reports . . . came from Air Force Reserve pilots based at Youngstown, [Ohio] who said they attempted to follow the object but that its speed—estimated at 100 miles an hour—was too slow for their jet trainers."

The Air Force, for its part, denied that any aircraft, jets or otherwise were sent after the UFO. In a letter from the Headquarters 911th Troop Carrier Group, Medium (Reserve) (CONAC), based at the Greater Pittsburgh Airport, Information Officer Eugene F. Rehrer wrote, "After the report was received a call was made to the Airport Tower at Greater Pittsburgh Airport. Nothing had been picked up on radar at the airport. The Air National Guard, also located at Greater Pittsburgh Airport had been called but not by this organization. F-102's [delta-winged fighters used by ADC at the time] were not scrambled to follow the UFO."

Of course, it could be pointed out that these comments refer only to the Greater Pittsburgh Airport and to F-102s. It seems from the descriptions given, and the locations given, that neither Pittsburgh nor F-102s were involved. That does not rule out other aircraft at other locations.

However, Colonel Hendricks, of the Youngstown Reserve, was interviewed on April 18. He said,

We have been erroneously quoted by the AP, also have been falsely quoted. Have had no contact with the media. In the initial release of a plane being two [sic] fast or two [sic] slow, nothing. I have attempted this morning to find out who in the organization may have had contact. Could find no one. News media had called last night and were informed that they had no information. Spoke with the writer of the *Cleveland Plain Dealer* ([identified in the letter only as] Bloomfield) who claims the Air Force planes were too fast. He doesn't know where the info came from. They were quering [sic] the AP wires. Youngstown did not have any aircraft airborne. Major [Quintanilla] asked him if there were any other units close. Air Force information flight in Cleveland. . . .

So the round of denials began. No one had any aircraft airborne and none of the radar facilities had anything unusual on their scopes. But there were deputy sheriffs who claimed to have seen some kind of aircraft attempting to close with the object. And our new stealth technology suggests that the lack of a radar return proves nothing. If we can fly aircraft over enemy anti-aircraft emplacements without being spotted, it stands to reason that an advanced technology might also be able to do that.

Weitzel, the NICAP investigator, could not find any answers to the problem. He wrote, "I checked in person at Sheriff's Office Base Radio Stations in Portage, Columbiana, and Mahoning counties, the Youngstown Police Department, Salem Police Department, and Chippewa Barracks, Pennsylvania State Police. Could not track down the source of rumors (and signed statements) about jet or radar reports. John Beighey, Rochester Police Radio Operator, denies hearing jet or radar reports such as Panzanella mentions, and is reluctant to discuss the event. Panzanella claims something may have come via phone-microphone, if Beighey had his button down; but there is still a conflict between Beighey's and Panzanella's testimony."

Weitzel thought it might be possible that the police radios had received, briefly, the aircraft radio transmissions, though they would have been on different frequencies. He thought this was highly unlikely. In the end, he had no explanation for the problem, but did accept the Air Force denials that they had any aircraft attempting intercepts. He thought it was possible that the witnesses had seen commercial jets in the area, that the jets had nothing to do with attempted intercepts, and that their presence was a coincidence. It was not a very satisfactory explanation.

The three police officers who had been involved in the chase, that is Spaur, Neff, and Panzanella, drove to the police station in Rochester, and called the Air Force at Pittsburgh. Spaur later said that some colonel had spoken to him briefly and then tried to persuade him that they had seen something conventional. Spaur was less than enthusiastic for that, and the colonel promised to forward the information on to Wright-Patterson Air Force Base. If the colonel had kept his promise, the response from the base, and from the officers of Project Blue Book, was lukewarm to nearly nonexistent.

According to Spaur, he received a phone call on April 18 from a "Mr." Quintanilla, who said, "Tell me about this mirage you saw." Again, according to Spaur, he was asked if it had been in view for more than a few minutes. Spaur said they had chased it across several counties and into Pennsylvania, and had it in sight for over half an hour. At that point, Spaur said the man lost interest in the conversation. The colonel had interviewed him longer and asked more questions.

Quintanilla called Spaur a second time and again questioned him about the length of the sighting. When the deputy assured Quintanilla that he had watched the object for more than a few minutes, and had in fact chased it, Quintanilla ended the conversation.

Less than a week later, in fact, on the following Friday, April 22, the Air Force announced the solution for the sighting. Quintanilla called the Portage County sheriff, Ross Dustman, and told him the case was resolved. His deputies had seen, first, an Echo communications satellite moving from northwest to southeast and when it was out of sight, Spaur had mistaken Venus for the same object. Spaur believed the object maneuvered in the sky because the highway changed directions, giving the illusion of movement. When Quintanilla finished, according to Dustman, he (meaning Dustman) "laughed out loud." The solution was ridiculous.

Dustman told reporters for the UPI, "I go along with my men. It was not a satellite and not Venus. I've seen Venus many times, but I never saw Venus fifty feet above a road and moving from side to side like this. . . . I have never seen Venus controlled like this seemed to be."

Spaur also had some words about the Air Force investigation and solution. "I don't know how much investigation [the Air Force] made, but evidently it wasn't a very lengthy one, or it didn't involve me. . . . I'm definitely sure that I wasn't chasing Venus or observing Venus and running wildly over the countryside. I'm not quite that bad off."

The Air Force statement failed to mention that there were other witnesses including Spaur's partner that night, Neff. Some of those other witnesses described events that were remarkably similar to those the police officers reported. About 5 A.M., two New Castle, Pennsylvania, couples, while driving just a few miles from the Ohio border, saw an object across a field to the west. They described it as a "hamburg" or an "ice cream cone" and that it was brilliant, "sort of like looking into a spotlight." They stopped the car and rolled down the windows, proving to themselves that it was not a reflection on the glass. At one point it flew across the road, and it always stayed about a quarter mile to a half mile in the air. Eventually it disappeared in the distance.

The whole explanation was so ridiculous, that almost no one accepted it. *Ravenna* [Ohio] *Record-Courier* reporter Carol Clapp told Weitzel that U.S. Congressman William Stanton wanted to know more about the sighting. Weitzel wrote a four-page letter outlining the problems with Blue Book's investigation and solution.

A few days later, Robert Cook, a Portage County judge, wrote to Stanton, telling him that the officers involved were men of integrity, and that he felt "it is grossly unfair to them for the Air Force to reach any conclusion in this matter until it has conducted a real and complete investigation."

Cook wrote that "Deputies Spaur and Neff said that they had a good look at the object and at times it was within one hundred feet of them. Chief Buchert took a picture of what he saw from a greater distance. . . . It is my further understanding that their [the Air Force] investigation of these sightings has merely consisted of telephone conversations with several of the eyewitnesses and an examination of the photographs taken by Chief Buchert. . . . The conclusion that the object sighted was the planet Venus is so ridiculous that the United States Air Force has suffered a great loss of prestige in this community."

Stanton, after receiving that communication, decided to take another step. He sent Weitzel's letter, as well as the results of his own investigation, to the Air Force commanding general. When he received no reply, he went to the Pentagon and spoke to Air Force Lieutenant Colonel John Spaulding, who conceded that Blue Book should have made an on-site investigation. He promised that such an investigation would be conducted shortly.

Maybe we should take a moment here to point out, once again, that the Air Force had the mission of investigating UFO sightings. Air Force regulations demanded it. Yet no one inside the Air Force seemed to care enough to do anything except deny and to try to prove that no intercept had been attempted. The only reason they responded to those questions was because they seemed to believe, based on the tone of the responses, that they were being unjustly accused of lying about the intercepts. I could point out that now they knew how it felt when a witness was told that he was too dumb to identify Venus in the morning sky.

The point is, however, that once again we have a case that provides good, solid information. No, it doesn't contain physical evidence, or rather, we have been told that it doesn't but it does have solid observations by police officers, made over a long period of time. Even with that, the Air Force chose to spend less than five working days investigating, and then conducted all their investigations over the telephone.

On May 10, about two weeks after the Air Force had tried to suggest satellites and Venus in combination, Quintanilla arrived in Ravenna to interview Spaur. Alerted by a message from Quintanilla, Spaur had called Weitzel and asked him to attend the meeting and to record it. Weitzel not only liked the idea, he tried to get both Panzanella and Huston to make the meeting, but both had to work. It strikes me as odd that Quintanilla didn't bother with this somewhat routine idea.

When Quintanilla arrived, he was met by Spaur, Sheriff Dustman, two reporters, Clapp and Tom Schley, Weitzel, and Dave Webb. Before the official interview began, Neff and Deputy Robert Wilson arrived. And then Quintanilla asked Weitzel and Webb to leave. Shortly after that the two reporters left, supposedly on their own. That left only Quintanilla and the police officers in the room with Weitzel's tape recorder which no one had bothered to turn off. So much for Air Force security.

It seems, however, that this wasn't really an investigation by the Air Force, but an attempt to push an idea off on the witnesses. Quintanilla tried to get Spaur to accept the Air Force explanation. He said, "I don't know whether you realize it or not, but there are at least thirty satellites that are visible to the naked eye. And these things have a northeasterly and a southeasterly component. . . . And I checked thoroughly. . . . And this is why I made the determination specifically, because of the directions which you *gave* me. That you had first spotted the satellite coming over, and then focused on Venus. Venus at night, that's a typical night, was at a magnitude of minus 3.9. Which is the brightest thing in the sky except for the moon."

Spaur responded, "Well, I don't know anything about it, but . . . I'm under the impression that . . . [you are saying] I have a misconception of . . ."

"No, you aren't, Dale. It's not a misconception, Dale. It's—you're not the first to chase that . . ."

"No," said Spaur, "I know damn well I wasn't chasing a satellite, first of all—"

Quintanilla interrupted then, and said, "You weren't chasing a satellite. I didn't say you were chasing a satellite."

Spaur continued, "I think that if it was in the atmosphere as close as this thing was, as large as it was, it would probably have burned up at that speed. Second of all, I'm under the impression that our satellites doesn't [sic] stop and go and go up and down . . ."

Quintanilla interrupted again. "Well, they zigzag. They don't zigzag 'cause a satellite is in perfect motion. But it gives you the illusion of zigzagging. It gives the illusion of movement. But it's not because the satellite itself is moving, it's because the eyeball does this. Your eyes, my eyes, his eyes . . ."

But the problem here is that Quintanilla is referring to autokinesis that occurs when someone stares at a point of light that isn't moving. Staring at bright stars, or Venus, at night, makes it seem that they are dancing around in the sky. But, if you look at the track of a satellite as it crosses the sky, the zigzag movement suggested by Quintanilla isn't in evidence. That attempt at convincing Spaur of his mistake is as transparent as all the others.

Failing to convince him of the satellite portion of the explanation, Quintanilla moved on to Venus. Spaur attempted to tell Quintanilla what he had seen that night. "Now, this, this thing, is this large—this big and this low. . . . I follow it, and I have Barney with me. We're going down the road. So you're gonna discount, well, there's two nuts. We're running Venus. Now Venus . . ."

Quintanilla interrupted again. "Now, now wait a minute . . ."

"Well, wait a minute," said Spaur. "Let me speak."

Quintanilla said, "You used the wrong word. . . . I'm an officer in the United States Air Force . . ."

"Right. You definitely are."

"And I don't call anybody a nut."

But it didn't stop there. Spaur said, "No. Okay. I have hallucinations, then. But this is what I've been saying . . ."

Quintanilla interrupted. "I didn't say you were having hallucinations . . ."

"What I'm trying to say is this. I'm going down the road. Now, this thing that I am following . . ."

But Quintanilla, who obviously has no interest in hearing the tale again, said, "And treat me with the same respect that I treat you."

"I will, sir. I am. I'll treat you with more respect than I've been treated in the last . . ."

That sort of describes the whole of the interview. Neither side wanted to concede a point to the other. Eventually Weitzel and the reporters were allowed to enter the room, and the situation didn't change. Weitzel and Quintanilla got into a nasty argument as Weitzel tried to suggest that the satellite-and-Venus explanation didn't fit the reported facts. Quintanilla was in the unenviable position of having to admit that he hadn't heard of some of the witnesses. Quintanilla finally excused himself.

Weitzel later said, "Several people from the radio and newspapers tried to get statements from Major Quintanilla and me that afternoon. The major had nothing to say, and I declined extensive comment until I could hear the entire tape recording. I did suggest, and now believe,

that Major Quintanilla had come to Portage County with his conclusions ready, and only listened politely, which on the whole he did, to
testimony. At no time while he was interviewing the men did anyone
see him taking notes. . . . The deputies and Sheriff Dustman were fed
up, and made no bones about their discouragement."

Weitzel's suggestion seems to be borne out by the lack of change in
the Air Force's conclusion. They had already issued their statement
about the solution for the sighting, and even though Spaur had mentioned the craft was close to the ground, even though they had talked
of it lighting the road under it, and even though it wasn't a point of
light, Quintanilla stuck to the conclusion it was Venus and a satellite.

The astronomer who had thought that Venus might provide part of
the explanation, based on hearing secondhand reports, eventually gave
up on the idea. William T. Powers, a systems engineer at the Dearborn
Observatory, Northwestern University, had originated the idea without talking to any of the witnesses. He eventually wrote to Spaur and
Neff, "Apparently I found out considerably more about this event than
the Air Force investigator did, because I cannot agree with the evaluation publicly released a few days after the sighting. What you reported to me could not possibly lead to such a conclusion: a satellite
satisfies none of the characteristics of your reported object. As a matter
of fact, Dr. Hynek agrees with this. He was not consulted before this
news release was put forth."

As a parenthetical note, it could be that Hynek was not consulted
after the "swamp gas" disaster. Hynek, on hearing about the sightings
in Michigan in March 1966, made an off-the-cuff remark that it
"sounded like swamp gas." Reporters hearing that, ran with the explanation. It resulted in a memo from the Air Force suggesting that Dr.
Hynek not issue any more statements because of the negative publicity.

Powers continued writing. "I thought at first that during the latter
part of your experience, after you had lost the object and then reac-
quired it, that you and Mr. Houston [sic] might have spotted Venus,
and thought it was the same object at a higher altitude: I spoke to
Major Quintanilla on the telephone at the time I gave him the results
of my telephone interview, and told him of this idea. Now I have
additional information, chiefly from Mr. William Weitzel, which ap-

pears to make that hypothesis incorrect. I now understand that you and other witnesses did notice Venus and the Moon, and saw the object in motion relative to them, as well as being able to see a shape. At no time, however, did I suppose that the earlier part of the sighting involved anything other than an airborne object."

It made no difference to Blue Book investigators. They had a theory to explain the sighting. It made no difference to them that the witnesses were talking of seeing an object, not a point of light, that it had been within a hundred feet of them, and had illuminated the highway. The purpose of Project Blue Book by this time was to explain UFO sightings and that is exactly what they had done.

Although there were attempts by several people to persuade the officers at Blue Book to change their opinion, it never happened. Hynek, the scientific consultant, even suggested the case be reevaluated as an unidentified. James McDonald called the satellite-and-Venus explanation an "absurdity."

McDonald, in fact, wrote, "The fact Officer Huston saw the object coming in out of the northwest sky clearly rules out his seeing Venus, yet at that time the first two officers had been following the object for a much longer time than Echo requires to transit the full sky. This, plus the four-witness descriptions of vertical ascent at the termination of the sighting are calmly swept aside . . ."

The facts of the case were overlooked and ignored as the Air Force worked to hammer the explanation into the hole they had created. What strikes me is that the witnesses reported the size and shape of the object, seeing it close to the ground, and watching it as it lifted into the sky. It was in sight long enough for them to get a good look at it. Yet all of this is ignored as the Air Force reported the various witnesses had seen a satellite and Venus.

If we go through the Air Force files, and I have done that, we can find dozens of cases of Venus being reported as a UFO. These are easy to find. The witness will talk of a bright point of light that seems to fly erratically, never far from the horizon. If it was a morning sighting, then the object disappears, slowly fading from view as the sun comes up; this is clearly Venus. If it is an evening sighting, with the object eventually lost on the horizon, this then, too, is Venus.

The point is, there are very distinctive descriptions that allow us to suggest Venus as the real culprit when appropriate. Yet, there isn't a case in which Venus is the answer and in which the witnesses provide a description of the object, suggest it was close to the ground, and who also see Venus in the sky where it should be.

Once again we have a case that has a label slapped on it, but we have no answer. The police officers saw something very unusual early that morning. They chased it until it lifted into the sky, disappearing. It was not Venus, a satellite, or any of the other mundane explanations that have been offered about it.

There is a postscript to this report that revolves around the lives of the men involved in the case. It has little to do with the Air Force investigation, though the answer offered by Quintanilla certainly made them look like they were not the brightest humans to ever walk the face of the planet.

Within six months of the sighting, Spaur had left law enforcement and was working as a painter. Spaur's marriage ended in divorce. One night he walked into the house, and for reasons that he said he did not understand, flew into a rage, grabbing his wife and shaking her. She filed charges and he spend a brief period in jail.

H. Wayne Huston resigned from the police force within months of the sighting. He moved to Seattle and became a bus driver. He told reporters that he had quit because of the sighting. He said that people laughed at him. He suggested that city officials didn't like police officers who saw flying saucers. Or maybe it was that city officials didn't care if police officers saw flying saucers, they just didn't want them to report those sightings to the Air Force.

Neff's wife said that the chase had changed him as well. He had been in a state of shock when she first saw him after the chase. Later he refused to talk about it, saying that he would not tell a soul if one landed in his backyard. According to his wife, he had been through the ringer.

These weren't the first, nor the last, police officers who had lost their jobs after reporting flying saucers. The list is long and almost endless. And, in a few cases it seems to be the result of an effort to discredit the officer who made the report.

But the facts remain. The police officers, in communications with their superiors, chased something across parts of Ohio and Pennsylvania on April 17. Other officers, hearing those radio messages, went out and saw the same thing. If Blue Book was a search for the truth, and for information, they would have done more than make a few telephone calls, and one "investigative" trip. They would have attempted to find out what really happened.

OCTOBER 24, 1968:

WHY NOT MINOT?

There are thousands of cases in the Project Blue Book files that seem to have plausible explanations attached to them. It seems as if the investigation conducted by Air Force officers has been complete so that there should be no reason to question them. Then there are cases in which the explanations become so convoluted that it is extraordinary that anyone was able to come up with the solution.

I am reminded of a scene in Joseph Wambaugh's *The Glitter Dome* in which the police officers are talking about the solution to a difficult case. They have finally be able to rule it a suicide and clear the books. Their explanation seems plausible, but it is clear from the dialogue that they worked very hard to make it seem plausible. It is also clear that neither officer accepts the answer as real. It just cleared the books. At the very end of the story, referring to a different investigation, one of them comments that they finally solved one.

In the Minot case, it seems as if the Air Force investigators were working very hard to provide a solution that would be acceptable to higher-ranking officers. At no time does it seem that they care if they have the correct solution, only that it is acceptable.

According to the Project Record Card, the conclusion for the sightings that took place are: "Ground-Visual: 1) Probable (Aircraft) (B-52). 2) Probable Astro (Sirius). Radar: Possible (Plasma). Air-Visual: Possible (Plasma)."

In the comments section, the investigating officer wrote, "The ground-visual sightings appear to be of the star Sirius and the B-52 which was flying the area. The B-52 radar contact and the temporary loss of UHF transmission could be attributed to plasma, similar to ball lightning. The air-visual from the B-52 could be the star Vega which was on the horizon at the time, or it could be a light on the ground, or possibly a plasma."

Anytime I see such a conglomeration of explanations, I have to stop to take a look at the case. If we had a situation in which UFOs had been sighted and reported in the days preceding it, I could believe that there were many people out looking and seeing what are later identified as common objects. But here we seem to have the sightings taking place with no real communication between the witnesses. Suddenly, on October 24, 1968 air police and maintenance crews on the ground, and the crew of a B-52 on a routine training mission, begin to see flying saucers.

In other cases, I have suggested that if we link the sightings, such as those by Kenneth Arnold and then Fred Johnson, we have a strong case that defies easy explanation. Here it seems that I am suggesting that we separate the cases. Not so. I'm suggesting that as the ground sightings are taking place, that the crew of the B-52 is not aware of it until alerted by the control tower. Their sighting, which is running concurrently with that on the ground, is probably linked. The key is that the B-52 crew did not know what was being seen from the ground.

According to the file, it seems that the first sighting was made about thirty minutes after midnight by Airman Isley. No first names are found in the file. He saw a bright light in the east that apparently was just hovering.

Two hours later, Airman First Class O'Connor sighted a bright light. At the same time, Staff Sergeant Smith reported that he had seen a bright star light.

At 0308 (that is, 3:08 A.M.) a series of sightings began by maintenance teams around the Minot area. O'Connor, the maintenance team chief, reported that all members of his team saw a lighted object that was reddish orange in color. O'Connor suggested it was a large object that had flashing green and white lights. According to the report, "After they entered N-7 LF [a field site designated November Seven] the object came directly overhead with the sound of jet engines."

The report continued,

SSgt. Bond the FSC at Nov Flt [Flt means "flight" and refers to a platoon-sized organization] stated that the object which looked to him as the sun, came near the handred antenna at Nov-1. It then moved to the right and he sent the SAT out to check and see what it was. The object then moved about one mile away with the Nov SAT following. They came within ½ mile from where it appeared to be landing. When it reached the surface the lights became dimmer and finally went out. After this they could see nothing. SSgt Smith at Oscar-1 saw the object separate into two parts and go in oposite [sic] directions and return and pass under each other. At this time Julelt Flt and Mike Flt Team observed the same things and described it the same way. The approximate grid coordinates of the apparently landing was AA-43. The entire observation period as near as can be determined was about 45 minutes.

At 0324 (3:29 A.M.) Staff Sergeant Wagla, Airman First Class Allis, and Airman First Class Deer sighted a UFO from one location. A minute later Staff Sergeant Halko, Airman First Class Jenkins, and Airman First Class Richardson sighted the UFO from a separate location. And ten minutes after that, the crew of a B-52 was brought into the case.

The transcript of the conversations between the tower and the aircraft are available in the Blue Book file. The times in the transcript are all in Greenwich Mean Time, but I have corrected them for local time in North Dakota so that it will be consistent with the times given for the sightings by ground maintenance and security personnel.

At 3:30 A.M., the controllers received the information that there was a UFO twenty-four miles to the northwest. At 3:34 A.M. "JAG-31"

(JAG Three One), a B-52 on a calibration check, requested a clearance and was at "Flight Level 200 (2000)."

At 3:34 A.M. the pilot asked, "MIB (Minot) approach control, does JAG-31 have clearance to WT fix [a designated point on the ground] at Flight Level 200?"

"JAG-31, roger, climb out on a heading of 290 climb and maintain 5000. Stand by for higher altitude. We're trying to get it from center now."

At 3:35 A.M., the controller asked, "And, JAG-31, on your way out to the WT fix request you look out toward your one o'clock position for the next fifteen or sixteen miles and see if you see any orange glows out there."

"Roger, roger . . . glows 31."

"Someone is seeing flying saucers again."

"Roger I see a . . ." The rest of the transmission from the aircraft is garbled.

At 3:52 A.M., the controller then radioed, "Three one, the UFO is being picked up by weathers radar also. Should be at our one o'clock position three miles now."

The pilot said, "We have nothing on our airborne radar and I'm in some pretty thick haze right now and unable to see out that way."

At 3:58 A.M., though the transmissions have nothing to do with the sighting of the UFO, there is a strange event. The pilot requested a straight TACAN approach, and received instructions from the controller about that. The pilot called, and then, apparently, the radio went dead. Although they could hear the instructions from the ground, they could no longer transmit. The controller asked them to "squawk ident" which meant to use the aircraft's transponder which would "paint" the controller's radar with a large, glowing blip for easy identification.

At 4:00 A.M., the controller again suggested, "JAG 31, if you hear me squawk ident . . . JAG 31 ident observed. Cleared for the approach attempt. Contact on frequency 271 decimal three and you're cleared for the low approach."

They continued to have radio troubles for another couple of minutes. At 4:02 A.M., they were again able to communicate easily.

The pilot said, "Our UFO was off to our left there when we started penetration [penetration refers to turning inbound for the low approach]."

"Roger. Understand you did see something on your left side.

"We had a radar return at about a mile and a quarter nine o'clock position for about the time we left 200 to about 14. . . ."

They discussed the troubles with the transmissions and then, at 4:03 A.M., the controller asked, "Affirmative. I was wondering how far out did you see that UFO?"

"He was about one and a half miles off our left wing at thirty-five miles when we started in and he stayed with us till about ten."

"I wonder if that could have been your radio troubles."

"I don't know. . . . But that's exactly when they started."

At 4:13 A.M., as they are working the "low approach" the controller asked, "JAG-31, are you observing any more UFOs?"

"Negative on radar. We can't see anything visually."

"JAG-31, roger. The personnel on from the missile site advise they don't see anything anymore, either."

Finally, at 4:21 A.M., the controller said, "JAG-31, [garbled] requests that somebody from your aircraft stop in at base ops after you land."

"Roger, 31. We'll give them a call."

What we have, then, is a group of sightings made by men on the ground, at the missile sites scattered around the Minot Air Force Base. There is a radar sighting on the ground, the "weathers" radar. Later, there is a visual sighting from the crew of the B-52, and there is a radar sighting from the aircraft as well. Although the first sightings began just after midnight and the last was made about four in the morning, they were not continuous. There were a number of sightings made by a number of men at various times at various locations.

Project Blue Book was alerted about the sightings that same day. In a "memo for the record" dated October 24, 1968, Lieutenant Marano began to receive telephone calls. He learned that the commander of the base at Minot, and Major General Nichols at 15th Air Force Headquarters, were interested in what had happened. Apparently a lieutenant colonel named Werlich had been appointed the local—meaning Minot—UFO officer. He would conduct the investigation.

The "memo for the record" explained the incident.

At about 0300 hours local, a B-52 that was about 39 miles north-west of Minot AFB and was making practice penetrations sighted an unidentified blip on their radar. Initially the target traveled approximately 2½ miles in 3 sec or about 3,000 mi/hr. After passing from the right to the left of the plane, it assumed a position off the left wing of the 52. The blip stayed off the left wing for approximately 20 miles at which point it broke off. Scope photographs were taken. When the target was close to the B-52 neither of the two transmitters in the B-52 would operate properly but when it broke off both returned to normal function.

At about this time a missile maintenance man called in and reported sighting a bright orangish-red object. The object was hovering at about 1,000 feet or so, and had a sound similar to a jet engine. The observer had stopped his car, but he then started it up again. As he started to move, the object followed him then accelerated and appeared to stop at about 6–8 miles away. The observer shortly afterward lost sight of it.

In response to the maintenance man's call, the B-52, which had continued its penetration run, was vectored toward the visual which was about 10 miles northwest of the base. The B-52 confirmed having sighted a bright light of some type that appeared to be hovering just over or on the ground.

Now comes one of the most interesting parts, and one that seemed to have slipped by the Air Force investigators at Blue Book. "Fourteen other people in separate locations also reported sighting a similar object. Also, at this approximate time, security alarm for one of the sites was activated. This was an alarm for both the outer and inner ring. When guards arrived at the scene they found that the outer door was open and the combination lock on the inner door had been removed."

With command emphasis on the sightings, and with more than one general officer interested in the case, it was "investigated" by Blue Book. I use the quotation marks because of a line in one of the "memos for the record." On October 30, 1968, Quintanilla, now a lieutenant colonel himself, had a telephone conversation with Colonel Pullen at SAC Headquarters. Asked if he had "sent anybody up to investigate the sighting," Quintanilla replied, "We did not send anybody up because I only have four people on my staff, myself, an assistant, a secretary, and an admin sergeant. I talked to Colonel Werlich for over thirty minutes and since this didn't appear unusual I didn't send anyone up."

What we have is a sighting that involved both ground and airborne radars. We have visual sightings to corroborate those returns from both the aircraft and people on the ground. In fact, there are people at separate locations who reported seeing the UFO, but according to Quintanilla, there was nothing unusual about the case. Just let the local boys look into it and then write it off.

This is in stark contrast to the way Ruppelt, during his tenure as the chief of Blue Book, operated. He'd fly around the country making personal investigations. A look at the files showed that he was in Lubbock to investigate the Lubbock lights, he was in Florida to investigate the case of the burned scoutmaster, and, had he been able to convince the Air Force bureaucrats in Washington, D.C., that he needed to stay overnight, he would have personally investigated the Washington National sightings in the days that followed them.

But now, fifteen years later, the case of a radar sighting, an airborne sighting with radar confirmation, wasn't unusual. Quintanilla, with his small staff, couldn't go to Minot to interrogate the various military witnesses himself. Instead, he sat in his office at Wright-Patterson, read the reports, written by others, made a telephone call or two, and then made his determination about the sighting.

In a November 1 "memo for the record," Lieutenant Marano noted, "Colonel Werlich, the Minot officer in charge of the investigation, said that he had already had the people fill out AF Forms 117," which were the long forms the Air Force used to gather UFO data. Werlich told Lieutenant Marano, "I monitored them while they filled them out, but I can't see where the navigator can help. . . ."

Later, in that same "memo," Lieutenant Marano noted, "The one we are mainly interested is the one that cannot be identified. The one of radar and the aircraft correlated pretty well."

Using maps, they attempted to identify the low-flying light that could have been on the ground. According to the report, "There is nothing there that would produce this type of light. The same for O'Conner and Nicely from November 7 [that is, two of the maintenance men from the silo designated N or rather November Seven] which is near Greno."

Later, in response to a question about the object on the ground, Marano was told, "They were able to see a light source while the 52 got in real close, then it disappeared."

The account, in the files, and the memos for record, are somewhat confusing. It seemed that they were suggesting that the men on the ground who saw the lights and then heard a roar like that of jet engines had seen the B-52. "Almost 80 percent were looking at the B-52. If you would look at an aircraft at 20,000 feet, then you wouldn't see much but I'm am [sic] to place logic in that it was there and what they saw was there. There is enough there that it is worth looking at. Nobody can definitely say that these people definitely saw the aircraft, but within reason they probably saw it."

What this seems to be suggesting is that the officers at Minot think the ground sightings might be of the B-52, but they're not sure. It's almost as if they are trying to convince themselves of the answer. But it also seems that they realize they are suggesting that the men stationed at Minot are incapable of identifying a huge bomber that is assigned to SAC, remembering, of course, that Minot is a SAC base. How could that many men, some of whom had been around SAC and B-52s for years, suddenly be incapable of recognizing the aircraft? It is an explanation that is ridiculous. The men, had they been looking at a B-52, would have identified it as such.

There is another factor here. Once again we don't have a highly charged environment where everyone has been talking about flying saucers for weeks. We have a number of men who look into the night sky and see something they can't identify. Had the answer been the B-52, it seems quite reasonable that the men would have identified it as such at the time of the sighting. Just how clever would they have to be to find that answer?

The Air Force investigators, having disposed of the ground-visual sightings, after a fashion, began to attack the radar aspect of the case. But there is an interesting statement in one of the "memos for the record" which, not surprisingly, is somewhat confusing. Apparently Colonel Werlich, in a telephone communication with Blue Book officers, said, "I only stated one radar in the message because there was only one radar set. The ECM [electric counter measures] equipment hadn't been used. RAPCOM [radar facility] was painting [meaning "operating"], IFF [identification friend or foe transponder] was operating in the airplane. It's a fairly good size blip. The object would have been covered by the blip. There is a Sage site [another radar facility] to the south. They do not remember any unidentified paints. The only one that I have is the one on the plane. The unusual part is the B-52 was in the middle of a sentence and the voice just quit transmitting right in the middle of the word . . ."

Werlich seems to be suggesting here that only one radar picked up the UFO, yet he also suggests that if it was close to the bomber, then the IFF equipment, which emits a signal so that the blip on the radar is huge and stands out for easy identification by the radar operator, would have covered the UFO. He also suggests that another site's radar operators don't remember any unidentified blips, which is a fairly weak statement.

But going back through the case file, there is a mention of the weathers radar but there is no identification of this site. In fact, someone added a penciled question mark above the notation for the weathers radar. If, as suggested in the file, the "weathers radar" picked up the blip, and we know that the B-52's radar had it for a number of minutes, then two different radar sets had "painted" it. One was on the ground and the other was airborne at the time.

The other interesting point made during this conversation was that the transmitters on the B-52 shut down. UFOs have often been associated with electromagnetic effects which seem to suppress electrical systems, causing cars to stall, lights to dim, and radios to fade. But this is a selective suppression of the electrical system. The only problem is that the transmitters of the UHF radios ceased to transmit. Apparently all other electrical systems on the aircraft continued to function properly.

Werlich said, "My personal opinion is that it couldn't be a malfunction because they transmitted before and afterwards. The aircraft was not checked out afterwards because the transmission [sic] was working."

In a proper investigation, the transmitter should have been checked for a short. The coincidence of the close approach of the UFO might have been just that, a coincidence. But a short would show up again at some point. There is no indication from the Blue Book record that such is the case. Of course, if it did, there is no reason for Werlich, or anyone else at Minot, to report that to Blue Book.

During the conversation another of the Air Force's old standbys, a temperature inversion, was mentioned a couple of times. Lieutenant Marano "then explained about the many astronomical bodies that were over the area at the time and when there is quite an inversion they are magnified even greater."

The Air Force investigators were now suggesting that not only couldn't their personnel identify a B-52 when it flew over them, now they couldn't identify stars. These ill-trained ground personnel, for some unexplained reason, began to see flying saucers all over the skies above Minot on October 24.

Then on November 1, 1968, in a memo for the record, it is reported, "Talked to Mr. Goff [whoever that is] . . . who is quite familiar with air-borne radars. Mr. Goff said that from the evidence at this time it would appear to him that the sightings may have been precipitated by some type of ionized air plasma similar to ball lightning. He felt that a plasma could account for the radar blip, loss of transmission, and some of the visual sightings. . . ."

This, to me, sounded like a reasonable solution to the problem. But it also sounded like someone trying to find an explanation for a case where none existed, so I called a friend who teaches physics at a major university. The first comment he made was most telling. If this is true, then why isn't the phenomenon reported more often?

What he was saying was that if plasma was a good explanation for this particular sighting, then we could expect to see similar things around other aircraft all the time. We could expect to have many reports of intermittent failures of transmitters, airborne radars plagued with plasma images, and reports of glowing plasmas following other aircraft. Yet this simply isn't the case.

During my discussion with the physicist, I kept asking about the glow, and how bright it would be. It began to sound as if we were talking about two different phenomena. What he was attempting to say was that plasmas don't glow unless there is another feature. I mentioned the glow around high power lines, and he said that the electricity could excite the plasma to make it glow, but that they didn't glow on their own. In other words, unless there was another mechanism there causing a glow, those on the ground, and in the plane, wouldn't have been able to see anything. The plasma, that is, the ionized air, would be the color of air.

The idea of the plasma causing the sightings seems to have impressed many of the people involved here. In a teletype message from Quintanilla to Colonel Pullen at SAC, he wrote, "It is my feelings, [sic] after reviewing preliminary information submitted by Monot [sic-obviously Minot], that UFO painted by B-52 on radar and also observed visually by IP [pilot] and personnel on the ground is probably a plasma of the ball-lightning class. Plasmas of this type will paint on radar and also affect some electronic equipment at certain frequencies."

He then made a statement that is contradictory. "Plasmas are not uncommon, however, they are unique and extremely difficult to duplicate in the laboratory."

Quintanilla finished with, "Also, because of durations, feel strongly that some security guards and maintenance crew were observing some first-magnitude celestial bodies which were greatly magnified by the inversion layer and haze which was present at Minot during the time of the UFO observations. . . . Consider the UFO reports as fairly routine, except for the plasma observation which is interesting from a scientific point of view. We will study this report in more detail when we receive the raw data from Minot."

Of course, the question springs to mind, Why? You have an answer and you certainly aren't going to change it. We've already seen how the facts of a case make little impact on the solution for it. Besides, by November 13, Quintanilla had his final solutions. He wrote, "The following conclusions have been reached after a thorough study of the data submitted to the Foreign Technology Division. The ground-visual sightings appear to be of the star Sirius and the B-52 which was flying in the area. The B-52 radar contact and the temporary loss of the UHF transmission could be attributed to a plasma similar to ball lightning. The air-visual from the B-52 could be the star Vega which was on the horizon at the time, or it could be a light on the ground, or possibly a plasma. . . . No further investigation by the Foreign Technology Division is contemplated."

Let's see if we understand all of this. The trained men on the ground, some of whom have been in the Air Force for a long time, saw Sirius through the inversion layer and were fooled by it. Some of the others saw a B-52 on a routine training mission and were unable to identify it as a B-52. Others still, saw some stars, through the inversion, and failed to identify them.

Apparently the radar sightings from the ground were not investigated because I see nothing in the file to indicate that Blue Book officers ever identified the "weathers radar." Had anyone at Blue Book asked, I'm sure the officers at Minot would have been able to identify the sighting. It is interesting that, according to the file, no one ever followed this particular lead.

And, let's see if we understand the explanation for the B-52 sighting. It could be Vega, a star seen through the inversion layer that magnified its size and brightness. Or, it could be a light on the ground, fooling the bomber crew because of the inversion layer. Or, it could be a plasma which might explain the radar return and the failure of the radios to transmit, if we can figure out how the plasma could selectively suppress the radio without affecting the other electronic equipment.

The answers provided in this case are no answers whatsoever. It is a combination of new buzzwords such as "plasma"; a belief that Air Force personnel, including bomber crews, are unable to recognize stars; and a suggestion that many of these same people can't recognize a B-52 when they see it. Here was a case that deserved more investigation but got none of that. And here is the proof for which we had been searching. Blue Book wasn't interested in investigating UFOs, they were interested in resolving UFO sightings. Once again, they made no on-site investigation but conducted it from their offices at Wright-Patterson.

In fact, that is pointed out in one of the "memos for the record." Colonel Werlich called Blue Book and said, "Thursday I called, with the personal opinion that we needed technical assistance at that time and that is what we requested and we didn't get it and we have tried to do what we could."

The Air Force explanations offered are not very good. That was why I called the physicist. I wanted to know what he thought about the plasma idea. He said, "They're reaching here. This just doesn't make good sense."

And that is exactly what I thought as I read the file. The Air Force investigators don't care what the solution is as long as they find one. Bringing in the plasmas sounds good, and for Air Force officers who know nothing about plasmas (just like the majority of us) it makes sense. But when the case file is reviewed, we find, just as we have before, that the explanation makes no sense. This should be labeled as an unidentified.

JANUARY 17, 1969:

THE LAST OF THE UNIDENTIFIEDS

In an example of how the Air Force can't win for losing, I thought we'd take a look at the last case submitted to Project Blue Book that was labeled as an unidentified. The Project Record card stated, "The most likely stimulus was a helicopter with an unusual lighting system. However, a check of the four airports in the area revealed that three definitely did not have any helo activity in the area and the other had destroyed flight records for that date and was therefore unable to say if any helicopter activity originated from their airfield that night. It is also possible that a light aircraft such as an aerial advertiser, the Goodyear blimp, or an aircraft doing infrared photography may have been the stimulus of the sighting. However, because it has not been definitely established that an aircraft of this type was in the area, the sighting is being carried as unidentified."

If that isn't a load of double-talk, I have never seen it. It might be a helicopter, but we can't find any records that one was flying. It might be an advertising plane, but again no records. And, of course, the time of the sighting, about four in the morning, tends to rule out an advertising plane. Who is awake at four to see the thing anyway? The same goes for the Goodyear blimp. And, finally, it might have been an airplane doing infrared photography, but again, no records.

Using the same logic, we could suggest that it was the space shuttle, though none had been built. Maybe it was an advanced-design fighter that had a single test flight. Maybe it was one of the *Apollo* capsules reentering the atmosphere, though we have no records.

The record card, once again, establishes the mind-set of the men who were doing the investigation. Here was a case that had no explanation that could be proven, but we're going to speculate about what it might have been to weaken the unidentified label. It makes no difference that there is not a single shred of evidence to support any of these suggestions, they're still tossed out as if giving them the substance of a typed line will somehow make them real.

According to a statement in the Project Blue Book files, Roman K. Lupton, of Crittenden, Virginia, was awakened at 3:24 A.M. on the morning of January 17, 1969, by an unusual sound. It was like the hum of an electric motor that was about to go bad. Lupton's wife said that she could hear the same, somewhat annoying sound.

According to Lupton, "I went to the bedroom window . . . looked in the direction of the sound for a few seconds before it came into sight. . . . I watched this object with lights all around the bottom move slowly forward with an up-and-down motion which was also slow, 30 miles per hour, varying not more than 25 feet up and down. It went forward over a yard light in my neighbors' yard next door, a little further forward and started in a banking left turn with the same speed and motion as before. At this point the object seems to tilt and turn instead of changing elevation—except for this banking motion it was the same as it had been previously. . . . At this time as it was turning, the blinking light was clearest and possibly could have been the first time I saw it. . . . At this point it went out of sight."

Lupton said that he had seen a series of windows around the bottom of the UFO that were all brightly lighted except one in the rear that blinked. The windows were rectangular and appeared translucent. They allowed the light out but Lupton couldn't see in, and each seemed to be surrounded by a glow or haze. Lupton could see the center of the craft in the light and said that it was solid, apparently metallic, and reflected some of the light.

Lupton asked his wife if she had seen the object and she said she had. Next he called the operator in Smithfield and was startled when she said that she could hear the sound in the background.

When the noise faded out, Lupton decided that he should alert someone in authority and finally asked the operator to place a call to Langley Air Force Base. He was connected to an airman who took UFO reports, and Lupton told him the same thing that he had told to the operator.

The next day, Lupton tried to find the operator that he had talked to hoping to establish some corroboration but failed to find her. Finally, on January 22, he spoke to the supervisor who told him that the only thing that the operator could have heard was some kind of aircraft. Lupton insisted, but the supervisor was equally insistent. The supervisor refused to supply the name of the operator or even let him talk to her.

Also on January 17, Lupton decided to try to find others who might have heard the noise. According to Lupton, "When I got home I started looking for someone. . . . The wife [of his next door neighbor] . . . remembered her mother saying she had heard something. Sure enough the lady and her three-year-old granddaughter both had heard it. The lady [Louise Bailey] stated 'it had awakened the girl [Robin Harvill] and both were frightened,' but the lady did not look out of her window to see what was making the sound. . . . She also stated that 'it sounded as if it were coming through the roof.' "

The next day, Lupton did the same thing and found another neighbor who said that she had heard the sound. Adrienne Carron (or Corron, it's spelled both ways in the Air Force file) said that "the sound was loud and varying and it was coming from almost right on the roof top" and it also frightened her four-year-old daughter, Evelyn.

In the letter that Lupton wrote to the Air Force about the experience, he listed all those who had heard the sound. What is interesting about the list is that the Air Force officers who reviewed the file left in all the names except a Sunday-school teacher, and a hint that someone else had reported the sound to Langley.

The Air Force eventually decided to investigate the case. Almost two months afterward, Lupton filed his report which included the standard Air Force Form 117, that is the UFO form, a NICAP form, a post card, and a road map. Lieutenant Colonel Everett M. Worthington wrote, "After discussing this sighting with Mr. Lupton, I attempted to bring into focus the similarity between his UFO sighting and a jet-powered helicopter. He was not receptive to this line of reasoning."

On April 7, after Lieutenant Colonel Worthington had completed his investigation and suggested a helicopter, Lieutenant Colonel Quintanilla wrote to a number of agencies around the Crittenden, Virginia, area asking if they had any helicopter traffic flying at that time of the morning. All the agencies except one responded they had no traffic in the area. The lone exception was the FAA which reported that such records were destroyed after fifteen days. They didn't know if there had been any helicopter traffic in the area because they no longer had their records.

The response from Fort Eustis was the most interesting. Not only didn't they have helicopters flying, Lurlene Martin, the flight-scheduling clerk at Felker Army Airfield, said that poor weather conditions had grounded all their aircraft at 9:30 P.M. and they did not resume flying until the following morning. That would seem to suggest poor weather throughout the region that would have kept all helicopter activity on the ground.

This one note, in the files, could be quite important only because it suggests that the weather was bad. The poor weather could have been localized and therefore not apply to a larger region. Air Force investigators didn't bother to find out. They had decided that Lupton saw a helicopter and tried to convince him of it.

The other question is, If it had been a helicopter, what kind was it? There was obviously a strange lighting configuration, and it would seem to me, that an investigation could have attacked the problem from that direction. Had they been able to locate a helicopter with a strange lighting configuration on it, that would have gone a long way to solving the case. Even if they couldn't prove the aircraft was flying on the date in question, the configuration of the lights would have been persuasive evidence. However, there is no indication in the file that the Air Force investigators tried that.

In the end, we are left with a case where one man apparently saw a strange object, and about a dozen others heard the sound it made. That would, of course, rule out hallucination. It does not prove that Lupton saw a flying saucer, just that he did see something strange.

It is too bad that the last unidentified UFO sighting in the Project Blue Book files had to be so nonspectacular. There were no photographs, radar tracks, or movies taken. It was just a sighting in the early morning caused by a low-flying, and very noisy, object.

What might be more important in this, the last of the Blue Book unidentifieds, is the reaction of the military. Rather than investigate the case, they spent time trying to convince the witness he had seen a helicopter when the evidence showed that no helicopters were flying in his area at the time. And even with those negative results, they noted on the Project Card that a helicopter was the most likely answer.

To that, all I can say is, Did I miss something?

SO, WHAT DO WE MAKE OF ALL THIS?

At the end of Project Blue Book in 1969, the Air Force released a "Fact Sheet" about its study of UFOs. It reported that Air Force investigators had studied 12,618 reports and identified all but 701. According to the Fact Sheet, "Of these total sightings, 11,917 were found to have been caused by material objects (such as balloons, satellites, and aircraft), immaterial objects (such as lightning, reflections, and other natural phenomena), astronomical objects (such as stars, planets, the sun and the moon), weather conditions, and hoaxes. As indicated only 701 reported sightings remain unexplained."

The question that must be asked is whether the 701 unexplained sightings are a significant number. It is a small number compared to the total of sightings reported. Air Force officers and scientists reviewing the data have suggested that had "complete" information been available, the sightings would have been explained. It was a failure on the part of those reporting the sighting, or on the part of the officers investigating the sighting to supply that complete data. Had they been able to do the "job" right, an explanation would have been found.

But let's look at the Air Force investigation as we have studied it. The Mantell case is particularly illustrative of a point. Mantell was killed chasing something that neither he, nor those on the ground who saw it, could explain. To all of them in 1947, it was something other than a natural phenomenon and it certainly wasn't a balloon. All were familiar with balloons and this thing was just too big.

Given the range of the sightings—that is, the object was seen in towns separated by something on the order of 175 miles—a single weather balloon could not account for the sighting. Whatever it was had to be huge and very high, or the sightings were unrelated.

The investigators finally settled on Venus as the culprit. Spotting Venus in the daytime, under the best conditions, is difficult. The weather reports suggested that the weather conditions were not the best. There was a layer of haze that should have obscured Venus, effectively ruling it out as a source of the sighting.

The investigators decided it was a weather balloon, though there seemed to be no evidence to support the claim. Finally, they decided on a combination of Venus and *two* weather balloons. It was a wholly unsatisfactory explanation. The case, in 1948, should have been labeled as "unidentified" because they didn't have a real explanation for it. It was, in fact, unidentified.

Now, looking back on it, reading the file, and knowing of the classified Navy project called Skyhook, we can see what the solution is. Mantell, as well as those on the ground, in those widely separated locations, saw a Skyhook balloon. The descriptions provided by the witnesses, as well the size and shape of the balloon, makes it clear. Today, the Mantell case should be written off as a Skyhook, but in 1948, it was unidentified.

The point here is that the Mantell case was not Venus, as the Air Force said, it was not a weather balloon as the Air Force said, and it was not a combination of weather balloons and Venus as the Air Force said. It was, in fact, a single balloon, of a type that was new and unknown to the majority of the people in the United States in 1948. The Air Force, in 1948, had no answer to the case, but they labeled it as "identified" nonetheless.

This tells us that, at one time, the Air Force was interested in labeling the cases but not solving them. By rushing to slap the label on the case, they harmed their own credibility when the actual solution was discovered. UFO believers, scientists, military officers, and the rest of us, would have been more accepting of their "final" solution had they not blunted the impact of it with a number of other, unacceptable answers.

In fact, by studying the trend in explanations, we can put together a history of the UFO project as it began in the summer of 1947. Ed Ruppelt, in his book, *The Report on Unidentified Flying Objects*, reported that the Pentagon was in a panic during the summer of 1947. There were reports of flying saucers all over the country, but officials didn't know what they were. There was a push for immediate answers. If flying saucers were real, and extraterrestrial, control of the sky was suddenly and completely gone. If they were real, then questions about an alien invasion became very real.

But that was the summer of 1947 when the phenomenon was still new. Ruppelt wrote, "As 1947 drew to a close, the Air Force's Project Sign had outgrown its initial panic and settled down to a routine operation." It meant that those at the top in the military and in the government had realized that alien invasion fleets were not standing by to land. In fact, some may have thought, after the summer, that if they waited long enough, the fad of flying saucers would end and there would be no reason to worry.

In the summer of 1948, it became clear that the Chief of Staff of the Air Force didn't believe that UFOs were extraterrestrial. A report sent to him was slapped back and those who had authored it found themselves searching for new work. The lieutenants and captains in the Air Force were smart enough to see that suggesting UFOs were real and extraterrestrial was not a way to advance their careers. Answers were what was wanted by the top brass and answers they supplied. UFO cases that had been puzzling for months were suddenly solved. The explanations might have flown in the face of the facts, but that didn't matter. The Chief of Staff wanted answers and those who expected to climb the military ladders were supplying them.

The only time that the official Air Force investigation progressed with what could be called objectivity was a short period from the end of 1951 to the very beginning of 1953. Is it any wonder, then, that about 40 percent of the cases listed as unidentified in the overall files came from that short period?

After that, in document after document, in report after report, and policy shift after policy shift, there is a single uniting thread. UFO sightings are to be explained. It doesn't matter if the facts must be ignored, the case is to be solved.

Take, as just a single example that we studied earlier, the report from Minot Air Force Base. The Air Force would have us believe that the men assigned to the Strategic Air Command are incapable of recognizing a B-52 when it flies over. The investigators would have us believe that these same men are incapable of recognizing the stars in the sky. And, to explain the radar returns, they would have us believe that plasmas, a phenomenon that had just come into the public arena, were responsible for those sightings. Those investigators would even ignore the fact that radars other than that on the aircraft were affected. Plasmas sounded like a wonderful answer in 1968.

Well, I found a physicist who knew something about plasmas, talked to him about the case, and was told the explanation was ridiculous. The Air Force officer who suggested plasmas was just looking for a way to write the case off. The plasma answer didn't make sense to the physicist. Of course, to other Air Force officers and to the news media and general public who knew nothing of plasma physics, the explanation sounded credible and that was all they wanted. An answer that would be believed. They knew that most of us would not have the time or the training to review the case closely. They provided a scientific-sounding explanation and slapped it on the file. Case closed.

What this tells us, as do some of the other cases we examined, such as that of the police officers who "chased Venus" or the private pilot who tried to intercept "Venus or a sun dog," was that the Air Force investigators were interested in nothing other than explaining the sightings reported to them. While the Air Force statement suggests that only 701 sightings were listed as unidentified, they don't mention all the others that are mislabeled. In my survey of the files, I found dozens of reports that seemed to have been "solved" in a fashion similar to that mentioned above.

This also suggests that even if the 701 sightings that were unexplained was not a significant number, when we add in those that had solutions that were less than accurate, the number increases. If we added only three hundred, a very conservative number, then we suddenly have a thousand sightings that aren't explained, or about one in twelve. Is that a significant number?

But let's take it even further, which we can. What the Air Force status sheet didn't tell anyone was that many of the cases were labeled as having insufficient data for a scientific analysis. Although there were few such cases in the beginning of the project, by the end many of them were labeled as such.

It should be pointed out here that calling a case "insufficient data" is not an explanation. It is merely a label. But, the point would be to keep the case out of the "unidentified" files. By doing so, they are not counted in the 701 sightings labeled as "unidentified."

In the course of this work, I reviewed a number of those cases. In some of them there just wasn't enough information to make a proper evaluation. If, for example, a single witness saw a bright light move across the sky at three o'clock in the morning, how could the Air Force be expected to "solve" the riddle? It could have been a meteor that was distinctive enough that it fooled the witness. What if it was a private plane with the landing lights on and the wind blowing hard enough to push the engine noise away from the witness? What if it was spotlights playing across a cloud? There simply isn't enough information and the Air Force investigators were right in labeling it as "insufficient data."

But the majority of the cases weren't like that. There was a great deal of accurate and precise information supplied by the witnesses. Sometimes there was more than one witness. The thickness of the file and the amount of the information seems to have overwhelmed the officers reviewing it. There was too much information, so that many of the old standby answers such as weather balloons or Venus just couldn't be bent to fit the mold. Rather than suggest an unexplained case, the report was stamped with "insufficient data."

In one case, one of the very last to labeled as "unidentified," the witness was furious when his case was deemed "insufficient data." He filled out one of the Air Force forms and then added a long statement to question 35, which asks for additional "information which you feel pertinent and which is not adequately covered in the specific points of the questionnaire or a narrative explanation of your sighting." He wrote, "It is a real mystery to me why you state in your August 21 missive, 'The information which we received is not sufficient for a scientific evaluation,' in consideration of the fact that the very thorough report which Lieutenant Foreman took and supposedly submitted to you contained far more definitive information . . . than could be elicited via your questionnaire."

The witness continued, adding that more information was available through Foreman's (that is, the Air Force officer who investigated) report than in the form that was being sent, but that their handling of the case "leads me to believe . . . that accusations of negligence heaped upon you . . . by some independent investigations in recent years my NOT be entirely unfounded."

Like the rest of us, this witness was left wondering what was missing from his reports and Lieutenant Foreman's. What data was needed so that a scientific analysis could be made? It seemed to him that a great deal of time and effort was going into the collection of data that when received and processed revealed nothing or was lacking in some critical area.

After evaluating the new information, and realizing that the witness had not only a good education but a technical background, they changed the status from "insufficient data" to "unidentified." The Air Force officers had found themselves in another of their famous holes.

But the case does raise an interesting question: What was left out of the questionnaire that should have been included? The Air Force, with the help of the Battelle Memorial Institute, had spent months designing the form to gather precisely the type of information that the Air Force would need to gather. Several different versions had been tried and then revised. Even top UFO critic and debunker Dr. Donald Menzel had supplied the Air Force with his thoughts on the questionnaire being used by them. Menzel wrote about the design of the questionnaire, "I don't know who is at fault, but the questionnaire seems cleverly designed to avoid asking the most vital questions and to get the wrong answers. In response to my repeated criticisms, the Air Force asked me to suggest revisions for the new printing. I spent several weeks detailing the revisions and giving my reasons therefore. But they adopted only a few of my suggestions, rejecting the remainder because they considered them to be an invasion of privacy."

Menzel was quick to point out other inadequacies. "The original questionnaire determined whether or not the person was wearing glasses, but did not find out whether a person who was not wearing glasses was supposed to be wearing them. I wanted to know how long it had been since the witness had had an eye examination. I even wanted to know the nature of the correction."

While it seems that Menzel was delving into areas that were personal and private, and may not have relevant to the investigation, it is also obvious that the Air Force questionnaire, from a scientific standpoint, was not complete. There were standard questions that should have been asked and that clearly were not.

Finally, it must be noted that a large number of the cases marked as "insufficient data" were marked so because the Air Force questionnaire had not been completed in what the Air Force officers thought was a reasonable amount of time. This was a complex document that ran to several pages, calling for some precise information. The Air Force officers, when confronted with a sighting, apparently felt it was sufficient to send out a questionnaire, but apparently never believed it necessary to make follow-up inquiries. If their form was not completed, then the case was written off as "insufficient data."

As just a single example, a photographic case on August 21, 1968, from Ottsville, Pennsylvania, is listed as "Visual: INSUFFICIENT DATA FOR EVALUATION," and "Photo: INSUFFICIENT DATA FOR EVALUATION." The note on the card said, "Neither the form 117 not [sic] the photo-data sheet was returned as of 9 Dec '68."

Here is a case in which photographs were taken. The Air Force investigators response was to send out a couple of forms and let it go. There is no indication that any type of follow-up was made. There is no indication that the officers tried to learn more about the case. What is evident here is that by 1968 they were content to let the witnesses come to them so that they could make their pronouncements. They weren't interested in investigating UFO sightings. They were interested in clearing the cases off the books and writing comments on the Project Cards that would satisfy the requirements of Air Force regulations. In the military this is known as filling in the squares. Color in enough of the squares and you can expect promotion, medals, and other rewards.

In a review of the number of sightings for the period of July 1–10, 1967, picked at random, I found that 10 of the 34 sightings were listed as "insufficient data." One of the sightings, from Lizelia, Mississippi, was listed as "unidentified." One was listed as being "unreliable," which meant the witness had made other UFO sightings. And one was listed as "confusing data."

All in all, there were 13 sightings that were "unexplained," though only one was listed as such. The other 12 were labeled, but they certainly weren't explained. That means that about 30 percent of the sightings have no explanation for them. Or, in other words, about 4,000 of the 12,000 Blue Book sightings are not explained.

Is that a significant number?

Let's stop for a moment and look at the "unreliable" reports. First, some of the cases were marked as "unreliable" simply based on the investigator's opinion. For example, the January 17, 1969, case from Bradenton, Florida, is marked as "unreliable." Under "Comments," the investigator wrote, "It would seem very strange if a fifteen-year-old boy could watch several disc-shaped objects as strange as he reported for a period of twenty minutes and not make an attempt to get witnesses to the event. It would also be strange if an object were as low as he reported, in a residential area, and be reported by only one observer."

There are a couple of problems with that analysis. First, it could be that the boy was so overwhelmed by what he was watching that he didn't think of finding corroborating witnesses. It could be that he didn't want to try to find them because he didn't want to miss anything outside. It could be that there was no one around him that could be a corroborating witness. We have all heard stories of professional photographers who, when surprised by a stunning sight, forget all about the cameras hanging around their necks.

It is the conclusion drawn by Air Force investigators that is not valid. They thought it strange they received only one report from that area. They didn't look for other observers but assumed that since no one reported the sighting, there were no other observers. It could be that others, knowing the Air Force's habit of belittling UFO observers, as we have seen time and again in the files we examined, didn't want to be subjected to a similar fate.

No, the Air Force's conclusions here are what are not reliable. They were seeking a way of eliminating reports from the files without regard to the truth.

Second, it seems to be the thinking of the Air Force officers that seeing a UFO was such a rare circumstance that no one would have the opportunity twice. If they did report UFOs on more than one occasion, that would mean that the witness was unfamilar with the sky and was therefore unreliable. No reason to investigate a case in which the witness couldn't distinguish between what was supposed to be in the sky and what wasn't supposed to be there.

Such thinking does make some sense. If a person can't recognize the stars, the moon, meteors, or in some cases, the lights on radio towers that had been in the area for years, why waste time and a questionnaire? The observer is unreliable.

Interestingly, that doesn't always hold true. Charles B. Moore made UFO reports to the Air Force project on two occasions. Both his sightings are labeled as "unidentified." His first sighting, near Array, New Mexico, isn't very spectacular. Moore, along with a crew from the General Mills corporation, and a naval officer, Douglas C. McLaughlin (misidentified in some reports as Robert or "R." McLaughlin according to an AFOSI document in the Project Blue Book file) were launching balloons. They had "released a 350-gram balloon about 1020 MST and were following it with a standard ML-47 David White theodolite." Moore made a reading at 10:30 A.M. and then took over at the theodolite.

According to his report, made to Project Grudge, he had looked up to view the balloon with the naked eye and spotted what he thought was the balloon. Moore wrote, "When the distance between the theodolite and the supposed balloon became apparent, I took over the theodolite and found the true balloon still there, whereupon I abandoned it and picked up the object after it came out of the sun. The object was moving too fast to crank the theodolite around; therefore, one of the men pointed the theodolite and I looked. The object was ellipsoid . . . white in color except for a light yellow of one side as though it were in shadow."

"The object," according to Moore, "was not a balloon and was some distance away. Assuming escape velocity, a track is enclosed which figures elevation above the station of about 300,000 feet over the observed period. If this is true, the flight would have probably gone over the White Sands Proving Ground [later White Sands Missile Range], Holloman Air Force Base, and Los Alamos."

They lost sight of the object in the distance, after watching it for about 60 seconds. They had made measurements using their equipment and a stopwatch but took no photographs.

Dr. Donald Menzel, of course, later did what the Air Force couldn't do in their investigation. He identified the object seen by Moore and his crew. According to Menzel, the object was a mirage. That is, Menzel believed it to be an atmospheric reflection of the true balloon, making it appear as if there were two objects in the sky instead of one. He was so sure of this that he told Moore about the solution.

Moore, however, is an atmospheric physicist. He is as qualified as Menzel to discuss the dynamics of the atmosphere, and, according to him, when interviewed on El Paso radio station KTSM, the weather conditions were not right for the creation of mirages. Since Moore was on the scene, and since his training qualified him to make judgments about the conditions of the atmosphere at the time of the sighting, his observations are more important than Menzel's wild speculations.

When Moore spoke to Menzel, the Harvard professor would not listen to what Moore had to say. Menzel had found what to him was a satisfactory solution for the sighting, and he didn't want to discuss it seriously, or have his conclusions challenged. Air Force investigators, however, left the sighting labeled as "unidentified."

Just over two years later, on October 11, 1951, Moore, still conducting balloon research with General Mills, along with a number of other people including J. J. Kaliszewski, Doug Smith, and Dick Reilly, spotted another UFO. The object came in high and fast, slowed, and then made slow, climbing circles for two minutes before it shot off to the east. A second one appeared, and using a theodolite, it was carefully observed as it flew across the sky.

Moore, then, according to the Air Force files, was one of those rare birds who had seen UFOs on two separate occasions. Both times he was able to make observations using his equipment. And, as mentioned, on both occasions, his sightings were not readily identifiable.

Moore, however, is not alone. Dr. Clyde Tombaugh, the only living human to have discovered a planet in our solar system, reported UFOs on more than one occasion. According to Tombaugh,

I saw the object about eleven o'clock at night in August 1949 from the backyard of my home in Las Cruces, New Mexico. I happened to be looking at the zenith, admiring the beautiful transparent sky of stars, when suddenly I spied a geometrical group of faint bluish green rectangles of light similar to the "Lubbock lights." [It should be noted that his report was written *after* the "Lubbock lights" case in September 1951.] My wife and her mother were sitting in the yard with me and they saw them also. The group moved south-southeasterly, the individual rectangles became foreshortened, their space of formation smaller (at first about one degree across), and the intensity duller, fading from view at about 35 degrees above the horizon. Total time of visibility was about three seconds. I was too flabbergasted to count the number of rectangles of light, or to note some other features I wondered about later. There was no sound. I have done thousands of hours of night sky-watching, but never saw a sight so strange as this. The rectangles were of low luminosity; had there been a full moon in the sky, I am sure they would not have been visible.

Naturally, Tombaugh's sighting, because of who he is, has caused a great deal of speculation. Donald Menzel wrote about it, praising Tombaugh as a scientist, but then, after a fashion, explaining that Tombaugh had been fooled because of a thin inversion layer over New Mexico that night.

Menzel, in his 1953 book *Flying Saucers* wrote, "But what were these mysterious lights? I can only hazard here the same guess I made about the Lubbock lights—that a low, thin layer of haze or smoke reflected the lights of a distant house or some other multiple source. The haze must have been inconspicuous to the eye, because Tombaugh comments on the unusual clarity of the sky." (Note that Tombaugh commented on the unusual clarity of the sky but Menzel postulates a "thin layer of haze." It seems to be a real contradiction.)

A year or two after his first sighting, Tombaugh had a second one that he reported to J. Allen Hynek, who reported it in a memo that was originally classified. According to that document, Tombaugh, "while at Telescope No. 3 at White Sands observed an object of minus-6 magnitude traveling from the zenith to the southern horizon in about three seconds. The object executed the same maneuvers as the nighttime luminous object he had seen earlier."

What this demonstrates is that the Air Force's criterion for rejecting the sightings of those who report UFOs more than once is flawed. It shouldn't be assumed that anyone seeing UFOs more than once is unreliable. Certainly, there are unreliable observers out there, but the criterion should be more than multiple sightings. The Air Force's rejection of sightings for that reason alone may have been proper, and it wasn't scientific.

This idea goes hand in hand with another. That is, the higher the education of the observer, and the more details provided for the sighting, the more likely it will be identified. A survey of the data showed that the opposite was true. Higher education and more information resulted in a lower number of the cases being solved. A light in the night sky, if an airplane can be found in the right place, is easy to explain. But a disc-shaped object, at high noon, with observers on the ground and in the air, is difficult to explain, unless you ignore some of the data. That is, of course, exactly what happened in the Salt Lake City case.

I have mentioned the name of Donald Menzel a number of times. He "solved" cases that others had left as "unidentified." He applied a skeptical eye to these cases, finding solutions where others could not. He challenged the observers, such as Charles B. Moore, inventing conditions that those at the scene never saw. He told Moore that he'd seen a mirage, but Moore, equally qualified, and on the scene, said he hadn't.

Menzel couldn't accept the fact there might be extraterrestrial visitors. Since there couldn't be, he knew that the answer for the "unidentified" cases had to lie elsewhere. This is not exactly good science, either.

In the paper he presented to the Symposium on Unidentified Flying Objects, sponsored by the American Association for the Advancement of Science, on December 26 and 27, 1969, he castigated Dr. James McDonald for what he considered to be mistakes in McDonald's research, his beliefs about UFOs, and for not reporting everything about a case so that he, McDonald, could present a persuasive argument for his opinions.

Menzel, writing about the Chiles and Whitted case, suggested, "He accuses me of 'glossing over the reported rocking of the DC-3.' Nonsense! There was no mention of such 'rocking' in the official report."

The statement by Menzel is interesting for a couple of reasons. As noted in the chapter on the Chiles and Whitted case, the newspaper articles do report that Chiles mentioned a buffeting of the aircraft. But, when I searched the statements made by both Chiles and Whitted to official investigators, including those they wrote themselves and contained in the official files, they mentioned nothing about the turbulence.

The only conclusion we can draw is that there was no turbulence. Where did McDonald get the idea? Clearly he did not have access to the official file, as did Menzel, because Menzel knew what was in the file. So McDonald's mistake seems to be that he didn't see the official file, and that wasn't his fault. Turbulence was mentioned in the newspaper reports about the sighting. That must be where McDonald got the idea.

By way of contrast, on the Salt Lake City case Menzel, who insisted that it was a sun dog, wrote, "During all this time ground observers reported no motion whatever."

Remember, Menzel clearly had access to the official files. I read them before writing the sections here, and, as mentioned, I selected parts of those official statements because they proved that the people on the ground did say they saw the object move. Menzel was clearly wrong here. He had to know the truth, but he spouted the party line nonetheless.

So, given that, who engaged in the worst "science"—Menzel or McDonald? Clearly it was Menzel. He had to know the truth, he had access to information that was prohibited to McDonald, but glossed over it in his rush to solve the sightings.

All this leads to still another question. Remember the date of the sympmosium was late December 1969. The Project Blue Book files were supposedly classified. How did Menzel know, in 1969, what was in the files? The answer is that he had read them. He was working for the Air Force. He was consulting for the Air Force. That explains how he knew what was in the files, and it explains why, out of all the people who had written books about UFOs, including former head of Project Blue Book Ed Ruppelt, only the galleys of Menzel's books were in the files. Portions of these galleys are in many of the case files.

It also tells us something about the makeup of the Air Force team who investigated UFOs. Menzel was a rabid debunker. In a letter to me, he lectured that all sightings could be explained, for the most part, by misidentifications of natural phenomena, delusion, or conventional craft seen in unconventional circumstances. In all the other cases, the sightings were the result of "damned liars." For a scientist, he didn't have a very scientific attitude.

We can also see, in his handling of the "Lubbock lights" case, where his mind-set was. While a persuasive argument can be made that the first of the sightings, by the professors on the porch, might be some sort of natural phenomenon, such an explanation fails to explain the photographs taken by Carl Hart, Jr. Menzel tried, as he had with other sightings, multiple explanations. This suggests, of course, that he doesn't have a clue and just wanted to explain them away. When his multiple explanations failed to gain much attention, he decided, with no evidence whatsoever, that the photographs were a hoax.

That attitude was reflected by the personnel in Project Blue Book. Hector Quintanilla went out of his way to suggest solutions to sightings that were ridiculous. When police officers chased a glowing object from Ohio to Pennsylvania, he decided it was a combination of *Echo I* and Venus. He made his assessment based on a telephone conversation with a single witness, asked only a couple of questions, and then ended his investigation. Only under congressional pressure and orders from the Pentagon did he make the trip from Dayton, Ohio, across the state to interview the witnesses.

The interview with the police officers was not an attempt to gather additional information. It was an attempt by Quintanilla to convince the witnesses that they had seen a satellite and Venus. He didn't seem to be interested in hearing how the object had been within a hundred feet of the witnesses, or how its illumination lighted the road under it. Quintanilla had "solved" the case, and solved it stayed.

What this tells, or rather confirms, is that the Air Force project was in the business of "solving" UFO sightings and not investigating them. It also tells us that an "unidentified" label was the kiss of death. The point was to reduce the number of "unidentified" cases to a point where they became statistically insignificant and that point could be made to the public. Air Force officials insisted that, with complete information, all cases would have been identified.

How can we be sure that this is the case? Remember the letter written by an officer about Air Force Regulation 200-2, "which essentially stipulates the following . . . to explain or identify all UFO sightings."

And, remember that Edward Trapnell, an assistant to the Secretary of the Air Force, suggested finding a civilian agency to study the problem and then conclude it the way the Air Force wanted it concluded. One of the stipulations was that the civilian agency had to say some positive things about the Air Force's handling of the UFO question, even though, as is obvious to us, their handling had been less than adequate.

We see then, after 1953, when the Robertson Panel had "studied" UFOs, and had made their recommendations, of stripping the mystery from the phenomenon, and public education, the emphasis shifted from investigation to explanation. Twist and manipulate the data until it was warped into a position that fit with what the Air Force wanted us to believe. They were the "authorities" on the topic. They had employed the best research techniques. And they had no "secret" information that would lead to conclusions other than UFOs don't exist.

Yet, when we look at the files, those files that they must have believed no one would ever see, we learn that the situation is different than we were told. There were secret studies, some of which concluded that UFOs were extraterrestrial, there were cases in which the solutions were not consistent with the facts, and there were cases in which the Air Force should have investigated but never did.

The Air Force mission, or rather the public mission, was to investigate UFOs. That should mean they would be very interested in the photographic cases. Here were reports where they weren't confined by the eyewitness testimony. There was something that could be measured and analyzed. Here was something they could see. And yet, it seems that they had no real interest in pursuing some of the best of the photographic cases.

On May 11, 1950, Paul Trent, a farmer living near McMinnville, Oregon, took two photographs of an object that hovered near his house. The pictures of the disc-shaped craft have foreground detail in them. Neither Trent nor his wife attempted to make any money from the pictures. They have been examined time and again by experts. William Hartmann analyzed them for the Condon Committee and wrote, "The is one of the few UFO reports in which all factors investigated, geometric, psychological, and physical, appear to be consistent with the assertion that an extraordinary flying object, silvery, metallic, disc-shaped, tens of meters in diameter, and evidently artificial, flew within sight of two witnesses. It cannot be said that the evidence positively rules out a fabrication, although there are some physical factors such as the accuracy of certain photometric measures of the original negatives which argue against fabrication."

Years later, UFO debunker Philip J. Klass would suggest that shadows under the eaves of the barn "proved" the picture was taken in the morning, rather than the evening, and that proved the case a hoax. Others wrote the shadows off to random light scattering and essentially unimportant.

But the real point here is a case that even the scientists with the Condon Committee found of sufficient interest that they analyzed the photographs. But not so the Air Force. The Project Blue Book files show that this case is "information" only. It is not a "real" case and doesn't even have an evaluation written after it.

It would seem to me, that if you are charged with determining what flying saucers are, that if a case came to your attention that had two good photographs to go with it, you would make an effort to learn more. It would seem to me that this sort of a case would be better than all those with single witnesses that the Air Force chased down. It would seem to me that the value of such a case would be higher than those where there is only the testimony of witnesses.

So, where are we, then? The Air Force files, contrary to what they would have us believe, are a treasure trove of old cases. I have attempted to separate the rumors from the facts by studying the reports as they were gathered decades ago. We can learn, just as Menzel suggested, that neither Chiles nor Whitted felt the aircraft was buffeted by turbulence, though such facts have been presented in the past.

We can learn, even though the Air Force claimed a solution to a specific case, that the solution didn't always fit the facts. The Minot Air Force Base report proved that.

We can learn that the Air Force argued that UFOs weren't real and that its officers had found no evidence to support any other conclusion, when such was not the case. While they claimed all but 701 sightings were "identified," we have learned that those 11,000-plus files might have been labeled, but a good third of them were never identified. It is a subtle but very real difference.

We can learn that controversial cases, such as the Hill abduction, the McMinnville photographs, or the Kelly-Hopkinsville attack, while in the files, were there as "information" only. Why would the Air Force investigators shy away from investigating these cases, but collect information about them? It is an interesting fact.

We can learn, by studying the cases, that the Air Force officers who knew the truth about what was in the files rarely, if ever, shared it with the general public or the media. Instead, they would make their proclamations, and without access to the data, it would be difficult for anyone to argue the point. Now, with that data firmly in hand, we can see, time and again, how the officers were less than candid.

We can learn that a true evaluation of the material in the case files has not been done. Here, I have only scratched the surface of what can be found in the files. If someone, or some organization, was to undertake a complete, and I think it must be objective, reevaluation of the files, what is found would be startling. Would they be able to prove that UFOs are alien spacecraft? I don't think so. But, it would certainly be a starting point and would reveal that something strange has been going on for over five decades.

We can learn that Blue Book was not the final authority on UFO-sighting investigations. We can see, by regulation and report, that other organizations including the CIA, the 4602d AISS, and other military units, held responsibility for investigating UFOs. The situation wasn't one of a single entity investigating the sightings, but one of multiple entities often investigating cases without coordinating with one another.

We can learn that Blue Book was not an objective investigation searching for answers, but a military organization with a specific mission. The investigations sometime got in the way of the mission. That was proven when Quintanilla was forced to go to interview the police officers who had chased UFOs.

The arguments from Project Blue Book turn out to be circular. There are no UFOs, therefore we can find no evidence that there are UFOs. Since we found no evidence that there are UFOs, there cannot be UFOs. But all they had to do was study their own files without letting their personal beliefs, or the beliefs of their superiors, influence them. What we have in the Project Blue Book files are dozens of cases that scream for proper scientific scrutiny. That has yet to happen.

What we can learn from the Project Blue Book files is that something very unusual has been happening since June 1947. It has been investigated, analyzed, studied, and considered, and no one has provided a good solution as yet. In fact, by studying these files, it seems that a solid case for the extraterrestrial hypothesis can be made. That surely is not what they wanted, but it's what they got.

What we can learn from the Project Blue Book files is that 701 may not be a significant number, but 4,000 is. Those who played the numbers game were keeping them artificially low so that it would seem that there was nothing to UFOs. We learn that they were wrong.

Project Blue Book, as well as its predecessors, was a sham from the beginning. They went through the motions of gathering the data, they filled reams of paper with meaningless thoughts, and they worked to convince us that there was nothing to flying-saucer reports. But when we were allowed to see the evidence, we saw what it showed. Flying saucers do exist, and the best evaluation suggests that they are extra-terrestrial in origin. That is what we can learn from Project Blue Book.

APPENDIX A:

THE LUBBOCK LIGHTS, THE WASHINGTON NATIONALS, AND THE LAS VEGAS UFO CRASH: AN ANALYSIS OF THE DATA

Over the years there have been a number of important cases that have received a great deal of attention. To understand the situation at Project Blue Book, it is necessary to understand those cases. Many of them show how the investigations progressed and how the solutions were determined. There are, however, a number of other cases that were well researched by Air Force investigators at the time they occurred. These other cases, for the most part, took place between August 1951 and January 1953.

In putting together the book, I wanted to deal with cases that were important to understanding the philosophy of the Air Force investigation without confusing the issue of what they were really attempting. Because of that, there were a couple of cases that I wanted to discuss, but that didn't fit the flow of the narrative elsewhere. For that reason, I combined the cases and put them here.

The following are three cases that were investigated in depth by Air Force officers. For the most part, they found what they believe to be explanations for the sightings. As happened in so many other aspects of the Air Force study, the facts do not directly support the conclusions drawn. This is, you might say, just additional ammunition for the case I have been attempting to make throughout the book.

In August 1951, a series of spectacular sightings, including a series of photographs, took place over Lubbock, Texas. This all happened about the time that Ed Ruppelt had taken over the leadership of Blue Book and was reorganizing it. Less than a year later, a series of sightings took place over Washington's National Airport. The explanations offered by the Air Force, and the investigation of the case, demonstrated the mind-set of the military at that time. And, about ten years later, the Air Force investigated a series of sightings that culminated in the apparent explosion of something near Las Vegas, Nevada.

The "Lubbock lights" story began on a hot August night as several professors from Texas Tech College (later University) sat outside. A group of dully glowing lights flashed overhead. They moved silently, crossed the sky rapidly, and seemed to be in some kind of loose, but organized, formation. They were only in sight for two or three seconds and none of the professors got a very good look at them.

The professors, W. I. Robinson, A. G. Oberg, and W. L. Ducker, discussed what they had seen, trying to figure out what it might have been. They also tried to determine what to do if the lights returned. An hour or so later, the lights reappeared, and this time the professors were ready.

The lights were softly glowing bluish objects in another loose formation. It seemed to the professors that the first group had been in a more rigid and structured formation than later groups.

To the professors the next logical move was to learn if anyone else had seen the objects. Ducker called the local newspaper and spoken to the managing editor, Jay Harris, who wasn't interested in the report. Ducker, however, convinced him that a story should be printed. Harris finally agreed but only if Ducker allowed his name to be used. Ducker refused.

But then, a few minutes later, Ducker called back and agreed. In fact, he could print the names of all the professors, but only if Harris called the college public-relations department and cleared it with them.

The newspaper story was successful in that one respect. There were others who claimed to see the lights that same night. That seemed to be some corroboration of the lights seen by the professors. But, the important sighting, at least in the minds of the Air Force officers who later investigated, was made by Joe Bryant of Brownsfield, Texas.

Bryant told Air Force officers that he was sitting in his backyard when a group of the dim lights flew overhead. He described them as having a "kind of a glow, a little bigger than a star." Not long after that, a second group appeared. Neither of the groups was in sort of a regular formation, a clue that the Air Force choose to ignore.

There was a third flight, but instead of flying over the house, they dropped down and circled the building. As he watched, one of them chirped and he recognized them immediately. He identified them as plover, a bird common in west Texas. When he read the account of the professors in the newspaper the next day, he knew immediately what they had seen. If he hadn't been able to identify the last flight, if one of the birds hadn't chirped, he would have been fooled too.

The professors, unaware of what Bryant had seen and believed, set out to obtain additional information. Joined by other professors and professionals including Grayson Meade, E. R. Hienaman, and J. P. Brand, they equipped teams with two-way radios, measured a base from the location of the original sightings, then staked out the area. They hoped for additional sightings along the baseline. Knowing the length of that line, the time of the sighting, and the location and direction of flight, they would be able to calculate a great deal of important and useful information that might tell them what they had been seeing.

The problem was that none of the teams ever made a sighting. On one or two occasions, the wives said, the men who had remained at one house or the other had seen the lights, but the men at the bases saw nothing. The plan of calculating the data fell apart.

Then, on August 31, the case took an amazing turn. Carl Hart, Jr., a nineteen-year-old amateur photographer, managed to take five pictures as the lights flew over his house in the middle of Lubbock. Lying in bed about ten o'clock, he saw the lights flash over. Knowing that they sometimes returned, he prepared for that. When the lights appeared a few minutes later, he was ready, snapping two pictures of them. Not long after that, a third group flew and he managed three additional pictures.

Jay Harris, Lubbock newspaper editor, learned about the pictures when a photographer who worked for him periodically called to tell him that Hart had used his studio to develop the film. Harris, the ever-reluctant newsman, suggested that Hart should bring the pictures by the office.

Naturally the newspaper feared a hoax. Harris, and the newspaper's lead photographer, William Hams, talked to Hart on a number of occasions over the next several hours. Harris bluntly asked if the pictures were faked. Hart denied it. When I spoke to Hart about forty years later, I asked him what he had photographed. I didn't want to accuse him of faking the pictures but I wanted to know if he had changed his mind with the passage of years. Hart told me that he still didn't know what he had photographed.

Hams later decided to try to duplicate Hart's pictures. From the roof of the newspaper office, he attempted to photograph, at night, anything that flew over. He thought, that if he could duplicate the pictures, he would be able to figure out what they showed. He waited, but all he saw was a flight of birds that were barely visible in the glow of the sodium-vapor lamps on the streets below him. The birds were dimly outlined against the deeper black of the night sky and flew in a ragged V-formation.

He took photographs of the birds, but when he developed the film, the image was so weak that he couldn't make prints. He repeated his experiment on another occasion but was no more successful. From his experience, he was convinced that what Hart photographed couldn't have been birds under any circumstances.

Air Force investigations were conducted throughout the fall of 1951. Investigators were dispatched from Reese Air Force Base on the west side of Lubbock. They spoke to Hart on a number of occasions. They forwarded copies of their reports to both Project Blue Book headquarters and to Air Force office of Special Investigation headquarters in Washington, D.C. Ed Ruppelt even made a trip to Lubbock to speak to the witnesses including Carl Hart.

During those interviews, Hart was advised of his rights under the

Constitution of the United States. The investigators were playing hard-ball with the teenager. They were trying to pick apart his story to prove that he had somehow faked the pictures. Between November 6 and 9, during still another investigation of the Lubbock lights, Ruppelt and AFOSI Special Agent Howard N. Bossert again interviewed Hart. In their report, they wrote, "Hart's story could not be 'picked apart' because it was entirely logical. He [Hart] was questioned on why he did certain things and his answers were all logical, concise, and without hesitation."

When I talked to the experts at Texas Tech about the possibility of birds, Loren Smith told me that there are ducks in the Lubbock area that fly in V-formations, but they are reddish maroon and have no white on them to reflect the lights. Although migratory birds do fly past Lubbock, it is later in the year. What this means is that there are no birds in the area that account for the photographs.

What we must do is separate the Hart photographs from the rest of the Lubbock case. In fact, we must look at all the sightings individually, realizing that a solution to one is not necessarily the solution to another or to all the reports.

First we have the sightings made by the professors. Clearly this was something that was unusual. They were unable to identify the lights. They then, using their scientific training, set about to find out what they had seen. Although their plan was good, the phenomenon did not cooperate with them. There were some facts obtained and these can lead us to some conclusions.

For example, they had originally estimated the objects as being very large and flying at a very high altitude. When they established their baselines, they never saw the objects again. The wives, however, reported the objects overhead. That would seem to indicate they were smaller and much lower than originally thought. In fact, it suggests they were much smaller and much lower. The door is open for birds, though the problem, once again, is the lack of a proper bird in the Lubbock area.

Or is it? Joe Bryant claimed that he saw the lights too, but that one of them, or several of them, swooped out of the sky to fly around his house. At that point he identified them as plover.

From Bryant's claim, the Air Force investigators extrapolated that all the Lubbock sightings could be explained by birds. In one of the reports, the investigators wrote, "It was concluded that birds, with streetlights reflecting from them, were the probable cause of these sightings. . . . In all instances the witnesses were located in an area where their eyes were dark-adapted, thus making the objects appear brighter."

The problem is, and one with which the Air Force investigators never dealt, was that similar sightings, that is, strings of lights in the night skies, were seen all over west Texas. From as far north as Amarillo to as far south as the Midland-Odessa area, reports of these sorts of sightings were made. Birds and the newly installed sodium-vapor lamps in specific areas of Lubbock do not provide an adequate explanation.

What is relevant here, however, is that Air Force officers made a long, complex investigation of the sightings. Ruppelt flew down from Wright-Patterson Air Force Base and officers and investigators were dispatched repeatedly from nearby Reese. They actually spoke to the witnesses in person, searched for evidence, analyzed the photographs, and conducted follow-up interviews. Ruppelt made it clear that he believed there to be a plausible, mundane explanation for the sightings, but never officially said what it was. Later, by searching his files, I learned that he thought, personally, the Lubbock lights were explained by fireflies.

Of course, that explanation didn't explain the photographs. Ruppelt wrote that he never found an explanation for them. "The photos were never proven to be a hoax but neither were they proven to be genuine." According to Ruppelt, "There is no definite answer."

Less than a year later Ruppelt and Project Blue Book would be involved in another series of sightings that had highly credible, multiple witnesses, and provide another type of physical evidence. This one would involve radar and air intercepts and would take place in the nation's capital.

It began late in the evening on July 19 when two radars at the Air Routing and Traffic Control Center (ARTC) picked up eight unidentified targets near Andrews Air Force Base. According to reports made by the controllers, these were not airplanes because they moved too fast. One object, according to the calculations made at the time, was tracked at 7,000 miles an hour.

About twenty minutes later, or just after midnight on July 20, the tower radars at Washington's National Airport tracked five objects. What this meant was that three radars at three different locations had solid targets that were not identified as aircraft.

One of the controllers at the ARTC called for a senior controller, Harry C. Barnes, who in turn called the National Airport control tower. They had unidentified targets on their scopes, as did the controllers at Andrews Air Force Base. They had already eliminated a mechanical malfunction as the cause, but with the objects on other scopes in other locations, there was no longer any question of their reality. The performance of the blips ruled out airplanes. All the men, including Barnes, were sure they were looking at solid objects based on their years of experience with radar. Weather-related phenomena wouldn't produce the same effect on all the radars at the widely scattered locations. In fact, if weather was the explanation, the targets would have varied from scope to scope.

Just after midnight, Airman Second Class Bill Goodman called the Andrews control tower to tell them he was watching a bright orange light about the size of a softball that was gaining and losing altitude as it zipped through the sky.

During this time, Goodman talked to Airman First Class William B. Brady, who was in the tower. Goodman told Brady that the object was to the immediate south. Brady saw a ball of orange fire. There were discrepancies between the physical descriptions given by Goodman and Brady, but the problems were relatively small. It can be argued that the discrepancies are the result of the points of view of the two observers.

Joseph DeBoves, who was also on the scene as a civilian control-tower operator at Andrews, said that Brady became excited during one of his telephone conversations, yelling, "There one goes." DeBoves believed that Brady was watching nothing more interesting than a meteor.

About two in the morning on July 20, the Radar Officer, Captain

Harold C. Way, at Andrews Approach Control, learned that the ARTC had a target east of Andrews. He went outside and saw a strange light which he didn't believe to be a star. Later, however, he went back out, and this time decided that he was looking at a star.

Bolling Air Force Base became involved briefly about the time Way went outside. The tower operator there said that he saw a "roundish" object drifting low in the sky to the southeast of Bolling. There were no radar confirmations of the sighting, and that was the last of the reports from that base.

The ARTC again told the controllers at Andrews that they still had the targets on their scopes. There is conflicting data because some of the reports suggest that the Andrews radar showed nothing, while other reports claim they did. Now DeBoves, and two others in the tower, Monte Banning and John P. Izzo, Jr., swept the sky with binoculars but could see no lights other than the stars.

The sightings lasted through the night, and during that time, the crews of several airliners saw the lights right where the radars showed them to be. Tower operators also saw them, and jet fighters were brought in for attempted intercepts. Associated Press stories written hours after the sightings claimed that no intercepts had been attempted that night but those stories were inaccurate. Documents in the Project Blue Book files, as well as eyewitnesses, confirm the attempted intercepts.

Typical of the sightings were those made by Captain Casey Pierman on Capital Airlines flight 807. He was on a flight between Washington and Martinsburg, West Virginia, at 1:15 A.M. on July 20, when he and the rest of the crew saw seven objects flash across the sky. Pierman said, "They were like falling stars without trails."

Capital Airline officials said that National Airport radar picked up the objects and asked Pierman to keep an eye on them. Shortly after takeoff, Pierman radioed that he had the objects in sight. He was flying at 180 to 200 miles per hour, and reported the objects were traveling at tremendous speed. Official Air Force records confirm this.

Another Capital Airlines pilot, Captain Howard Dermott, on Capital flight 610, reported a single light followed him from Herndon, Virginia, to within four miles of National Airport. Both the ARTC and the National tower confirmed that an unidentified target followed the aircraft to within four miles of landing. At about the same time, an Air Force radar at Andrews AFB was tracking eight additional unknown objects as they flew over the Washington area.

One of the most persuasive sightings came early in the morning when one of the ARTC controllers called the Andrews Air Force Base control tower to tell them that there was a target south of the tower, over the Andrews radio range station. The tower operators looked to the south where a "huge fiery-orange sphere" was hovering. This again was later explained by the Air Force as a star.

Just before daylight, about four in the morning, after repeated requests from the ARTC, an F-94 interceptor arrived on the scene, but it was too little, too late. All the targets were gone. Although the flight crew made a short search of the local area, they found nothing unusual and returned to their base quickly.

During that night, apparently the three radar facilities only once reported a target that was seen by all three facilities. There were, however, a number of times when the ARTC radar and the Washington National tower radars had simultaneous contacts. It also seems that the radars were displaying the same targets that were seen by the crews of the Capital Airlines flights. What it boils down to is that multiple radars and multiple eyewitnesses were showing and seeing objects in the sky over Washington.

Air Force intelligence, including ATIC and the officers assigned to Project Blue Book, had no idea that these sightings had taken place. They learned of the Saturday night–Sunday morning UFO show when the information was published in several newspapers on Monday. Ruppelt, on business in Washington and unaware of the sightings, reported, "I got off an airliner from Dayton and I bought a newspaper in the lobby of Washington National Airport terminal building. I called Major Dewey Fournet, but all he knew was what he read in the papers."

Ruppelt wanted to stay in Washington to investigate the case but the bureaucracy got in the way. Ruppelt's orders didn't allow for an overnight stay. He tried to get them amended, but failed. He was warned that if he remained in Washington, even if on official business, he would be considered as absent without leave. Ruppelt had no choice but to return to Ohio without talking to anyone about the sightings.

A week later, almost to the minute, with the same crew on duty, the UFOs returned. About 10:30 P.M the same radar operators who had been on duty the week before, again spotted several slow-moving targets. This time the controllers carefully marked each of the unidentifieds. When they were all marked, they called the Andrews AFB radar facility. The unidentified targets were on their scope too.

An hour later, with targets being tracked continually, the controllers called for interceptors. Al Chop, the Pentagon spokesman for the UFO project, told me that he was in communication with the main basement command post at the Pentagon. He requested that interceptors be sent. As a civilian, he could only make the request and then wait for the flag officer (general or admiral) in command at the Pentagon to make the official decision.

As happened the week before, there was a delay, but by midnight, two F-94s were on station over Washington. At that point, the reporters who had assembled to observe the situation were asked, by Chop, to leave the radar room at National Airport because classified radio and intercept procedures would be in operation.

Although that fact was well reported, Ruppelt in his book, wrote, "I knew this was absurd because any radio ham worth his salt could build equipment and listen in on any intercept. The real reason for the press dismissal, I learned, was that not a few people in the radar room were positive that this night would be the big night in UFO history— the night when a pilot would close in on and get a good look at a UFO—and they didn't want the press to be in on it."

Major Dewey Fournet, the Pentagon liaison between the UFO project in Dayton and the intelligence community in Washington, was at National Airport. Also there were Al Chop, public-information officer, and Naval Lieutenant Holcomb, an electronics specialist assigned to the Air Force Directorate of Intelligence.

With those men watching, as well as the controllers at various facilities using various radars, the F-94s arrived. And the UFOs vanished from the scopes immediately. The jets were vectored to the last known position of the UFOs, but even though visibility was unrestricted in the area, the pilots could see nothing. The fighters made a systematic search of the area, but since they could find nothing, they returned to their base.

Chop told me, "The minute the first two interceptors appeared on our scope all our unknowns disappeared. It was like they just wiped them all off. All our other flights, all the known flights were still on the scope. . . . we watched these two planes leave. When they were out of our range, immediately we got our UFOs back."

Later, Air Force officers would learn that as the fighters appeared over Washington, people in the area of Langley Air Force Base, Virginia, spotted weird lights in the sky. An F-94 in the area on a routine mission was diverted to search for the light. The pilot saw it and turned toward it, but it disappeared "like somebody turning off a lightbulb."

The pilot continued the intercept and did get a radar lock on the now unlighted and unseen target. That was broken by the object as it sped away. The fighter continued the pursuit, obtaining two more radar locks on the object, but each time the locks were broken.

The scene then shifted back to Washington National. Again the Air Defense Command was alerted and again fighters were sent. This time the pilots were able to see the objects, vectored toward them by the air traffic controllers. But the fighters couldn't close on the lights. The pilots saw no external details, other than lights where the radar suggested that something should be seen.

After several minutes of failure to close on a target, one of them was spotted loping along. A fighter piloted by Lieutenant William Patterson turned, kicked in the afterburner, and tried to catch the object. It disappeared before Patterson could see much of anything.

Interviewed the next day, Patterson said, "I tried to make contact with the bogies below one thousand feet, but they [the controllers] vectored us around. I saw several bright lights. I was at my maximum speed, but even then I had no closing speed. I ceased chasing them because I saw no chance of overtaking them. I was vectored into new objects. Later I chased a single bright light which I estimated about ten miles away. I lost visual contact with it. . . ."

Al Chop remembered this intercept, as did Dewey Fournet. Chop said, "The flight controllers had directed him to them [the unknowns]. We had a little cluster of them. Five or six of them and he suddenly reports that he sees some lights. . . . He said they are very brilliant blue-white lights. He was going to try to close in to get a better look . . . he flew into the area where they were clustered and he reported they were all around him."

Chop said that he, along with the others in the radar room, watched the intercept on the radarscope. What the pilot was telling them, they could see on the radar.

Patterson had to break off the intercept, though there were still lights in the sky and objects on the scope. According to Chop, the pilot radioed that he was running low on fuel. He turned so that he could head back to his base.

Chop said that the last of the objects disappeared from the scope about the time the sun came up. Ruppelt later quizzed Fournet about the activities that night. According to Ruppelt, Fournet and Holcomb, the radar expert, were convinced the targets were solid, metallic objects. Fournet told Ruppelt that there were weather-related targets on the scopes, but the controllers were ignoring them. Everyone was convinced that the targets were real.

At 4:00 P.M., in Washington, D.C., Major General John A. Samford, Chief of Air Intelligence, held a press conference. Of that press conference, Ruppelt wrote, "General Samford made an honest attempt to straighten out the Washington National sightings, but the cards were stacked against him. He had to hedge on many answers to questions from the press because he didn't know the answers. This hedging gave the impression that he was trying to cover up something more than just the fact his people fouled up in not fully investigating the sightings. Then he brought in Captain Roy James from ATIC to handle all the queries about radar. James didn't do any better because he'd just arrived in Washington that morning and didn't know very much more about the sightings than he'd read in the papers. Major Dewey Fournet and Lieutenant Holcomb, who had been at the airport during the sightings, were extremely conspicuous by their absence. . . ." As was the Pentagon spokesman on UFOs, Al Chop.

From that point, it seems that there was an explanation for the Washington National sightings. Samford, during the conference, backed up by the radar expert, James, suggested that there was a temperature inversion over Washington. That became the explanation for the radar sightings but the truth is that there is no explanation. The temperature inversion simply doesn't work, especially when it is remembered that there were both radar and visual observations. But the Air Force officers were happy. The news media had an answer and the sightings could be ignored. Ironically, the sightings were carried as "unidentified" in the Project Blue Book files.

Ten years later, long after Ed Ruppelt had left Blue Book and the Air Force, there was another series of sightings, this time in the desert Southwest. The object interacted with the environment, it was seen on radar, and fighters from two separate Air Force bases were scrambled to intercept. Project Blue Book officers would explain the sightings but as happened so often in the past, that explanation is inadequate.

According to the Project Blue Book record cards, on April 18, 1962, an object came in over "Cuba and apparently landed in rough terrain west of Eureka, Utah. Bright enough to trip photo electric cells which controlled city streetlights." Air Force investigators believed that the case was explained by a meteor.

Just sixteen minutes later there was another major sighting over Las Vegas, Nevada. According to the Project Blue Book record card, it was a "Radar sighting. Blip. Speed of object varied. Initial observation at 060 no elevation. Disappearance at 105 degrees at 10,000 feet altitude. Heading tentatively northeast, however disappeared instantly to south. Observed by search and height radars. No visual."

The Air Force investigator noted on the record card, "There is insufficient data in the report to form a valid conclusion. Speed, changes in course, and altitude not included. Appearance on both search and height finder confirms that some object was there. Track characteristic indicate a possible balloon as the source."

But the problem with that is the *Las Vegas Sun*. The banner headline claimed, BRILLIANT RED EXPLOSION FLARES IN LAS VEGAS SKY. The article told of "a flaming sword" that started a ground search for a weird unidentified flying object. According to the newspaper, an "Air Force spokesman said that radar tracked the object to the Mesquite

[Nevada] area . . . Spokesman for the 28th Air Division in Reno said the power at Eureka [Utah] 40 miles west of Provo was knocked out from the impact and word of the strange landing was held up until power was restored."

Deputy Walter Butt, of the Clark County, Nevada (Las Vegas), Sheriff's Department led a search-and-rescue unit into the Spring Mountain area to look for wreckage. When I spoke to him in November 1988, he told me that they searched through the night using jeeps and when the sun came up, they continued using aircraft. They didn't find anything of importance. When no one reported a missing aircraft, they called off the search.

During my investigation of the case, I spoke to a number of people in the Eureka area. It is true that the city streetlights went out, and one or two parroted the Air Force explanation of photoelectric cells reacting to an extremely bright meteor. But such an explanation does not explain localized failures of lights nor does it explain car engines that stalled.

Among the first to sight the object was Sheriff Raymond Jackson of Nephi, Utah, not that far from Eureka. According to him, he was on Main Street and "heard kind of a roar." He glanced up and saw a yellow-white flame going west, heard a series of loud booms, and the lights in Nephi went out. Jackson noted specifically that it was the lights in the doctor's office, but said, "All the lights went out temporarily."

From Nephi, the object traveled to the northwest, toward Eureka which is about thirty miles away. It flew over Bob Robinson and Floyd Evans. Robinson told me he was traveling south of Eureka when they stopped for a moment and both men climbed out of the truck. Robinson saw the light in the southwest and pointed it out. Evans thought it was a jet aircraft.

The object, according to Robinson, approached them rapidly and passed directly overhead. Robinson said that he thought it was no higher than five hundred feet. It was a flaming object and he thought he could see a series of square windows on the craft, almost hidden in the glow of it.

Robinson said that both men were frightened by the experience.

They dived under the truck for protection. The engine of the truck began to sputter and run roughly as the object approached. The headlights dimmed, but didn't fade completely. When the object disappeared in the west, the lights brightened and the engine smoothed out, running normally.

What was interesting here was that we had two reports that seemed to be linked but which the Air Force investigators had separated. Yet the newspaper article put them back together. If that was true, then something very interesting happened.

The Air Force report on the Eureka end of the case, dated April 19, provided some interesting information. There was a lengthy report from Captain Herman Gordon Shields, who was interrogated at Hill Air Force Base by Douglas M. Crouch, Chief of the Criminal Investigations Section. Shields said that he had seen something from the cockpit of the aircraft he was piloting. It was an intense illumination from above. He thought it was another aircraft, and looked in its direction. He saw a long object that he said was shaped like a cigarette. "The fore part, or lower part of the object, was very bright, intense white such as a magnesium flare. The second half, the aft section, was a clearly distinguishable yellowish color."

Others in the area reported to the Air Force that they had seen something strange. A man in Silver City, Utah, saw a glowing ball of light about the size of a soccer ball.

Some time after the sighting, the Air Force dispatched Lieutenant Colonel Robert Friend, then chief of Project Blue Book, and Dr. J. Allen Hynek to the scene. They spent a day in Utah, searched for the meteor, and found nothing. They offered a reward for it but had no takers.

There were also reports in the files that suggested that jet fighters had been scrambled from two locations. Planes were sent up from both Nellis Air Force Base in Las Vegas, and Luke Air Force Base near Phoenix. The fighters didn't catch the object.

On September 21, 1962, Major C. R. Hart, of the Air Force Office of Public Information, wrote to an unidentified New York resident, "The official records of the Air Force list the 18 April 1962 Nevada sighting to which you refer as 'unidentified, insufficient data.' . . . The phenomena was not intercepted or fired upon."

We could read that letter and decide that it was strictly true. It could be that the Air Force spokesman was suggesting that the jet fighters scrambled and had not been able to find the object, though they searched for it. Therefore the object was not intercepted, though the attempt was made. However, no matter how you slice it, the letter is misleading.

So, what do we have here? We have an object that was seen crossing the United States. We have a report of a craft heading west as it passed over Utah, but one that, when spotted in Reno, was going toward the southeast. We have a craft that was tracked on radar and which disappeared from the scope in a flash. And, we have dozens of reports from witnesses who saw the object in Utah and Nevada, including those who talked about a "flaming sword."

If we link those two cases, and there is no reason not to link them, then we have a UFO report that is inexplicable. A meteor does not swoop close to the ground to turn out lights and stall truck engines. A meteor does not make a long, looping turn. And a meteor is not visible on radar. The ionized trail it leaves might be, the meteor itself is not.

If, on the other hand, we separate the cases by suggesting events on two separate days as the Air Force did, we have two cases that are easy to explain. The master index for Project Blue Book lists the Nellis Air Force Base end of the case on April 18 and the Eureka, Utah, end as April 19. If that is true, then the cases are explainable as separate events.

However, what the Air Force investigators did was list one by the local time, which is early evening on April 18, and the other by Greenwich Mean Time, which is early morning on April 19. By converting the Greenwich time back to local time, and compensating for the fact that Utah is in the Mountain Time Zone and Nevada in the Pacific, we learn that the sightings took place within sixteen minutes of one another. These weren't two events on two days, but a single event on one day.

What has the examination of these cases taught us about the Air Force investigation of UFOs? When the "Lubbock lights" case began in August 1951, at the time the UFO project was being reorganized, a real effort was made to learn what was going on. Repeated investigations and extensive interviews were carried out. Ruppelt himself made his way to Lubbock to talk to the principals in the case. He made the effort to learn what was going on and gathered data from different experts in his attempts to find the truth.

The photographs, which provided a form of physical evidence, were carefully analyzed. The validity of the photographs rested on the shoulders of a nineteen-year-old photographer. To be fair, it must be pointed out that the vast majority of teenage males who have submitted UFO pictures to the Air Force or the media have faked them. In this case, however, there is absolutely no evidence that a hoax was involved. Even more than forty years after the event, Carl Hart, Jr., maintained he doesn't know what he photographed.

In the end, however, Air Force investigators accepted the explanation as birds. While it is clear that Joe Bryant's sighting is explainable as birds, there is no reason to extrapolate from it. There is no evidence that what the college professors saw were birds. And certainly the photographs don't show birds. In other words, the Air Force investigators were able to label the case but were not able to solve it. A more honest answer is that the Lubbock lights are unidentified.

During the Washington Nationals, there were highly trained professionals making the sightings. The men were trained in the use of radar, knew what weather-related propagation looked like, and believed they were seeing something real. When airline pilots were called and asked to spot the objects, they saw lights where the radar said they should be.

More importantly, when jet interceptors arrived on the scene, the UFOs seemed to react to them, something that weather-related phenomena would not do. In one case, as the jets arrived, all the UFOs disappeared. When the jets departed the area, the UFOs returned. That suggests something other than weather.

On the second night the Pentagon liaison officer for Project Blue Book, Dewey Fournet, was present. Al Chop, the Pentagon spokesman for Project Blue Book, was present. Both saw the blips on the radar screens. Both watched the attempted intercepts. Both knew that what was happening had nothing to do with weather or temperature inversions.

Yet forty-eight hours later, as General Samford briefed reporters, neither man was at the press conference. Instead Samford relied on an Air Force captain, an expert on radar, who had not been on the scene during the sightings. His explanations sounded good, he was an expert, but he had not been there during the sightings so he didn't *know*.

It is Ed Ruppelt's discussion of the case that provides us with the best clues. Ruppelt candidly wrote that some of the Air Force personnel, both officers and enlisted men, were pressured to alter their testimonies. What had been seemingly inexplicable sightings of objects in the sky, became nothing more than stars. This implies that even in the summer of 1952, as some officers tried to conduct real investigations, others were attempting to suppress the data. There would be no other reason to pressure witnesses to change their stories.

By 1962, when the Las Vegas UFO explosion took place, all attempts at independent and objective investigation ceased. We've seen in other cases how the Air Force investigators split sightings into many components and then dealt with them individually. This is an old military tactic. Split the enemy forces and then attack them in detail. It means that it is easier to defeat a company than it is a regiment. If you can take on the regiment a company at a time, you can defeat it a company at a time.

If we can split the UFO sightings into their components, we can explain each of the components. The explanation of a meteor is ridiculous when the whole of the Eureka–Las Vegas case is examined. However, a meteor can explain the Eureka end of it if there is no linkage to the Las Vegas sighting. A meteor becomes a plausible explanation.

And the Las Vegas end is "explained" as "insufficient data." Just what does that mean? Well, it means they found no explanation for it, but they were able to label it. And what additional information did they need? They had a time, a date, a location, and very precise information about the directions and altitudes. They even had a number of eyewitnesses, had anyone at Project Blue Book or Nellis Air Force

Base bothered to read the newspaper. Of course, had they done that, they would have had additional and unanswerable questions with which to deal.

These three cases all have a single common denominator and that is the attempt to find an explanation, any explanation. Each was labeled with an explanation that doesn't stand up to any sort of objective scrutiny. The holes for the explanations are many. But it does reveal the nature of the investigation, even when there were attempts to objectively investigate. It demonstrates that the real motivation wasn't to find the truth but to label the cases. How else to explain what happened in these instances? How else to explain solutions that make no sense when the evidence, available to the investigators, is examined?

Yes, I spoke to people thirty and forty years after the fact. Yes, in that time memories can change and confabulation is a real consideration. But I also had access to the files prepared when the events were fresh in the minds of the witnesses, and I could see if confabulation had taken place. I could see if stories had changed, been altered over time, or embellished.

And events, especially frightening events, stand out in the mind. Bob Robinson talking of the craft flashing overhead is interesting, but the sputtering of the truck engine and the dimming of the lights is even more so. Raymond Jackson's comments about the lights in the doctor's office are interesting as well. Both suggest that the UFO was interacting with the environment under it and photoelectric cells on streetlights had nothing to do with it.

These cases are illustrative. They show us what was going on at the official UFO project. They show us that objective investigation did not take place. They show us that there was a scramble for answers regardless of the facts in the case. And they show us that the high-ranking Air Force officers were not above applying pressure to people so that a solution would seem to be more likely.

There is one other thing that we can see here. As I conducted my investigations, sometimes as much as forty years after the sightings, I was able to find additional witnesses. I was able to interview men and women who had made sighting reports and to find additional witnesses. Even in the limited time that I had, on the limited budget I had, I could talk to many different people about the case. The question that springs to mind is why couldn't the Air Force investigators do that? They had access to the same information resources that I did. They could have used the telephone the way I did. And, in many cases they were on the scene with days or weeks of the sightings, yet failed to find what I did. Doesn't that really speak volumes about the way the investigation was conducted? Doesn't that suggest that truth was not the motivation? Doesn't that suggest, just as we have done all along, that Air Force and official investigators were doing something other than searching for the truth?

APPENDIX B:

THE BLUE BOOK "UNIDENTIFIEDS"

In 1975 I learned, wholly by accident, that the Project Blue Book files had been declassified and were open for public review. This was back when the files were housed at Maxwell Air Force Base and before they had been microfilmed. Robert Charles Cornett and I spent days in the files, going through the index, writing down all the "unidentified" cases, many of the photo-and physical-evidence cases, and any others that caught our attention. We included the names of the witnesses, still much in evidence in those files.

Sometime later, the files were moved to the National Archives in Washington, D.C., and were microfilmed. Before the microfilming was done, a number of Air Force officers read each file, attempting to black out the names of all the witnesses. When the files were rereleased to the public and made available on microfilm, it seemed that one of the most critical pieces of evidence had been removed.

When I learned about the sanitization, I thought I had a record that was unique in the UFO field. I could put the names back in. Don Berliner, of the Washington-based Fund for UFO Research, seems to have had the chance to see the files when they first appeared at the National Archives. He did the same thing I did and he, too, could put the names back. Like me, he spent days going through the files, writing down the names of the witnesses. Don, much to his credit, apparently could think of no way to cash in on the information. He posted a great deal of it in one of the UFO newsgroups on the Internet. Apparently he thought that it might be of use to other researchers who hadn't had the access to the files that he did.

But there is one other point that should be made here. As I read the case files for this work, there wasn't one in which I didn't find the names of those witnesses. In other words, the Air Force officers who had the job of blacking out the names, did a very poor job of it. In every case I was interested in, I could find the names of the witnesses somewhere in the Blue Book file.

For example, in the Chiles and Whitted case of 1948, I found a statement written by Chiles for the Air Force. The officer responsible had removed Chiles' name from both the return address and the signature block of his letter. That same officer had removed all references to Chiles or Whitted in the body of the text. What he or she didn't do was remove it from the all-capital-letters statement on the top of the letter. In big, bold letters, it said, "STATEMENT OF CAPTAIN CLARENCE S. CHILES." And, throughout that case, I found additional references to both Chiles and Whitted, including a number of newspaper articles in which both men were named.

Along with the Chiles and Whitted case, there were a number of other sightings that seemed to be related to it. That same Air Force officer worked very hard to take out all the names of those witnesses, except for a handwritten chart of all the sightings from late July 1948 that included the locations, times, directions, and other information, and, of course, the names of every single witness in this case. That's right, a chart that contained all the names.

In the Kenneth Arnold case there was a transcript of a telephone interview with him. The Air Force officers had taken out Arnold's name at the beginning of the statements made by Arnold. But, again, at the top, in big, black letters, someone had written. "ARNOLD CASE."

Finding the names in the Florida scoutmaster case was somewhat more difficult. I could find the scoutmaster's name, but only the last name of one of the scouts until I reached the end. There was a clipping that contained the names and ages of each of the Boy Scouts. As I wrote the chapter, I thought about leaving the names out because they were, after all, just boys. And then I realized that each of them, eleven or twelve in 1952, were now older than I am.

That was the thing I found so ridiculous. They would so carefully remove the names from the reports, letters, and other documents, and then leave them in the newspaper articles that accompanied so many of the cases. In some files they had blacked out the names in the clippings, but always left enough information that, if I hadn't found them elsewhere in the file, I could have tracked down the newspaper or magazine to learn who the witnesses were.

It became something of a joke to me. How far would I have to read before I could find the names? In the Salt Lake City "daylight disc" case, I only found one name in the file itself, but the newspaper clippings that followed contained all the names. It was difficult from the information in the file to determine who had made which statement, but there was just enough that I could put it together.

So the work that I had thought of as unique was not. It had been duplicated by Don Berliner. And, had neither of us done it, we could have figured out from the files the names of those who were the witnesses. I'm happy that the Air Force officers didn't take their jobs seriously. They could have, with a little additional work, made it impossible to figure out who the witnesses were. In some cases, that could have been a deadly blow to the work that needs to be done.

What follows are most of the "unidentifieds" from the files with many of the names plugged back in. The list also contains some additional cases that the Air Force believed they had solved, though I don't accept their analysis. For those that aren't in Blue Book as an "unidentified" I have included the Air Force solution. Please don't construe that as an acceptance of the Air Force claim. It is a mere reporting of the information.

June 24, 1947: Mount Rainier, Washington. 3:00 P.M. Kenneth Arnold watched as nine crescent-shaped objects flashed among the mountain peaks "like saucers skipping on a pond." Air Force conclusion: Mirage.

June 24, 1947: Cascade Mountains, Washington. 3:00 P.M. Fred Johnson. Saw a number of "disc-shaped" craft overhead and noticed that his compass was spinning wildly.

July 3, 1947: Harborside, Maine. 2:30 P.M. Astronomer John Cole of South Brooksville, Maine, watched 10–15 seconds while ten very light objects, with two dark forms to their left, moved like a swarm of bees to the northwest. A loud roar was heard.

July 4, 1947: Over Emmet, Idaho. 8:17 P.M. United Air Lines Captain E. J. Smith, First Officer Ralph Stevens, and Stewardess Marty Morrow all watched for 12–15 minutes while four objects with flat bottoms and rough tops moved at varying speeds, with one high and to the right of the others.

July 6, 1947: Fairfield-Suisan Air Base, California. Captain and Mrs. James Burniston watched for one minute while one object having no wings or tail rolled from side to side three times and then flew away very fast to the southeast.

July 7, 1948: Phoenix, Arizona. William Rhodes watched a "heel-shaped" object that circled near his home. Took two photographs of the object which disappeared a few minutes later. Air Force conclusion: Hoax.

July 8, 1947: Muroc Air Base, California. 9:30 A.M. First Lieutenant Joseph McHenry, Technical Sergeant Ruvolo, Staff Sergeant Nauman, and Janette Scotte watched for an unstated length of time while two silver disc-shaped or spherical objects apparently made of metal flew a wide circular pattern. One of them later flew a tighter circle.

July 9, 1947: Meridian, Idaho. 12:17 *Idaho Statesman* aviation editor and former (AAF) B-29 pilot Dave Johnson watched for more than 10 seconds from an Idaho Air National Guard AT-6 while a black disc, which stood out against the clouds, made a half-roll and then a stair-step climb.

July 10, 1947: Harmon Field, Newfoundland, Canada. Between 3:00 and 5:00 P.M. Three ground crewmen, including Mr. Leidy, of Pan American Airways, watched briefly while one translucent disc-or wheel-shaped object flew very fast, leaving a dark blue trail. It then ascended and cut a path through the clouds.

July 29, 1947: Hamilton Air Base, California. 2:50 P.M. Assistant Base Operations Officer Captain William Rhyerd and ex–AAF B-29 pilot Ward Stewart watched for unknown length of time while two round, shiny, white objects with estimated 15–25-foot diameters, flew 3 or 4 times the apparent speed of a P-80, also in sight. One object flew straight and level. The other weaved from side to side like an escort fighter.

September 3, 1947: Oswego, Oregon. 12:15 P.M. Mrs. Raymond Dupui watched for unknown length of time as twelve to fifteen round, silver objects flew an unstated pattern.

October 1947: Dodgeville, Wisconsin. Unidentified witness watched for one hour while an undescribed object flew circles.

October 14, 1947: Eleven miles north-northeast of Cave Creek, Arizona. Noon. Fighter pilot J. L. Clark, a civilian pilot named Anderson, and an unidentified third man watched 45–60 seconds while one 3-foot flying wing-shaped object, which looked black against the white clouds and red against the blue sky, flew straight at an estimated 380 miles per hour, at 8,000–10,000 feet, from northwest to southeast.

April 5, 1948: Holloman Air Force Base New Mexico. Afternoon. Geophysics lab balloon observers Alsen, Johnson, and Chance saw two irregular, round, white or golden objects. One made three loops then rose and disappeared rapidly. The other flew in a fast arc to the west during the 30-second sighting.

July 24, 1948: Robins Air Force Base, Georgia. 1:50 A.M. Maintenance ground crewman Walter Massey saw a cigar-shaped craft that flashed overhead. He thought that he saw a flame coming from the rear.

July 24, 1948: Near Montgomery, Alabama. 2:45 A.M. Eastern Airlines pilots Clarence S. Chiles and John B. Whitted watched a bright light head for their airliner and pass on the right. The craft was cigar-shaped and had a double row of windows along it. A flame shot out of the back. Air Force conclusion: Astro: Fireball.

July 29, 1948: Indianapolis, Indiana. 9:08 A.M. James Toney and Robert Huggins, both employees of a rug-cleaning firm, watched a single shiny aluminum object, shaped something like an airplane's propeller, with 10–12 small cups protruding from either blade. Estimated size: 6–8 feet long, 1.5–2 feet wide. The object glided across the road a few hundred feet in front of their vehicle and apparently went down in a wooded area. Sighting lasted a few seconds.

July 31, 1948: Indianapolis, Indiana. 8:25 A.M. Mr. and Mrs. Vernon Swigert; he was an electrician. The object was shaped like a cymbal, or domed disc; about 20 feet across and 6–8 feet thick, and was white without any shine. It flew straight and level from horizon to horizon in about 10 seconds, shimmering in the sun as if spinning.

July or August 1948: In the vicinity of Marion, Virginia. Shortly after sunset, Max Abbott, flying a Bellanca Cruisair four-passenger private airplane, watched a single bright white light as it accelerated and turned up a valley.

September 23, 1948: San Pablo, California. Noon. Sylvester Bentham and retired U.S. Army Colonel Horace Eakins saw two objects, one of which was a buff or gray rectangle with vertical lines and the other a translucent "amoeba" with a dark spot near the center. The arms of the "amoeba" undulated. Both objects traveled very fast.

October 15, 1948: Fusuoka, Japan. 11:05 P.M. Pilot Halter and radar operator Hemphill of a P-61 "Black Widow" night fighter tracked up to six objects on radar, only one seen visually. It was a dull or dark object shaped like a dirigible with a flat bottom and clipped tail end. Six seen on radar separately. Pilot attempted to close on visual object, but it dove away fast.

December 3, 1948: Fairfield-Suisan Air Force Base, California. 8:15

P.M. An Air Force sergeant and a control tower operator watched a single round, white light that flew for 25 seconds with varying speed, bouncing motion, and finally a rapid erratic climb.

January 4, 1949: Hickam Field, Hawaii. 2:00 P.M. U.S. Air Force Captain Paul Storey saw one flat white, elliptical object with a matte top circle while oscillating to the right and left, and then sped away.

January 27, 1949: Cortez-Bradenton, Florida. 10:20 P.M. Captain Sames, acting chief of the Aircraft Branch, Eglin Air Force Base, and Mrs. Sames watched for 25 minutes while a cigar-shaped object as long as two Pullman cars and having seven lighted square windows, and throwing sparks, descended and then climbed with a bouncing motion at an estimated 400 miles per hour.

March 17, 1949: Camp Hood, Texas. 7:52 P.M. The witnesses included guards of the 2nd Armored Division. While awaiting the start of a flare-firing, they watched for an hour while eight large green, red, and white flarelike objects flew in generally straight lines.

April 3, 1949: Dillon, Montana. 11:55 A.M. Construction company owner Gosta Miller and three other unnamed persons observed one object shaped like two plates attached face-to-face with a matte bottom and a bright aluminum top. It was about 20 feet in diameter, 4–5 feet in thickness. It rocked or rotated in six cycles, descended, rocked, flew, rocked.

April 4, 1949: Merced, California. 10:20 P.M. William Parrott, former Air Force pilot, watched one generally round object with a curved bottom and dull coloring. The object gave off a clicking sound until overhead. Parrott's dog reacted.

April 24, 1949: Arrey, New Mexico. 10:30 A.M. General Mills meteorologist and balloon expert C. B. Moore and others on a balloon launch crew saw one white, round ellipsoid, about 2.5 times long as wide. Donald Menzel believed this to be a mirage.

April 28, 1949: Tucson, Arizona. 5:45 P.M. Howard Hann, Mr. Hubert, and Tex Keahey observed one bright, sausage-shaped object for 40 minutes while it rolled and flew fast.

May 5, 1949: Fort Bliss, Texas. 11:40 A.M. Army officers Major Day, Major Olhausen, and Captain Vaughn saw two oblong white discs, flying at an estimated 200–250 miles per hour, make a shallow turn during the 30-to 50-second observation.

May 6, 1949: Livermore, California. 9:35 A.M. C. G. Green saw two shiny, disc-like objects rotate around each other and bank. Then one shot upward with a gray trail and rejoined the other.

May 9, 1949: Tucson, Arizona. 2:30 P.M. Master Sergeant Troy Putnam observed as two round, flat silvery objects, estimated to be 25 feet in diameter, flew 750–1,000 miles per hour in a banked but steady manner.

May 27, 1949: South-central Oregon. 2:25 P.M. Joseph Shell, ferrying SNJ trainer for North American Aviation, from Red Bluff, California, to Burns, Oregon. Five to eight oval objects, twice as long as wide, and one-fifth as thick. They flew in trail formation, with an interval equal to 3 or 4 times their length, except that the second and third were closer together.

July 24, 1949: Mountain Home, Idaho. Noon. Henry Clark, manager of a flying service, flying a Piper Clipper. Seven delta-shaped objects, 35–55 feet in span, 20–30 feet long, 2–5 feet thick; light-colored except for a 12-foot diameter dark circle at the rear of each. They flew in a tight formation of twos with one behind, and made a perfect but unbanked turn. During the 10-minute sighting, they displayed decreasing smooth oscillations. Clark's engine ran rough during the sighting, and upon landing was found to have all its spark plugs burned out.

July 30, 1949: Mount Hood, Oregon. 9:00 P.M. Northwest Airlines captain Thrush, two Portland control tower operators, and one flying instructor watched as one object with one white light and two red lights, maneuvered and hovered.

February 5, 1950: Teaticket, Massachusetts. 5:10 P.M. Marvin Odom, former U.S. Navy fighter pilot, U.S. Air Force Lieutenant Philip Foushee, pilot from Otis Air Force Base, and two others saw two thin, illuminated cylinders, one of which dropped a fireball, maneuver together and then disappear high and fast after 5 minutes.

February 24, 1950: Albuquerque, New Mexico. 1:55 P.M. Municipal Airport Weather observers Luther McDonald and Harrison Manson saw one white, slightly elongated oval and watched it for 1.5 minutes through a theodolite while it flew straight and level.

February 25, 1950: Los Alamos, New Mexico. 3:55 P.M. Twelve Atomic Energy Commission security inspectors watched as one cylinder with tapered ends, silver and flashing, flew slow and then fast, fluttered and oscillated, and changed course. Observations by individuals varied from 3 seconds to 2 minutes.

March 3, 1950: Selfridge Air Force Base, Michigan. 11:05 P.M. Lieutenant Frank Mattson observed as one intense, dull yellowish light descended vertically, then flew straight and level very fast for 4 minutes.

March 20, 1950: Stuggart, Arkansas. 9:26 P.M. Chicago and Southern Airlines Captain Jack Adams and First Officer G. W. Anderson, Jr., saw one 100-foot circular disc with 9–12 portholes along the lower side emitting a soft purple light, and a light at the top which flashed three times in 9 seconds, and which flew at not less than 1,000 miles per hour. It was seen for 25–35 seconds.

March 27, 1950: Motobo, Okinawa. 10:30 A.M. USAF radar operator Corporal Bolfango tracked an object on radar for 2 minutes while it was stationary and then moved at 500 miles per hour.

March 28, 1950: Santiago, Chile. 3:15 P.M. Master Sergeant Patterson, of the office of the U.S. Air Attaché, observed one white object for 5–10 seconds through binoculars while it flew high and fast, crossing 30 degrees of sky.

March 29, 1950: Marrowbore Lake, Tennessee. 7:00 A.M. Real-estate salesmen Whiteside and Williams saw 6–12 dark objects shaped like 300-pound bombs, estimated to be 5 feet long. Flew 500 miles per hour and descended, making a noise like wind blowing through the trees.

April 8, 1950: Kokomo, Indiana. 2:00 A.M. Earl Baker saw one gray metallic disc, 50 feet in diameter, 15 feet thick; toy top–shaped with a "conning tower" at the top and three ports on the rim giving off a blue light. It hovered for 2 minutes, then flew away. Baker was roused from sleep by his dog.

April 14, 1950: Fort Monmouth, New Jersey. 2:30 P.M. Army Master Sergeant James observed four rectangular, amber objects, about 3 feet by 4 feet, which changed speed and direction rapidly; the group of objects rose and fell during the 3-to 4-minute sighting.

April 23, 1950: Red Bud, Illinois. 3:58 P.M. Sighting made by photographer Dean Morgan, Mr. and Mrs. Greene, and Donald Gene. Morgan photographed the object that was seen by the Greenes and Gene. The object hovered, and then shot away. Air Force conclusion: Not a case, information only.

May 7, 1950: Nine miles south of Ely, Nevada. 6:45 P.M. Mr. and Mrs. George Smith and their grandson watched as one silvery white object hovered at 100 feet altitude, moved back and forth for 10 minutes, and then flew up and away. Air Force conclusion: No investigation.

May 24, 1950. Holloman Air Force Base, New Mexico. Morning. Photos taken by two stations on Videon Camera. Two different objects and triangulation could not be effected. Photos sent to Dr. Marichi at Cambridge. Air Force conclusion: Insufficient data, file incomplete.

June 21, 1950: Hamilton Air Force Base, California. 1:35 A.M. Corporal Garland Pryor and Staff Sergeant Ellis Lorimer saw a disc–shaped object shooting a blue flame and traveling at over 1,000 miles per hour. Air Force conclusion: Insufficient data. Report not in file. Case will be evaluated if file is located.

June 27, 1950: Texarkana, Texas. 7:50 A.M. Terrell and Yates, employees of Red River Arsenal, saw one object, bright, shaped like two dishpans face-to-face, fly straight and level, fast, for 4–5 seconds.

July 13, 1950: Redstone Arsenal, Alabama. 5:00 P.M. Two skilled Arsenal employees including Mr. Washburn saw one object, shaped like a bowtie, which looked like polished aluminum. Flew straight and level, then one triangle rotated a quarter turn in the opposite direction and returned to its original position. The object then made a right-angle turn and accelerated away after at least 30 seconds.

August 4, 1950: Approximately 100 miles southeast of New York City. 10:00 A.M. Ship's Master Nils Lewring, and Chief Mate Jacob Koelwyn, Third Mate, of M/V Marcala saw one 10-foot cylindrical object at 50–100 feet altitude, flying with a churning or rotary motion, accelerated at the end of the 15-second sighting.

August 20, 1950: Nicosia, Cyprus. 1:30 P.M. U.S. Air Force MATS liaison officer Lieutenant William Ghormley, Colonel W. V. Brown, and Lieutenant Colonel L. W. Brauer watched as one small, round, bright object flew fast, straight, and level for 15–20 seconds.

August 25, 1950: Approximately 250 miles southwest of Bermuda. 8:00 P.M. B-29 radarman Staff Sergeant William Shaffer reported radar observation, plus possible blue streak 3 minutes later. B-29 followed unidentified target, then passed it at a quarter-mile distance; target followed for 5 minutes, then passed B-29 and sped away. Total time of tracking: 20 minutes.

August 30, 1950: Sandy Point, Newfoundland, Canada. 1:30 P.M. Three local employees, including Kaeel and Alexander, of the Air Force Base watched as a dark, barrel-shaped object, with a pole down from it into the water, flew at 3–5 miles per hour and at 15–20 feet altitude for 5 minutes.

September 3, 1950: Spokane, Washington. 2:00 P.M. Major R. J. Gardiner, Mrs. Gardiner, and a neighbor (Major saw three objects, others saw one) see metallic bronze discs, 20–30 feet long 2–6 feet thick. They moved independently and erratically for 5 minutes.

September 20, 1950: Kit Carson, Colorado. 10:49 A.M. The witness is identified only as a reliable source. Witness saw two large, round, glowing objects and three smaller, internally lit objects. Two hovered for one minute, moved, and three smaller ones came from behind or within the two larger objects, and all sped upward and away.

September 21, 1950: Provincetown, Massachusetts. 9:52 A.M. MIT research associate and Air National Guard Major M. H. Ligda reports radar tracking of one object during MIT tracking of USAF flight of F-84 or F-86 jet fighters. Object speed was 22 miles per minute (1,200 miles per hour); made turn of 11–12 Gs' acceleration during one-minute observation.

October 15, 1950: Oak Ridge, Tennessee. 3:20 P.M. Atomic Energy Commission Trooper Rymer, J. Moneymaker, and Captain Zarzecki saw two shiny silver objects shaped like bullets or bladders. They dove with a smoke trail and one vanished. The other hovered at 5–6 feet altitude, 50 feet away, then left and returned several times somewhat farther away.

October 15, 1950: Pope Air Force Base, North Carolina. Witness identified only as Daniel. Listed as "unidentified" in index, but no other data available.

October 15, 1950: Pope Air Force Base, North Carolina. Witness: Woodward. Same as previous observation.

October 23, 1950: Bonlee, North Carolina. 12:42 P.M. Ex–U.S. Air Force pilot Frank Risher saw one aluminum object shaped like a dirigible or Convair C-99 cargo plane, with three portholes. It arrived from the southeast, hovered 3–5 seconds, and flew away to the south-southeast at end of the 40-second sighting.

November 5, 1950: Oak Ridge, Tennessee. 11:55 A.M. Fairchild Aircraft illustrator Don Patrick. One translucent object, light gray with dark core, shaped like a pear or bean. Flew for 5–10 minutes with rapid, darting movements.

December 2, 1950: Nanyika, Kenya. 10:50 A.M. Mr. and Mrs. L.

Scott saw one pearly, iridescent object with a flattened top; it spun while hovering and made a sound like bees buzzing.

December 6, 1950: Fort Myers, Florida. 5:00 P.M. Harry Lamp and four boys, using 10-power binoculars saw one 75-foot object, 3–4 feet thick, with a bubble on top; it was silver with a red rim, having two white and two orange jets along it. The center revolved when the object hovered. It flew away very fast.

December 11, 1950: Ten miles northwest of Gulcana, Alaska. 10:13 P.M. The crew of Northwest Air Lines flight 802 saw two white flashes, followed by a dark cloud which rose and split in two.

January 8, 1951: South of Fort Worth, Texas. 10:45 P.M. Mr. and Mrs. W. J. Boggus, plus unidentified drivers and passengers in other cars, stopped to watch two groups of red and green lights in triangular formations, which were stationary and then moved.

January 12, 1951: Fort Benning, Georgia. 10:00 P.M. U.S. Army Second Lieutenant A. C. Hale. One light with a fan-shaped wake remained motionless like a star about 20 minutes and then sped away.

January 16, 1951: Artesia, New Mexico. Time unknown. Sighting made by two members of a balloon project from the General Mills Aeronautical Research Laboratory, the manager of the Artesia Airport, and three pilots. The balloon crew was observing their 110-foot balloon at an altitude of 112,000 feet when a dull white, round object was spotted. It appeared larger than the balloon, but made no movement. Later, the balloon crew and the others saw two objects from the airport that were flying side by side. They circled the balloon and flew away to the northeast. The second observation lasted about 40 seconds.

February 1, 1951: Johnson Air Base, Japan. 5:10 P.M. Pilot and radar operator of F-82 night fighter saw one amber light make three or four 360-degree turns to the right, reverse toward the F-82, and then climb out of sight.

February 21, 1951: Durban, South Africa. 4:55 A.M. Three men in a truck, and several other persons, none of whom are named, saw a dark red, torpedo-shaped object with a darker center, fly straight and level.

February 26, 1951: Ladd Air Force Base, Alaska. 7:10 A.M. U.S. Air Force Sergeant J. B. Sells saw one dull gray, metallic object, estimated to be 120 feet long and 10–12 feet thick, as it hovered, puffed smoke, and sped away after about a minute.

March 10, 1951: Chinnampo, Korea. 9:51 A.M. U.S. Air Force B-29 bomber crew, including scanners and tail gunner, watched as a large red-yellow glow burst and became blue-white. No further information in files.

March 13, 1951: McClellan Air Force Base, California. 3:20 P.M. U.S. Air Force First Lieutenant B. J. Hastie and Mrs. Rafferty see a cylinder with twin tails, 200 feet long and 90 feet wide, turn north and fly at incredible speed.

March 15, 1951: New Delhi, India. 10:20 A.M. Twenty-five members of a flying club, including the chief aerial engineer and his two assistants, saw one metallic cigar-shaped object with white exhaust which turned black when it accelerated to an estimated 1,000 miles per hour and made a large loop.

June 1, 1951: Niagara Falls, New York. 4:20 A.M. Master Sergeant H. E. Sweeney and two enlisted men watched one glowing yellow-orange, saucer-shaped object with arc-shaped wings, as it flew straight up. It was seen for 30–40 seconds.

July 24, 1951: Portsmouth, New Hampshire. Hanscom Air Force Base operations officer Captain Cobb and Corporal Fein saw one 100–200-feet tubular object, five times long as it was wide, with fins at one end, and grayish-colored with many black spots. It flew 800–1,000 miles per hour at 1,000–2,000 feet altitude, leaving a faint swath.

August 25, 1951: Albuquerque, New Mexico. 9:58 P.M. Sighting made by Sandia Base security guard Hugh Young and his wife. A flying wing-shaped craft passed over their heads at an estimated 800–1,000-feet altitude with no sound. Size was estimated at one and a half times the wingspan of a B–36 bomber, or about 350 feet. There were dark, chordwise stripes on the underside, and 6–8 pairs of soft, glowing lights on trailing edge of the "wing." Speed was estimated at 300–400 miles per hour. The object was seen for about 30 seconds.

August 31, 1951: Matador, Texas. 12:45 P.M. Mrs. Tom Tilson and one or two other women, saw one pear-shaped object with the length of a B-29 fuselage (100 feet), aluminum or silver, with a port or some type of aperture on the side. It moved with the smaller end forward, drifting slowly at about 150 feet altitude, then headed up in a circular fashion and out of sight after a few seconds.

September 6, 1951: Claremont, California. 7:20 P.M. Staff Sergeant W. T. Smith and Master Sergeant L. L. Duel saw six orange lights in an irregular formation, which flew straight and level into a coastal fog bank after 3–4 minutes.

September 14, 1951: Goose Bay, Labrador, Canada. 9:30 P.M. Technical Sergeant W. B. Maupin and Corporal J. W. Green saw three objects tracked on radar. Two were on a collision course, then one evaded to the right upon the request, by radio, of one of the radar operators. No aircraft were known to be in the area. A third unidentified track then joined the first two. The sighting lasted more than 15 minutes.

October 2, 1951: Columbus, Ohio. 6:00 P.M. Battelle Memorial Institute graduate physicist Howard Cross saw one bright oval with a clipped tail fly straight and level, fading into the distance after one minute.

October 3, 1951: Kadena, Okinawa. 10:27 P.M. Radar operators Sergeant M. W. Watson and Private Gonzales, and one other sergeant see one large, sausage-shaped blip tracked at an estimated 4,800 miles per hour.

October 9, 1951: Terre Haute, Indiana. 1:42 P.M. CAA chief aircraft communicator Roy Messmore at Hulman Municipal Airport observed one round silver object as it flew directly overhead, reaching the horizon in 15 seconds.

October 9, 1951: Paris, Illinois. 1:45 P.M. Similar to event at Terre Haute (15 miles southeast). It was originally listed as "unidentified" but was eventually reclassified.

October 11, 1951: Minneapolis, Minnesota. 6:30 A.M. Sighting made by General Mills balloon researchers, including aeronautical engineer J. J. Kaliszewski, aerologist Charles B. Moore (his second "unidentified" UFO report), pilot Dick Reilly in the air, and Doug Smith on the ground. The flight crew saw the first object, a brightly glowing one with a dark underside and a halo around it. The object arrived high and fast, then slowed and made slow climbing circles for about two minutes, and finally sped away to the east. Soon they saw another one, confirmed by ground observers using a theodolite, which sped across the sky. Total time first object was seen was 5 minutes; second was seen for a few seconds.

November 18, 1951: Washington, D.C. 3:20 A.M. Crew of Capital Airlines DC-4 flight 610 and Andrews Air Force Base senior air traffic controller Tom Selby saw one object with several lights, which followed the DC-4 for about 20 minutes and then turned back.

November 24, 1951: Mankato, Minnesota. 3:53 P.M. U.S. Air Force and Air National Guard pilots W. H. Fairbrother and D. E. Stewart in F-51 Mustangs saw one milky white object shaped like Northrop flying wing; estimated 8-foot wing span. Flew straight and level for 5 seconds.

December 7, 1951: Sunbury, Ohio. 4:30 P.M. Amateur astronomer Carl Loar observed one silvery sphere, seen through telescope; two specks sighted at sides. Object seemed to explode and was replaced by a dark cloud and many specks.

December 7, 1951: Oak Ridge, Tennessee. 8:15 A.M. Atomic Energy Commission guard J. H. Collins saw one 20-foot square object, white-gray but not shiny, flew above ridge to clouds and back again twice.

January 16, 1952: Artesia, New Mexico. Carried as an "unidentified" in the Project Blue Book files.

February 11, 1952: Pittsburgh, Pennsylvania. Carried as an "unidentified" in the Project Blue Book files.

February 23, 1952: Sinuiji, North Korea. Witnesses saw a cylindrical-shaped bluish object that disappeared by fading out.

March 20, 1952: Queen Anne's City, Maryland. Sighting was an orange-yellow light in horizontal flight that made two vertical jumps.

March 23, 1952: Yakima, Washington. Radar sighting of object and a jet fighter was scrambled for an intercept. Ground radars also picked up the object.

March 24, 1952: Point Conception, California. Radar observation made by Hancock.

March 29, 1952: Misawa Air Force Base, Japan. Carried as an "unidentified" in the Project Blue Book files.

March 5, 1952: Duncanville, Texas. Object observed by radar maintenance mechanic.

April 5, 1952: Miami, Florida. The witness observed four objects pass the full moon. One object was more plainly seen, was about half the moon's diameter, and had a sharply defined leading edge.

April 6, 1952: Temple, Texas. 2:59 P.M. Disc-shaped objects in a circular formation.

April 12, 1952: North Bay, Ontario. 11:30 P.M. A round, amber-colored object came in from the south. It flew at twice the speed of an F-86 at low level. It stopped and reversed direction.

April 14, 1952: Memphis, Tennessee. 6:30 P.M. Witness saw an inverted bowl with vertical slots. It flew straight and level and had red glowing exhaust.

April 14, 1952: La Crosse, Wisconsin. 12:35 P.M. Witnesses watched object traveling in straight and level flight, change position in a V-formation.

April 15, 1952: Santa Cruz, California. 7:40 P.M. Two circular objects were seen in straight and level flight. Project Card noted that the witness, Hays, appeared to be reliable.

April 17, 1952: Longmeadow, Massachusetts. 8:30 P.M. The object is described as star-colored and star-shaped. It made erratic movements including rapid climbs and dives. Although this sounds suspiciously like a very bright star, the Project Blue Book files carried it as an unidentified.

April 17–18, 1952: Yuma Test Station, Arizona. A white, circular object flew across the sky leaving a white vapor trail behind it.

April 18, 1952: Bethesda, Maryland. 1:30 A.M. Witness sighted orange-yellow lights in a V-formation that flew straight and level.

April 18, 1952: Corner Brook, Newfoundland. 10:10 P.M. The witness saw a round, yellowish gold object that seemed to disappear and then come back. What is interesting is that the witness had published an article the day before debunking UFOs.

April 18, 1952: Japan. Object was seen on radar.

April 22, 1952: Okinawa. The crew of a B-29 reported they saw three elliptical-shaped objects, about two to three feet long, maneuvering erratically.

April 24, 1952: Bellevue Hill, Vermont. 5:00 A.M. The crew of a C-124 saw three circular objects, bluish in color, as they flew in straight and level flight.

April 24, 1952: Milton, Massachusetts. 2:30 P.M. Witness named Burn saw two dark red objects of a "flat, square shape" as they traveled in "wobbly" flight, climbed, leveled out, and then climbed again.

April 24, 1952: Clovis, New Mexico. 8:10 P.M. An Air Force flight surgeon saw many orange-amber lights flying in a formation described as a "blob."

April 27, 1952: Roseville, Michigan. 4:14 P.M. A number of civilians saw four oval-and cigar-shaped objects that turned over and changed shape as they flew and performed a variety of maneuvers.

April 27, 1952: Yuma, Arizona. 8:30 P.M. An Air Force staff sergeant and his wife saw a bright red, disc-shaped object as it came and went. It made a rapid climb. They may have seen one object eight times or eight objects one time.

April 29, 1952: Marshall, Texas. 3:30 P.M. Witness saw a round, white object in straight and level flight.

April 29, 1952: Near Goodland, Kansas. 10:00 P.M. Witness reported a fan-shaped object, white, in straight and level flight.

May 1, 1952: Moses Lake, Washington. An Atomic Energy Commission employee watched a silver object in straight and level flight.

May 1, 1952: George Air Force Base, California. 5:50 P.M. Several Air Force officers and enlisted men watched five flat, white, disc-shaped objects make a sudden 90-degree turn and disappear.

May 5, 1952: Tenafly, New Jersey. UFO witnessed by Judson. Carried as an "unidentified" in the Project Blue Book files.

May 7, 1952: Kessler Air Force Base, Mississippi. 12:15 P.M. Four Air Force personnel saw about ten objects that were cylindrical-shaped and looked to be made of aluminum, dart in and out of the clouds.

May 9, 1952: George Air Force Base, California. 10:30 A.M. Witnesses on the ground and a pilot of an F-86 saw one silver-colored, round object that disappeared to the north. This was one of a series of sightings at the base on May 9, 11, 13, 14, 20. Some were "identified" and many were marked as "insufficient data."

May 10, 1952: Ellenton, South Carolina. 11:45 P.M. A number of civilians watched four objects, yellow in color and disc-shaped, which flew straight and level for a short period. One object was reported to have pulled up to avoid other objects on the ground.

May 14, 1952: Puerto Rico. 7:00 P.M. An attorney, among others, reported two objects, orange in color, spherical, one of which darted around.

May 20, 1952: Houston, Texas. 10:10 P.M. Three Air Force navigators watched an orange-white light coming toward them. The object flew straight except for one turn.

May 25, 1952: Walnut Lake, Michigan. 11:15 P.M. Seven civilians including a witness named Hoffman; reported a white–yellow-orange moon-shaped object, which they followed in a car for thirty minutes.

May 28, 1952: Saigon, RVN. 10:30 A.M. A civilian reported a single white-silver, disc-shaped object that was in sight for two minutes.

May 28, 1952: Albuquerque, New Mexico. 1:30 P.M. A city fireman reported two sightings of a light silver–and–light brown, circular object that came in from the northeast at high speed, stopped to circle, and then climbed out of sight.

May 29, 1952: San Antonio, Texas. 7:00 P.M. An Air Force pilot watched a single object that he described as "tubular" for about eight minutes.

June 1, 1952: Rapid City, South Dakota. Carried as an "unidentified" in the Project Blue Book files.

June 1, 1952: Walla Walla, Washington. Carried as an "unidentified" in the Project Blue Book files.

June 2, 1952: Bayview, Washington. Carried as an "unidentified" in the Project Blue Book files.

June 5, 1952: Lubbock, Texas. Witnessed by Bacon. Carried as an "unidentified" in the Project Blue Book files.

June 5, 1952: Albuquerque, New Mexico. Carried as an "unidentified" in the Project Blue Book files.

June 5, 1952: Offutt Air Force Base, Nebraska. Carried as an "unidentified" in the Project Blue Book files.

June 6, 1952: Kimpo Air Force Base, Japan. Carried as an "unidentified" in the Project Blue Book files. It was also noted in the Master Index that the case file was missing.

June 7, 1952: Albuquerque, New Mexico. Carried as an "unidentified" in the Project Blue Book files.

June 8, 1952: Albuquerque, New Mexico. Witnessed by Markland. Carried as an "unidentified" in the Project Blue Book files.

June 9, 1952: Minneapolis, Minnesota. Carried as an "unidentified" in the Project Blue Book files. It is also noted in the Master Index that the case file was missing.

June 12, 1952: Fort Smith, Arkansas. Carried as an "unidentified" in the Project Blue Book files.

June 12, 1952: Marrakech, Morocco. Carried as an "unidentified" in the Project Blue Book files.

June 13, 1952: Middletown, Pennsylvania. Witnessed by Thomas. Carried as an "unidentified" in the Project Blue Book files.

June 15, 1952: Louisville, Kentucky. Witnessed by Duke. Carried as an "unidentified" in the Project Blue Book files.

June 16, 1952: Walker Air Force Base, Roswell, New Mexico. Carried as an "unidentified" in the Project Blue Book files.

June 17, 1952: McChord Air Force Base, Washington. Carried as an "unidentified" in the Project Blue Book files.

June 17, 1952: Cape Cod, Massachusetts. Carried as an "unidentified" in the Project Blue Book files.

June 18, 1952: Columbus, Wisconsin. Carried as an "unidentified" in the Project Blue Book files.

June 18, 1952: Pontiac, Michigan. Witnessed by Hoffman. Carried as an "unidentified" in the Project Blue Book files.

June 19, 1952: Goose Air Force Base, Labrador, Newfoundland, Canada. Labeled as a radar case. Carried as an "unidentified" in the Project Blue Book files.

June 19, 1952: Yuma, Arizona. Carried as an "unidentified" in the Project Blue Book files.

June 20, 1952: Korea. Carried as an "unidentified" in the Project Blue Book files.

June 21, 1952: Kelly Air Force Base, Texas. Carried as an "unidentified" in the Project Blue Book files.

June 22, 1952: Korea. Carried as an "unidentified" in the Project Blue Book files.

June 23, 1952. Spokane, Washington. Carried as an "unidentified" in the Project Blue Book files.

June 23, 1952: McChord Air Force Base, Washington. Carried as an "unidentified" in the Project Blue Book files.

June 23, 1952: Kirksville, Missouri. Carried as an "unidentified" in the Project Blue Book files. It is also noted in the Master Index that the case file is missing.

June 23, 1952: Oakridge, Tennessee. Carried as an "unidentified" in the Project Blue Book files.

June 23, 1952: New Owensboro, Tennessee. A contractor named Depp heard a sound like an aircraft and looked up to see two round objects, described as looking like soap bubbles, flying one behind the other. They disappeared in about five seconds.

June 25, 1952: Tokyo, Japan. Carried as an "unidentified" in the Project Blue Book files.

June 25, 1952: Chicago, Illinois. Carried as an "unidentified" in the Project Blue Book files.

June 25, 1952. Japan, Korea area. Carried as an "unidentified" in the Project Blue Book files.

June 26, 1952. Terre Haute, Indiana. Carried as an "unidentified" in the Project Blue Book files.

June 26, 1952: Pottstown, Pennsylvania. Carried as an "unidentified" in the Project Blue Book files.

June 27, 1952: Topeka, Kansas. Sighting made by military witnesses. A pilot saw one object that hovered and pulsated. Carried as an "unidentified" in the Project Blue Book files.

June 28, 1952: Lake Kishkonoug, Wisconsin. One silver-white sphere was observed over the lake. The object made a 180-degree turn and became elliptical during the turn and then a sphere.

June 28, 1952: Nagoya, Honshu, Japan. Military witnesses saw a single, blue object that was elliptical. Carried as an "unidentified" in the Project Blue Book files.

June 29, 1952: O'Hare Airport, Chicago, Illinois. Witnesses saw one oval object which was very bright and smooth like highly polished silver. After a time, object moved at a high rate of speed and disappeared like a lightbulb being shut off.

July 3, 1952: Selfridge Air Force Base, Michigan. Carried as an "unidentified" in the Project Blue Book files.

July 3, 1952: Chicago, Illinois. Carried as an "unidentified" in the Project Blue Book files.

July 5, 1952: Norman, Oklahoma. Carried as an "unidentified" in the Project Blue Book files.

July 6–12, 1952: Governors Island, New York. Amateur photographer Neff was making time exposures and didn't see the object until the film was developed.

July 9, 1952: Colorado Springs, Colorado. Sighting witnessed by military personnel. Carried as an "unidentified" in the Project Blue Book files.

July 12, 1952: Annapolis, Maryland. Sighting witnessed by Mr. Washburn. Carried as an "unidentified" in the Project Blue Book files.

July 13, 1952: Kirksville, Missouri. An object was seen on military radar, and the case file is accompanied by scope photographs. Carried as an "unidentified" in the Project Blue Book files.

July 14, 1952: Norfolk, Virginia. Witnessed by Nash. Carried as an "unidentified" in the Project Blue Book files.

July 18, 1952: Miami, Florida. UFO witnessed by Raymer. Carried as an "unidentified" in the Project Blue Book files.

July 20, 1952: Lavalette, New Jersey. Witnessed by Spoomer. Carried as an "unidentified" in the Project Blue Book files.

July 21, 1952: Holyoke, Massachusetts. Witnessed by Burgess. Carried as an "unidentified" in the Project Blue Book files.

July 22, 1952: Between Boston and Provincetown, Massachusetts. 10:47 P.M. The pilot and the radar operator of a U.S. Air Force F-94 jet interceptor saw one round blue light pass the F-94, spinning.

July 22, 1952: Trenton, New Jersey. 10:50 P.M. to 12:45 A.M. (July 23). Crews of several U.S. Air Force F-94 jet interceptors from Dover Air Force Base, Delaware made thirteen visual sightings and one radar tracking of blue-white lights during two hours.

July 23, 1952: Pottstown, Pennsylvania. 8:40 A.M. The two-man crews of three U.S. Air Force F-94 jet interceptors saw a large silver object, shaped like a long pear with two or three squares beneath it, flying at 150–180 knots, while a smaller object, delta-shaped or swept back, flew around it at 1,000–1,500 knots.

July 23, 1952: Altoona, Pennsylvania. 12:50 P.M. Two-man crews of two Air Force F-94 jet interceptors at 35,000–46,000 feet altitude saw three cylindrical objects in a vertical stack formation flying at an altitude of 50,000–80,000 feet.

July 23, 1952: South Bend, Indiana. 11:35 P.M. U.S. Air Force pilot Captain H. W. Kloth watched as two bright blue-white objects flew together; the rear one then veered off after about 9 minutes.

July 24, 1952: Carson Sink, Nevada. 3:40 P.M. Air Force Lieutenant Colonels McGinn and Barton, flying in a B-25 bomber, watched three silver, delta-shaped objects, each with a ridge along the top, cross in front of and above the B-25 at high speed, in 3–4 seconds.

July 26, 1952: Washington, D.C. 8:00 P.M. until after midnight. Sightings made by radar operators at several airports, and airline pilots. Many unidentified blips were tracked by radar all over the Washington area, at varying speeds. Pilots spotted unidentified lights.

July 26, 1952: Kansas City, Missouri. 12:15 A.M. Sighting made by U.S. Air Force captain H. A. Stone and men in control towers at Fairfax Field and Municipal Airport. One greenish light with red-orange flashes was seen for one hour as it descended in the northwest from 40 degrees elevation to 10 degrees elevation.

July 26, 1952: Andrews Air Force Base, Maryland. This was a continuation of the extensive sightings and radar tracking reports reported throughout the Washington, D.C., area, all night long.

July 26, 1952: Kirtland Air Force Base, New Mexico. 12:05 A.M. Airman First Class J. M. Donaldson, saw eight to ten orange balls in a triangular or V-formation which flew very fast for 3–4 seconds.

July 26, 1952: Williams, California. Case missing from official files.

July 27, 1952: Selfridge Air Force Base, Michigan. 10:05–10:20A.M. Three B-29 bomber crewmen on ground watched as many round, white objects flew straight and level, very fast; two at 10:05, one at 10:10, one at 10:15, and one at 10:20. Each was seen for about 30 seconds.

July 27, 1952: Wichita Falls, Texas. 8:30 P.M. Mr. and Mrs. Adrian Ellis saw two disc-shaped objects, illuminated by a phosphorus light. They flew at an estimated 1,000 miles per hour for 15 seconds.

July 28, 1952: Heidelberg, West Germany. 10:20 P.M. Sergeant B. C. Grassmoen and WAC Private First Class A. P. Turner watched one saucer-shaped object, having an appearance of light metal and giving off shafts of white light. It flew slowly, made a 90-degree turn, and climbed away fast after 4–5 minutes.

July 28, 1952: McGuire Air Force Base, New Jersey. 6:00A.M. Ground

Control Approach radar operator Master Sergeant W. F. Dees, and persons in the base control tower, tracked on radar a large cluster of very distinct blips. The visual observation was of oblong objects having neither wings nor tail, which made very fast turns and at one time were in echelon formation.

July 28, 1952: McChord Air Force Base, Washington. 2:15 A.M. Technical Sergeant Walstead and Staff Sergeant Calkins of the 635th AC&W Squadron saw a dull, glowing blue-green ball, the size of a dime at arm's length, fly very fast, straight, and level.

July 29, 1952: Osceola, Wisconsin. 1:30 A.M. Radar operators on ground and the pilot of a F-51 Mustang in flight saw several clusters of up to ten small radar targets and one large target. The small targets moved from the southwest to the east at 50–60 knots, following each other. The large one moved at 600 knots. The pilot confirmed one target.

July 29, 1952: Langley Air Force Base, Virginia. 2:30 P.M. Sighting made by U.S. Air Force captain T. G. Moore, of the military air traffic control system. One undescribed object flew at an estimated 2,600 miles per hour, below 5,000 feet altitude, toward the air base for about 2 minutes.

July 29, 1952: Langley Air Force Base, Virginia. 2:50 P.M. Sighting made by Mr. Moore and Gilfillan electronics representative W. Yhope. One radar target was tracked moving away, stopping for 2 minutes, again moving very, very fast.

July 29, 1952: Merced, California. 3:44 or 3:45 P.M. Herbert Mitchell and one employee watched one dark, discus-shaped object, trailed by a silvery light two lengths behind, as it tipped on its side, dove, hesitated, and then circled very fast during the 2-minute sighting.

July 29, 1952: Wichita, Kansas. 12:35 P.M. Air Force shop employees Douglas and Hess at Municipal Airport saw one bright white circular object with a flat bottom fly very fast, and then hover 10–15 seconds over the Cessna Aircraft Company plant, during the 5-minute sighting.

July 29, 1952: Ennis, Montana. 12:30 P.M. U.S. Air Force persons, alerted that UFOs were coming from the direction of Seattle, Washington saw two to five flat, disc-shaped objects, one of which hovered for 3–4 minutes, while the others circled it.

July 30, 1952: Albuquerque, New Mexico. 11:02 P.M. U.S. Air Force First Lieutenant George Funk saw an orange light which remained stationary for 10 minutes.

July 30, 1952: San Antonio, Texas. 10:00 A.M. E. E. Nye and one other person watched as one round, white object flew slowly and then sped away after 20–30 minutes.

August 1, 1952: Lancaster, California. 1:14 A.M. Sheriff's deputies and other persons, one named Mallette, saw two brilliant red lights hover and maneuver for 5 minutes.

August 2, 1952: Lake Charles, Louisiana. 3:00 A.M. U.S. Air Force first lieutenant W. A. Theil and one enlisted man saw one red ball with a blue-flame tail fly straight and level for 3–4 seconds.

August 4, 1952: Phoenix, Arizona. 2:20 A.M. U.S. Air Force airman first class W. F. Vain saw one yellow ball which lengthened and narrowed to a plate shape, then flew straight and level for 5 minutes.

August 4, 1952: Mount Vernon, New York. 11:37 A.M. One woman and two children saw one object, shaped like a lifesaver or donut, emit black smoke from its top and make a 15-foot arc in 1.5 minutes.

August 5, 1952: Haneda Air Force Base, Japan. 11:30 P.M. Sighting made by USAF F-94 jet interceptor pilots First Lieutenant W. R. Holder and First Lieutenant A. M. Jones, and Haneda control tower operators. Airborne radar tracked a target for 90 seconds. Control tower operators watched for fifty to sixty minutes while a dark shape with a light flew as fast as 330 knots (380 mph), hovered, flew curves, and performed a variety of maneuvers.

August 6, 1952: Tokyo, Japan. This is a continuation of the Haneda Air Force Base sightings.

August 6, 1952: Port Austin, Michigan. Case missing from official files.

August 7, 1952: San Antonio, Texas. 9:08 A.M. Mrs. Susan Pfuhl saw four glowing white discs: one made a 180-degree turn, one flew straight and level, one veered off, and one circled during the 70-minute sighting.

August 9, 1952: Lake Charles, Louisiana. 10:50 A.M. USAF Airman Third Class J. P. Raley. One disc-shaped object flew very fast and then hovered for 2 seconds during a 5–6 minute sighting.

August 13, 1952: Tokyo, Japan. 9:45 P.M. Sighting made by USAF Marine Corps pilot Major D. McGough. One orange light flew a left orbit at 8,000 feet and 230 miles per hour, spiraled down to no more than 1,500 feet, remained stationary for 2–3 minutes and went out. An attempted interception was unsuccessful.

August 18, 1952: Fairfield, California. 12:50 A.M. Three policemen watched one object change color like a diamond, and change directions during the 30-minute sighting.

August 19, 1952: Red Bluff, California. 2:38 P.M. Ground Observer Corps observer Albert Lathrop saw two objects, shaped like fat bullets, which flew straight and level, very fast, for 25 seconds.

August 19, 1952: West Palm Beach, Florida. 9:30 P.M. Scoutmaster Sonny Desvergers claimed to have seen a flying saucer up close. It launched a red mist that burned him slightly. Air Force conclusion: The best hoax in UFO history.

August 20, 1952: Neffesville, Pennsylvania. 3:10 A.M. Bill Ford and two others saw an undescribed object fly at 500 feet altitude for several minutes.

August 21, 1952: Dallas, Texas. 11:54 P.M. Jack Rossen, ex–artillery observer, saw three blue-white lights hover then descend, and then, one and a half minutes later, one of them descended further.

August 23, 1952: Akron, Ohio. 4:10 A.M. USAF Second Lieutenant

H. K. Funseth, a ground radar observer, and two U.S. Navy men saw a single pulsing amber light that was seen to fly straight and level for 7 minutes.

August 24, 1952: Hermanas, Mexico. 10:15 A.M. Georgia Air National Guard F-84G jet fighter pilot Colonel G. W. Johnson saw two 6-foot silver balls in abreast formation; one turned gray rapidly, the other slowly. One changed to a long gray shape during a turn. The sighting lasted about 10 minutes.

August 24, 1952: Tucson, Arizona. 5:40 P.M. Mr. and Mrs. George White watched one large round, metallic, white light with a vague lower surface, as it flew slowly, then fast with a dancing, wavering motion, for about one minute.

August 24, 1952: Levelland, Texas. 9:30 P.M.; 10:30 P.M. Mr. and Mrs. Elmer Sharp saw a single object, shaped like a spinning top, changing color from red to yellow to blue, and with a fiery tail, which hovered for 20 minutes, whistling, then flew away. It, or another like it, returned an hour later.

August 25, 1952: Pittsburg, Kansas. 5:35 A.M. Radio station musician William Squyres saw a single dull aluminum object, shaped like two meat platters face-to-face, estimated at 75 feet long, 45 feet wide, and 15 feet thick. Through a window in the front section shone a blue light; the head and shoulders of a man could be seen. The midsection had numerous windows through which could be seen some kind of regular movement. A series of small propellers were spaced close together along the outer edge of the object, revolving at high speed. The object was hovering about 10 feet above the ground, 100 yards off the road, with a slight rocking motion. It then ascended vertically with a sound like a large covey of quail starting to fly at the same time. Vegetation showed signs of having been disturbed under the object.

August 25, 1952: Holloman AFB, New Mexico. 3:40 P.M. Civilian supervisor Fred Lee and foreman L. A. Aquilar watched a single round silver object fly south, turn and fly north, make a 360-degree turn and fly away vertically after 3–5 minutes.

August 26, 1952: Lathrop Wells, Nevada. 12:10 A.M. Sighting made by USAF Captain D. A. Woods. One large, round, very bright object with a V-shaped contrail having a dark cone in the center, flew very fast, hovered, and made an instantaneous 90-degree turn, followed by a gentle climb and finally sudden acceleration.

August 28, 1952: Chickasaw and Brookley AFB, Alabama. 9:30 P.M. Sighting made by USAF control tower operators, officer from USAF Office of Special Investigations, and others. Six objects, varying from fiery red to sparkling diamond appearance, hovered and flew erratically up and down for one hour and fifteen minutes.

August 29, 1952: Colorado Springs, Colorado. 8:35 P.M. Pilot C. A. Magruder saw three objects, 50 feet in diameter, 10 feet high, aluminum with red-yellow exhaust, as they flew in trail at an estimated 1,500 mph for 4–5 seconds.

August 29, 1952: West of Thule, Greenland. 10:50 A.M. Two U.S. Navy pilots flying a P4Y-2 patrol plane saw three white disc-shaped or spherical objects hover, then fly very fast in a triangular formation, in 2–3 minutes.

September 1, 1952: Marietta, Georgia. 10:50 P.M. An ex–Air Force B-25 gunner saw two large white, disc-shaped objects with green vapor trails fly in trail formation, merge, and fly away very fast.

September 1, 1952: Marietta, Georgia. 10:30 P.M. One unidentified person using binoculars saw two large objects shaped like spinning tops and displaying red, blue, and green colors, fly side by side, leaving a sparkling trail for 30 minutes.

September 1, 1952: Atlanta, Georgia. 9:43 P.M. Mrs. William Davis and nine other persons saw one light, similar to the evening star, move up and down for a long period of time.

September 1, 1952: Marietta, Georgia. 10:30 P.M. Mr. Bowman (ex–artillery officer) and twenty-four others saw a red, white, and blue-green object which spun and shot off sparks for 15 minutes.

September 1, 1952: Yaak, Montana. 4:45 A.M. Visual sighting by two

USAF enlisted men; radar tracking seen by three men using an AN/FPS-3 radar set. Two small, varicolored lights became black silhouettes at dawn; flew erratically.

September 2, 1952: Chicago, Illinois. 3:00 A.M. Radar tracker Turason (ground control approach) at Midway Airport. Forty targets flew in miscellaneous directions, up to 175 miles per hour. Two seemed to fly in formation with a DC-6 airliner.

September 3, 1952: Tucson, Arizona. 9:00 A.M. Civilian pilots McCraven and Thomas saw one shiny, dark ellipse make three broad, curving sweeps in 1.5 minutes.

September 6, 1952: Lake Charles AFB, Louisiana. 1:30 A.M. Technical Sergeant J. E. Wilson and two enlisted men saw one bright, starlike light move about the sky for 2 hours.

September 6, 1952: Tucson, Arizona. 4:55 P.M. Ex-congresswoman Mrs. Isabella King and Bill McClain saw one orange teardrop-shaped object whirl on its vertical axis, descend very fast, stop, and retrace its path upward while whirling in the opposite direction.

September 7, 1952: San Antonio, Texas. 10:30 P.M. Chemist J. W. Gibson and others see one orange object or light (the color of 2,000 feet) explode into view. It was seen from three to twenty seconds by various observers.

September 9, 1952: Rabat, French Morocco. 9:00 P.M. E. J. Colisimo, a civilian illustrator with USAF Intelligence sees one disc with lights along part of its circumference, fly twice as fast as a T-33 jet trainer, in a slightly curved path for 5 seconds.

September 12, 1952: Allen, Maryland. 9:30 P.M. Mr. and Mrs. David Kolb, of the Ground Observer Corps, using binoculars. One white light with a red trim and streamers flew northeast for 35 minutes.

September 13, 1952: Allentown, Pennsylvania. 7:40 P.M. Private pilot W. A. Hobler, flying a Beech Bonanza, saw one object, shaped like a fat football, of a flaming orange-red color, descend and then pull up in front of the witness's airplane.

September 14, 1952: Santa Barbara, California. 8:40 P.M. USAF C-54 transport pilot Tarbutton saw one blue-white light travel straight and level, then go up. It was seen for 30 seconds.

September 14, 1952: North Atlantic, between Ireland and Greenland. Military persons from several countries aboard ships in the NATO "Operation Mainbrace" exercise. Among the sightings: one blue-green triangle was observed flying 1,500 mph; three objects in a triangular formation gave off white light exhaust at 1,500 mph.

September 14, 1952: White Lake, South Dakota. 7:00 P.M. Ground Observer Corps observer L. W. Barnes, using binoculars, saw one red cigar-shaped object, with three puffs behind it, fly west, then south, and then was gone. Seen for thirty to forty minutes.

September 14, 1952: Ciudad Juarez, Mexico. 11:30 P.M. to 1:20 A.M. (September 15). Consulting engineer R. J. Portis and three others saw six groups of twelve to fifteen luminous spheres or discs, which flew in formations varying from arcs to inverted Y's, very fast.

September 14, 1952: Olmstead AFB, Pennsylvania. Time not known. Witness: Pilot of Flying Tiger Airlines airplane N67977. One blue light flew very fast on a collision course with the airliner.

September 16, 1952: Portland, Maine. 6:22 P.M. Sighting made by the crew of U.S. Navy P2V Neptune patrol plane, visually and via radar. A group of five lights was seen at the same time a long, thin blip was being tracked on radar. The sighting lasted 20 minutes.

September 16, 1952: Warner Robins AFB, Georgia. 7:30 P.M. Three USAF officers and two civilians saw two white lights fly abreast, at 100 mph, for 15 minutes.

September 17, 1952: Tucson, Arizona. 11:40 A.M. Mr. and Mrs. Ted Hollingsworth saw two groups of three large, flat, shiny objects fly in tight formations; the first group slow, the second faster. Seen for 2 minutes.

September 23, 1952: Gander Lake, Newfoundland, Canada. Pepperell AFB operations officer and seven other campers saw one bright white light, which reflected on the lake, and flew straight and level at 100 mph for 10 minutes.

September 24, 1952: Charleston, West Virginia. 3:30 P.M. Sighting made by the crew of USAF B-29 bomber. A lot of bright, metallic particles or flashes, up to 3 feet in length, streamed past the B-29 for 15 minutes.

September 26, 1952: Four hundred miles north-northwest of Azores Islands. 11:16 P.M. The pilot, copilot, engineer, and aircraft commander of a USAF C-124 transport plane saw two distinct green lights to the right and slightly above the C-124, and at one time the lights seemed to turn toward the plane. The lights alternated leading each other during more than one hour of observation.

September 27, 1952: Inyokern, California. 10:00 P.M. Two couples, using a 5× telescope, watched a single large, round object, which went through the color spectrum every 2 seconds, and was seen to fly straight and level for 15 minutes.

September 29, 1952: Rochester, England. 3:55 P.M. Report came via the Rochester Police Department. Two flat objects hovered for 3 minutes, and then sped away.

September 29, 1952: Southern Pines, North Carolina. 8:15 P.M. U.S. Army Reserve First Lieutenant C. H. Stevens and two others saw one green ellipse with a long tail, which orbited for 15 minutes.

September 29, 1952: Aurora, Colorado. 3:15 P.M. USAF Technical Sergeant B. R. Hughes saw five or six circular objects, bright white but not shiny, circle in trail formation for 5–6 minutes.

October 1, 1952: Shaw AFB, South Carolina. 6:57 P.M. USAF First Lieutenant T. J. Pointek, pilot of an RF-80 reconnaissance jet, watched as one bright white light flew straight, then vertical, then hovered, and then made an abrupt turn during a 23-minute attempted intercept.

October 1, 1952: Pascagoula, Mississippi. 7:40 P.M. Sighting made by Mr. and Mrs. C. C. McLean and one other person. One round, milky-white object, shaped like a powder puff, hovered for 5–10 minutes then flew away very fast in an arc. A loud blast was heard at the start of the 22-minute sighting.

October 7, 1952: Alamagordo, New Mexico. 8:30 P.M. USAF Lieutenant Bagnell. One pale blue oval, with its long axis vertical, flew straight and level for 4–5 seconds, covering 30 miles in that time.

October 10, 1952: Otis AFB, Massachusetts. 6:30 P.M. A USAF staff sergeant and enlisted men saw one blinking white light move like a pendulum for 20 minutes, and then shoot straight up.

October 17, 1952: Taos, New Mexico. 9:15 P.M. Four USAF officers watched one round, bright blue light move from north to northeast at an elevation of 45 degrees for 2–3 seconds and then burn out.

October 17, 1952: Killeen, Texas. 10:15 P.M. Ministers Greenwalt and Kluck saw ten lights, or a rectangle of lights, move more or less straight and level for 5 seconds.

October 17, 1952: Tierra Amarilla, New Mexico. 11 P.M. One military person (no detail) saw one white streamer move at an estimated 3,000 mph in an arc for 20 seconds.

October 19, 1952: San Antonio, Texas. 1:30 P.M. Ex-USAF aircrewman Woolsey observed three circular aluminum objects, one of which was olive-drab–colored on the side, which flew in a rough V-formation. One object flipped slowly, another object stopped, during the 3-to 4-minute sighting.

October 19, 1952: Five hundred miles south of Hawaii. 6:58 P.M. The crew of USAF C-50 transport plane saw one round yellow light, with a red glowing edge, estimated at 100 feet in diameter, fly at 300–400 knots.

October 21, 1952: Knoxville, Tennessee. Sighting made by persons at an airport weather station. Six white lights flew in a loose formation for 1–2 minutes, and made a shallow dive at a weather balloon.

October 24, 1952: Elberton, Alabama. 8:26 P.M. Sighting was made by USAF Lieutenant Rau and Captain Marcinko, flying a Beech T-ll trainer. One object, shaped like a plate, with a brilliant front and vague trail, flew with its concave surface forward for 5 seconds.

October 29, 1952: Erding Air Depot, West Germany. 7:50 A.M. USAF Staff Sergeant Anderson and Airman Second Class Max Handy saw one round object, silhouetted against a cloud, fly straight and level and smooth at 400 mph for 20 seconds.

October 31, 1952: Fayetteville, Georgia. 7:40 P.M. Sighting made by USAF Lieutenant James Allen. One orange, blimp-shaped object, 80 feet long and 20 feet high, flew at treetop level, crossed over Allen's car (at which time his radio stopped playing), then climbed out at 45 feet and tremendous speed at the end of a one-minute sighting.

November 3, 1952: Laredo AFB, Texas. 6:29 P.M. Two control tower operators, including Lemaster, saw one long, elliptical, white-gray light which flew very fast, paused, and then increased speed during a 3-to 4-second observation.

November 4, 1952: Vineland, New Jersey. 5:40 P.M. Housewife Mrs. Sprague saw two groups of two to three whirling discs of light fly toward the southeast over a period of 30 seconds.

November 12, 1952: Los Alamos, New Mexico. 10:23 P.M. A security inspector saw four red, white, and green lights fly slowly over a prohibited area for 15 minutes.

November 13, 1952: Opheim, Montana. 2:20 A.M. Radar tracking by USAF 779th AC&W station. An unexplained track was followed for 1 hour, 28 minutes, at 158,000 feet altitude (30 miles) and a speed of 240 mph.

November 13, 1952: Glasgow, Montana. 2:43 A.M. U.S. Weather Bureau observer Earl Oksendahl saw five oval-shaped objects, with lights all around them, fly in a V-formation for about 20 seconds. Each object seemed to be changing position vertically by climbing or diving as if to hold formation. Formation came from the northwest, made a 90-degree turn overhead, and flew away to the southwest.

November 15, 1952: Wichita, Kansas. 7:02 A.M. USAF Major R. L.

Wallander, Captain Belleman, and Airman Third Class Phipps watched one orange object varied in shape, as it made jerky upward sweeps with 10-to 15-second pauses during a 3-to 5-minute sighting.

November 24, 1952: Annandale, Virginia. 6:30 P.M. L. L. Brettner watched as one round, glowing object flew very fast, made right-angle turns, and reversed course during a one-hour sighting.

November 27, 1952: Albuquerque, New Mexico. 12:10 P.M. Sighting made by the pilot and the crew chief of USAF B-26 bomber. A series of black smoke bursts (4-3-3-4-3), similar to antiaircraft fire, was seen over a 20-minute period.

November 30, 1952: Washington, D.C. Sighting made by one operator at Washington National Airport. Radar trackings similar to those of July 26, 1952.

December 8, 1952: Ladd AFB, Alaska. 8:16 P.M. Pilot First Lieutenant D. Dickman and radar operator First Lieutenant T. Davies in USAF F-94 jet interceptor (s/n 49-2522) saw one white, oval light which changed to red at higher altitude, flew straight and level for 2 minutes, then climbed at phenomenal speed on an erratic flight path. Sighting lasted 10 minutes.

December 9, 1952: Madison, Wisconsin. 5:45 P.M. Captain Bridges and First Lieutenant Johneon, in a USAF T-33 jet trainer, saw four bright lights, in diamond formation, which flew at 400 mph and were passed by the T-33 at 450 mph during the 10-minute sighting.

December 28, 1952: Marysville, California. Case missing from official files.

January 1, 1953: Craig, Montana. 8:45 P.M. Warner Anderson and two women saw a single silver, saucer-shaped object with a red glowing bottom, fly low over a river and then climb fast in a horizontal attitude.

January 8, 1953: Larson AFB, Washington. 7:15 A.M. Men from the 82nd Fighter-Interceptor Squadron, including the squadron commander, none of whom were airborne, watched a single green, disc-shaped or round object fly southwest for 15 minutes, with a vertically bobbing motion and sideways movements, below clouds.

January 10, 1953: Sonoma, California. 3:45 or 4:00 P.M. Retired Colonel Robert McNab, and Mr. Hunter of the Federal Security Agency, saw a single flat object, like a pinhead, make three 360-degree right turns in 9 seconds, make abrupt 90-degree turns to the right and left, stop, accelerate to original speed and finally fly out of sight vertically after 60–75 seconds.

January 17, 1953: Near Guatemala City, Guatemala. 3:55 P.M. Geologist-salesman J. J. Sackett watched as one brilliant green-gold object, shaped like the Goodyear blimp, with its length twice its height, flew 400 mph straight and level, stopped, then went straight up with one stop. Sighting lasted 22 seconds.

January 28, 1953: Port Mugu, California. 1:00 P.M. R. W. Love, owner of Love Diving Company, engaged in retrieving radio-controlled drones. An 18-to 20-foot white, flat disc flew straight and level, overhead, for 6 minutes.

January 28, 1953: Corona, California. 6:05 P.M. USAF Technical Sergeant George Beyer. Five 25-foot green spheres flew in V-formation, then changed to trail formation at which time the end objects turned red. Sighting lasted 12 minutes.

January 28, 1953: Albany, Georgia. Sighting made by radar maintenance personnel. Radar tracked one stationary target for 20 minutes. A visual sighting about the same time was later explained.

February 3, 1953: Keflavik, Iceland. 5:25 P.M. Radar operators tracked four unidentified targets for 24 minutes.

February 4, 1953: Yuma, Arizona. 1:50 P.M. U.S. Weather Bureau observer Stanley Brown, using a theodolite, saw one white, oblong object, which was tracked flying straight up, leveling off, and being joined by a second, similar object. The second twice flew away and returned to the first. After 5 minutes, both were lost to sight behind clouds.

February 17, 1953: Port Austin, Michigan. 10:04 P.M. Sighting made by two officers and three airmen of USAF AC&W squadron, visually and by radar. Visual object appeared to be larger and brighter than a star and changed color; it was seen to move slowly for 5 minutes, until 10:09 P.M. Radar picked up a target at 10:08 P.M. moving in a similar direction for 17 minutes, at similar speed.

February 20, 1953: Pittsburg–Stockton, California. Number 1, time unknown; number 2, 10:30 P.M. Sighting made by USAF B-25 bomber pilots. Number 1 was a bright yellow light seen for 8 minutes. Number 2 was a bright light which flew on a collision course, dimmed, and climbed away fast.

February 24, 1953: Sherman, Texas. 7:43 P.M. Warrant officer and Mrs. Alden. Two bright red, round objects with big halos flew in small circles, climbed, and faded during a 3-to 7-second sighting.

February 27, 1953: Shreveport, Louisiana. 11:58 A.M. A USAF airman/private pilot watched as five yellow discs made circular turns, fluttered; three of them vanished, the other two flew erratic square turns for a total of 4 minutes.

March 11, 1953: Hackettstown, New Jersey. 4:00 A.M. Mrs. Nina Cook, an experienced private pilot and wife of a Pan Am flight engineer, saw a large light, blinking 10–15 times per minute, moving up and down along a mountain range.

March 14, 1953: North of Hiroshima, Japan. 11:45 P.M. Radar and visual observation by ten crew members of a U.S. Navy P2V-5 patrol plane. Groups of 5–10 colored lights, totaling 90–100, slowly moved aft off the left side of the airplane, as detected visually and by airborne radar for 5 minutes.

March 21, 1953: Elmira, New York. 3:05 P.M. Ground Observer Corps observation post. Six discs in a group flew high and fast for a few seconds.

March 25, 1953: San Antonio, Texas. 3:05 P.M. USAF Captain and

Mrs. D. E. Cox saw several lights, some of which moved straight, others which made 360-degree turns for 1.5 hours.

March 27, 1953: Mount Taylor, New Mexico. 7:25 P.M. Pilot of USAF F-86 jet fighter at 600 knots. One bright orange circle flew at 800 knots and executed three fast rolls. Pilot chased object for 4 minutes.

March 29, 1953: Spooner, Wisconsin. 3:45 P.M. L. C. Gillette saw one aluminum, circular object fly high and fast, twice reversing its course.

April 30, 1955: Travis County, Texas. A military witness watched four black objects, about the size of a pencil eraser held at arm's length, flying in a cluster, disappearing to the west.

May 4, 1955: Keflavik Airport, Iceland. Military witnesses watched ten round objects, looking like oxidized silver, that flew in the general area but were in no formation. They flew in very erratic patterns.

May 23, 1955: Cheyenne, Wyoming. Midnight. Military witnesses watched four objects in a side-by-side formation.

July 29, 1955: Columbus, Nebraska. Witness saw five objects, four of which were orange and one white, appearing as flashing lights.

August 11, 1955: Iceland. Witnesses watched about a dozen objects that seemed to change shape from cigar-shaped to egg-shaped. Formation changed while the witnesses watched.

August 23, 1955: Arlington, Virginia. Witness watched a number of orange flat, disc-shaped objects which were very high and in very rapid flight.

August 27, 1956: Juniata, Pennsylvania. A witness watched a single circular object with a plastic dome protruding from the top. The object climbed to about 20,000 feet by climbing vertically. It disappeared by fading from sight.

September 4, 1956: Dallas, Texas. Military and civilian witnesses watched a single object that was "star"-shaped but the size of a dime held at arm's length. The object flashed from white to red and disappeared traveling to the west.

September 14, 1956: Highland, North Carolina. Witness saw fourteen objects, about the size of a grapefruit, colored yellow to a deep red, flying in a formation. The objects flew from the southwest to the east and then to the northeast and then returned.

November 1, 1956: North of St. Louis, Missouri. Military observer watched a single object that was described as a round light that was a very light yellow. The witness believed the object moved at more than 1,200 mph.

November 30, 1956: Charleston Air Force Base, South Carolina. An Air Force pilot and navigator saw one object as it appeared to be about a hundred feet above the water. They believed that the object, which they could give no shape, color, or size for, was about ten miles from them.

December 31, 1956: Guam. An Air Force interceptor pilot saw a single object as it passed under his aircraft. Pilot attempted to intercept but was unable to gain on it. Finally broke off because of low fuel. The UFO was white, round, and had blinking white lights.

April 25, 1957: Ringgold, Louisiana. 2:30 A.M. Witness saw a single object that was crescent-shaped and colored a bright red.

June 12, 1957: Milan, Italy. 7:30 P.M. Witness watched a single object as it zigzagged from the east, and descended over the city. It seemed to rotate on its axis.

July 27, 1957: Longmont, Colorado. Civilian saw one object as it maneuvered for ten minutes. Case was submitted eight years later by Hynek.

July 29, 1957: Cleveland, Ohio. Civilian airline pilot reported a single object that was a brilliant yellow, dimmed, and returned to its brilliance.

July 29, 1957: Oldsmar, Florida. 11:45 A.M. Civilian saw a single object that was a pale yellow ball of fire. The object exploded into multicolored lights upon hitting the water.

September 20, 1957: Kadena Air Force Base, Okinana. 8:00 P.M. Military witness saw a single object that was oval-shaped and glowed like a fluorescent light. It made no sound.

October 8, 1957: Seattle, Washington. Military witnesses watched two round white objects maneuvering in the sky. They were in sight for 25–30 seconds.

November 2, 1957: Levelland, Texas. A series of sightings that included the sheriff, Weir Clem, other police officers, and several unrelated witnesses began when Pedro Saucido saw a bright red, egg-shaped object on the ground. Throughout the next several hours, others reported the object, which stalled their cars and affected the electrical system. Air Force conclusion: Ball lightning.

November 6, 1957: Boerne, Texas. An official Project Blue Book case that was labeled as an "unidentified."

November 6, 1957: Radium Springs, New Mexico. An official Project Blue Book case that was labeled as an "unidentified."

November 8, 1957: Merrick, Long Island, New York. 10:10 A.M. Mrs. L. Dinner saw a bar-shaped object, 3.5 feet long, which gave off blue flashes and made a swishing sound. No further data.

November 26, 1957: Robins Air Force Base, Georgia. 10:07 A.M. Three control tower operators, one weather observer, and four others watched a single silver, cigar-shaped object suddenly vanish after minutes.

November 30, 1957: New Orleans, Louisiana. 2:11 P.M. Witnesses: Three U.S. Coast Guardsmen. One round object turned white, then gold, then separated into three parts and turned red. Sighting lasted 20 minutes.

December 13, 1957: Col Anahuac, Mexico. 9:35 A.M. R. C. Cano watched as fourteen or fifteen circular, tapered discs, very bright, flew in a formation like a stack of coins, then changed to an inverted-V formation. Sighting lasted 20 minutes.

December 17, 1957: Near Grand Junction, Colorado. 7:20 P.M. F. G. Hickman, seventeen, saw one round object change from yellow to white to green to red; red tail was twice as long as the body.

March 14, 1958: Healdsburg, California. 8:45 A.M. Mr. and Mrs. W. F. Cummings and one other saw a 3-foot round black object touch the ground and then take off. Watched for 2 minutes.

April 14, 1958: Lynchburg, Virginia. 1:00 P.M. Air Force Major D. G. Tilley, flying a C-47 transport plane, watched one gray-black rectangular object rotate very slowly on its horizontal axis for 4 seconds.

May 9, 1958: Bohol Island, Phillipine Islands. 11:05 A.M. A Phillipine Airlines pilot saw an object with a shiny, metallic surface fall and spin for 1.5 minutes.

June 14, 1958: Pueblo, Colorado. 10:46 A.M. Airport weather observer O. R. Foster, using a theodolite, watched a single object shaped like Saturn less the bottom part. It was silver with no metallic luster, and flew overhead for 5 minutes.

June 20, 1958: Fort Bragg, North Carolina. 11:05 P.M. Battalion communication chief Sergeant First Class A. Parsley saw one silver, circular object, its lower portion seen through a green haze, as it hovered, then oscillated slightly, then moved at great speed. He watched it for 10 minutes.

August 17, 1958: Warren, Michigan. 7:05 P.M. A. D. Chisholm saw one extremely bright object shaped first like a bell, then like a saucer, which hovered for 5 minutes, flipped over, and sped away to the west-southwest. Sighting lasted 6–10 minutes.

September 1, 1958: Wheelus Air Force Base, Libya. 12:15 A.M. Sightings made by Philco technical representative A. M. Slaton. One round, blue-white object flew at varying speeds. First sighting lasted 2 minutes, second lasted 1.5 minutes.

October 2, 1958: Stroudsburg, Pennsylvania. 2:30 P.M. Naturalist Ivan Sanderson saw one dull-gray object, shaped like a pickle with a flat bottom, which flew erratically and made loops for 15 seconds.

October 27, 1958: Lock Raven Dam, Maryland. 10:30 P.M. Phillip Small and Alvin Cohen saw one large, flat, egg-shaped object which affected a car's electrical system and caused a burning sensation on one of its occupants.

November 3, 1958: Minot, North Dakota. 2:01 P.M. Master Sergeant William R. Butler, medic, saw one bright green object, shaped like a 10-cent piece, and one smaller, silver round object. The first object exploded, then the second object moved toward the location of the first at high speed.

March 26 or 27, 1959: Corsica, Pennsylvania. 12:45 P.M. T. E. Clark saw one dark red, barrel-shaped object, 20 feet long, 6–7 feet high, descend below some trees during the 3-minute sighting.

June 18, 1959: Edmonton, Alberta, Canada. 9:30 P.M. A. Cavelli and R. Blessin, using 7× binoculars, watched as one brown, cigar-shaped object came from below the horizon, ascending to 40–50 degrees above the horizon in 4 minutes.

June 30, 1959: Patuxent River Naval Air Station, Maryland. 8:23 P.M. Sighting made by Navy Commander D. Connolly. One gold, oblate-shaped object, nine times as wide as it was thick, metallic and with sharp edges, flew straight and level for 20–30 seconds.

July 25, 1959: Irondequoit, New York. 1:00 P.M. Technical illustrator W. D. Neva watched as one thin, crescent moon–shaped object with a small white dome in the center, flew at tremendous speed for 5–10 seconds.

August 10, 1959: Goose Air Force Base, Labrador, Canada. 1:28 A.M. Sighting made by Royal Canadian Air Force pilot Flight Lieutenant M. S. Mowat, on the ground. One large, starlike light crossed 53 degrees of sky in 25 minutes.

September 13, 1959: Gills Rock, Wisconsin. 1:05 A.M. R. H.

Daubner watched as one round yellow light, with eight blue lights within it, and then five larger red lights, flew very fast vertically while making a pulsating jet noise. Sighting lasted 10 minutes.

September 13, 1959: Bunker Hill Air Force Base, Indiana. 4:00 P.M. At least two control tower operators and the pilot of a Mooney private airplane saw one pear-shaped object, colored white, cream, and metallic, with a trail under it. The object showed little movement during 3 hours. Attempted intercept by a U.S. Air Force T-33 jet trainer failed.

October (third or fourth week) 1959: Telephone Ridge, Oregon. 9:15 P.M. Sighting made by department-store manager C. A. Cissman. One bright light approached, hovered about 30 minutes, and then was up and gone in 2 seconds.

October 4, 1959: Quezon, Phillipine Islands. 9:25 P.M. U.S. Navy Lieutenant C. H. Pogson and Chief Petty Officer K. J. Moore saw one large round or oval object, changing from red to red-orange, which flew straight and level for 15 minutes.

October 6, 1959: Lincoln, Nebraska. 8:15 P.M. Lieutenant Colonel L. Liggett (Selective Service) and wife. One round, white-yellow light made several abrupt turns and flew very fast for 2 minutes.

October 19, 1959: Kansas. 9:25 P.M. Sighting made by Captain F. A. Henney, engineering instructor at the U.S. Air Force Academy, who was flying a T-33 jet trainer. One bright yellowish light came head-on at the T-33; the pilot avoided it and the light dimmed. Sighting lasted 30 seconds.

November 18, 1959: Crystal Springs, Mississippi. 6:25 P.M. J. M. Porter watched as a row of red lights flew slowly, then speeded up immensely. Sighting lasted 5–6 minutes.

February 27, 1960: Rome Air Force Base, New York. 6:27 P.M. Control tower officer Captain J. Huey and four other tower operators saw one light trailing a white fan shape, which made a mild descent for 3–4 minutes.

March 4, 1960: Dubuque, Iowa. 5:55 P.M. Charles Morris watched three elliptical-shaped objects make a slight climb for 4 minutes. Film exposed during sighting showed no images of the objects.

March 23, 1960: Indianapolis, Indiana. 3:35 A.M. Mr. and Mrs. E. I. Larsen observed a series of balls, arranged like an X with one diagonal line; seen for three-quarters of a minute.

April 12, 1960: LaCamp, Louisiana. 9:00 P.M. Monroe Arnold saw one fiery-red disc which exploded four or five times. Analysis of paint samples from explosion proved inconclusive. Sighting lasted 2–3 seconds.

April 17, 1960: Richards-Gebauer Air Force Base, Missouri. 8:29 P.M. Sighting made by U.S. Air Force Major J. G. Ford and Link representative A. Chapdelaine, using a 48× telescope. One reddish glow made an odd orbit for 2.5 minutes.

April 25, 1960: Shelby, Montana. 7:00 to 10:00 P.M. Mrs. M. Clark watched as five circular objects flew in trail formation, hovered and accelerated, and made sharp turns. Case file includes other reports from Mrs. Clark for the previous 3 years.

July 19, 1960: St. Louis, Missouri. 8:30 P.M. T. L. Ochs saw one round, bright red light which flew overhead, stopped and hovered, and then backed up. Sighting lasted 20 minutes.

August 23, 1960: Wichita, Kansas. 3:24 A.M. Boeing aeronautical engineer C. A. Komiske saw one round object with yellow lights coming from what looked like three triangular windows at bottom. Object was dull orange. Flew in an arc for 2 minutes.

August 29, 1960: Crete, Illinois. 4:05 P.M. Farmer Ed Schneeweis saw one shiny, round, silver object fly straight up very fast for 18 seconds.

September 10, 1960: Ridgecrest, California. 9:50 P.M. Mr. and Mrs. M. G. Evans saw two light-gray glowing objects, saucer-or boomerang-shaped, which swished when accelerating.

October 5, 1960: Mount Kisko, New York. 7:37 P.M. E. G.

Crossland saw one bright, starlike light move across 120 degrees of sky in 20 seconds.

November 27, 1960: Chula Vista, California. 7:30 P.M. Mr. and Mrs. L. M. Hart watched as one orange-red point of light made huge circles and stopped during the 20-to 30-minute sighting.

November 29, 1960: south of Kyushu, Japan. 6:38 P.M. Sighting made by U.S. Air Force Lieutenant Colonel R. L. Blwlin and Major F. B. Brown, who were flying a T-33 jet trainer. One white light glowed and paralleled the course of the T-33 for 10 minutes.

February 27, 1961: Bark River, Michigan. 10:15 P.M. Mrs. LaPalm saw one fiery-red, round object, preceded by light rays, slow and descend while her dog howled.

Spring 1961: Kemah, Texas. Case missing from official files.

April 24, 1961: Two hundred miles southwest of San Francisco, California. 3:34 A.M. Aircraft commander Captain H. J. Savoy and navigator First Lieutenant M. W. Rand, on a U.S. Air Force RC-121D patrol plane, saw one reddish white, round object or light, similar to a satellite. Observed for 8 minutes.

May 22, 1961: Tyndall Air Force Base, Florida. 4:30 P.M. Mrs. A. J. Jones and Mrs. R. F. Davis watched as one big silver-dollar disc hovered and revolved, then suddenly disappeared after 15 minutes.

June 2, 1961: Miyako Jima, Japan. 10:17 P.M. First Lieutenant R. N. Monahan and Hazeltine Electric Company technical representative D. W. Mattison saw one blue-white light fly an erratic course at varying speed, in an arclike path, for 5 minutes.

July 7, 1961: Copemish, Michigan. 11:00 P.M. Nannette Hilley saw one large ball fly slow, and split into four after 45 minutes. Four flew in close formation, descended, and flew away to the west. Total sighting lasted 1 hour.

July 11, 1961: Springfield, Ohio. 7:45 P.M. Ex–air navigator G. Scott,

Mrs. Scott, and neighbors watched as one round, bright light, like shiny aluminum, passed overhead in 20 minutes.

July 20, 1961: Houston, Texas. 8:00 A.M. Sighting made by Trans-Texas Airlines Captain A. V. Beather, who was flying a DC-3, plus a vague report from ground radar. Two very bright white lights or objects flew in trail formation for 30 minutes.

August 12, 1961: Kansas City, Kansas. 9:00 P.M. College seniors J. B. Furkenhoff and Tom Phipps saw one very large oval object with a fin extending from one edge to the center; it looked like a sled with lighted car running-boards. It hovered at 50 feet altitude for 3–5 minutes, then flew straight up and east.

November 21, 1961: Oldtown, Florida. 7:30 P.M. C. Locklear and Helen Hatch saw one round, red-orange object which flew straight up and faded after 3–4 minutes.

November 23, 1961: Sioux City, Iowa. 9:30 P.M. F. Braunger. One bright red star flew straight and level for 15 minutes.

December 13, 1961: Washington, D.C. 5:05 P.M. C. F. Muncy, ex-U.S. Navy pilot W. J. Myers, and G. Weber. One dark diamond-shaped object with a bright tip flew straight and level for 1–3 minutes.

February 25, 1962: Kotzbue, Alaska. 7:20 P.M. One U.S. Army private, six anonymous civilians. One red light, trailed 30 seconds later by a blue light. Sighting lasted 5 minutes.

March 1, 1962: Salem, New York. 10:35 P.M. Mrs. L. Doxsey, 66. One gold-colored box flew straight and level across the horizon for 3–4 minutes.

March 26, 1962: Ramstein Air Base, West Germany. 1:35 P.M. USAF Captain J. M. Lowery, from an unspecified aircraft. One thin, cylindrical object—one-third snout, two-thirds tail fins—flew at an estimated Mach 2.7 for 5–8 seconds.

March 26, 1962: Naperville, Illinois. 11:40 P.M. Mrs. D. Wheeler, Claudine Milligan watched as six or eight red balls, arranged in a rectangular formation, became two objects with lights by the end of the 15-minute sighting.

March 26, 1962: Westfield, Massachusetts. 10:45 P.M. Many unidentified young people watched as one large red ball flew or fell down, then went back up during a 3-to 10-minute sighting.

April 4, 1962: Wurtland, Kentucky. 0150Z. G. R. Wells and J. Lewis, using 117× telescope saw one small object changing brightness; it gave off smoke but remained stationary like a comet for 6 minutes. Case missing from official files.

June 21, 1962: Indianapolis, Indiana. 4:00 A.M. Lieutenant Colonel H. King and tail gunner Master Sergeant Roberts, aboard a B-52 heavy jet bomber, saw three bright, starlike lights: First one was seen; 10 seconds later, two more were seen. Total sighting took 3 minutes.

June 30, 1962: Richmond, Virginia. 9:00 A.M. Sighting made by thirteen-year-old Meadors. One red, starlike light was seen for an unspecified length of time. No further details in files.

July 19, 1962: Bayhead, New Jersey. 9:30 P.M. C. T. Loftus and H. Wilbert saw four or five lights dart about the sky for 7–10 minutes.

July 29, 1962: Ocean Springs, Mississippi. 11:20 P.M. Mr. and Mrs. M. O. Barton saw one bright cherry-red, diamond-shaped object fly slow, hover, and make fast half loops for 10 minutes.

August 18, 1962: Bermuda. 5:00 P.M. Radio station owner M. Sheppard and chief announcer A. Seymour saw three dull-white, egg-shaped objects waver as they moved for 20 minutes.

September 21, 1962: West-southwest of Biloxi, Mississippi, in the Gulf of Mexico. 7:37 P.M. Fishing-boat captain S. A. Guthrie saw two objects, red and black with orange streaks, one as big as the moon, and the other smaller. They arced across the sky for 13 minutes.

October 23, 1962: Farmington, Utah. 3:00 P.M. R. O. Christensen watched one gray-and-silver ball, trailing what looked like twine with two knots in it, as it swerved, and climbed away at a 45-degree angle, making a sound like a flock of ducks (rushing air).

November 17, 1962: Tampa, Florida. 9:00 P.M. F. L. Swindale, college graduate and ex–Marine captain watched as three bright, starlike lights approached, hovered, and bounced, then faded after 11–15 minutes.

May 18, 1953: New Plymouth, New Zealand. 10:30 P.M. Sighting made by C. S. Chapman, fifteen. One white, fuzzy, flashing light hovered and darted around for 4 minutes.

May 22, 1963: Pequannock, New Jersey. 10:45 P.M. Myra Jackson watched as four pink wheels spun or rolled very fast from east to west in succession, each taking about one second.

June 15, 1963: Two hundred miles north of Venezuela. 10:39 A.M. Third Mate R. C. Chamberlin, of S/ Thetis. One luminous disc traveled at 1.5 times the speed of a satellite for 3–4 minutes.

Summer 1963: Middletown, New York. 9:30 or 10:00 P.M. Grace Dutcher saw eight to ten lights move at random, then in an oval formation, then singly, during the one-minute sighting.

July 1, 1963: Glen Ellyn, Illinois. 8:00 P.M. R. B. Stiles, eleven, using a theodolite, saw one light, the size of a matchhead at arm's length, flash and move around the sky for 1.5 hours.

August 11, 1963: Warrenville, Illinois. 10:00 P.M. R. M. Boersma saw one light move around the sky for 20 seconds.

August 13, 1963: St. Gallen, Switzerland. 8:04 P.M. A. F. Schelling watched as one fireball became a dark object after 4 minutes, and then a bigger glow a minute later, and finally exploded.

September 14, 1963: Susanville, California. 3:15 P.M. Sighting made by E. A. Grant, veteran of thirty-seven years training forest-fire lookouts for the U.S. Forest Service. One round object intercepted a long object and either attached itself to the latter or disappeared. Sighting lasted 10 minutes.

September 15, 1963: Vandalia, Ohio. 6:00 P.M. Mrs. F. E. Roush saw two very bright gold objects—one shaped like a banana and the other like an ear of corn. One remained stationary, the other moved from west to north during 10 minutes.

October 4, 1963: Bedford, Ohio. 3:32 P.M. R. E. Carpenter, fifteen, saw one intense oblong light with tapered ends and surrounded by an aqua haze, flash and flicker while stationary for 15 seconds.

October 23, 1963: Meridian, Idaho. 8:35 P.M. Several unnamed students saw one object shaped like a circle from below and like a football from the side, which hovered low over the observers, making a deep, pulsating, loud, extremely irritating sound, for 6 minutes.

October 24, 1963: Cupar Fife, Scotland. Sighting made by A. McLean (age twelve) and G. McLean (eight). One light moved for an unspecified length of time. No further details in files. Note: Project Blue Book chief Major H. Quintanilla told the youngsters, in a letter, that this was "one of the most complete" of the unexplained cases for the year.

December 11, 1963: McMinnville, Oregon. 7:00 A.M. W. W. Dolan, professor of mathematics and astronomy, and dean of the faculty of Linfield College, saw one bright, starlike light hover, slow, dim, and flash in one minute.

December 16, 1963: Eight hundred miles north of Midway Island, Central Pacific. 5:05 P.M. Unspecified persons aboard a military aircraft saw one white light blink 2–3 times per second as it moved very fast across the sky for 15 seconds.

April 3, 1964: Monticello, Wisconsin. 9:00 P.M. Mr. and Mrs. R. Wold watched four huge red lights in a rectangular formation, with a white light above, which were near the ground, tilted, and flew away after 3–4 minutes.

April 11, 1964: Homer, New York. 6:30 P.M. Physiotherapist W. B. Ochsner and wife watched as two cloudlike objects darkened; one shot away and returned during the 30-to 45-minute sighting.

April 24, 1964: Socorro, New Mexico. 5:45 P.M. Socorro policeman Lonnie Zamora watched an object with flames underneath descend toward the desert. Two small humanoids observed near the vertical oval on the ground. Later he watched the object take off with a roar, go silent, and fly away. Burning and charred brush was found at the landing sight.

May 9, 1964: Chicago, Illinois. 10:20 P.M. J. R. Betz, U.S. District Court reporter, saw three light-green, crescent-shaped objects, about half the apparent size of the moon, fly very fast in tight formation from east to west, oscillating in size and color, for 3 seconds.

May 18, 1964: Mount Vernon, Virginia. 5:15 P.M. Civil engineer F. Meyers saw one small, glowing white oval split twice after moving from the right of the moon around to the left. Sighting lasted 17 minutes.

May 26, 1964: Cambridge, Massachusetts. 7:43 P.M. P. Wankowicz, Royal Air Force pilot and ex-Smithsonian satellite tracker, saw one thin, white ellipsoid (3.5 times as long as wide) fly straight and level for 3–4 seconds.

May 26, 1964: Pleasantview, Pennsylvania. 11:00 P.M. Sighting made by Reverend H. C. Shaw. One yellow-orange light, shaped like the bottom of a ball, was spotted in a field and chased down the road for 2 miles.

June 13, 1964: Toledo, Ohio. 9:15 P.M. B. L. English, announcer for radio station WTOD saw three glowing white spheres, glowing red on their sides, move slowly, hover and then move in circles very fast, all the while making a low, rumbling sound.

June 29, 1964: Lavonia, Georgia. B. E. Parham noticed a brilliant light in the sky, moving toward him at a 45-degree angle. He felt a burning sensation on his arms. Air Force conclusion: The phenomena was determined to be St. Elmo's fire. The report was not forwarded to the investigating office at Wright-Patterson since it was evaluated on the spot.

July 16, 1964: Fifteen miles south of Houghton Lake, Michigan. 11: 15 P.M. Northern Air Service pilot K. Jannereth spotted four white lights in a stepped-up echelon formation, which were joined by two more. They closed in on the airplane, then rapidly slowed and flew along with it for a total of 5 minutes.

July 20, 1964: Littleton, Illinois. 4:45 A.M. J. J Winkle saw one round-topped, flat-bottomed object with a 60-foot diameter and a long acet-ylene-colored flame shooting downward, which flew straight and level, made a half loop, then rose up. Sighting lasted one minute.

July 27, 1964: Norwich, New York. 7:30 P.M. Duabert, engineering supervisor, saw one aluminum sphere with a luminous ring, which remained stationary for 4–5 minutes.

July 27, 1964: Denver, Colorado. 8:20 P.M. A. Borsa saw one white ball of fire, the size of a car, which climbed slowly, then speeded up. Sighting lasted 2–3 minutes.

August 10, 1964: Wake Island (north of Marshall Island, Pacific Ocean). 5:16 A.M. Sighting made by aircraft commander Captain B. C. Jones and navigator First Lieutenant H. J. Cavender, in a parked U.S. Air Force C-124 transport plane. One reddish, blinking light approached the runway, stopped, and made several reverses during 2 minutes.

August 15, 1964: New York, New York. 1:20 A.M. S. F. D. Alessandro saw one 10-by 5-foot bullet-shaped object with wavy lines on the rounded front part and six pipes along the straight rear portion, which made a *whishhh* sound.

August 15, 1964: Yosemite National Park, California. 8:15 A.M. E. J. Haug, of the San Francisco Orchestra and the San Francisco Conservatory of Music, and C. R. Bubb, a high school mathematics teacher, spotted three bright silver, round objects, in a stack formation, which flew very fast, changing positions within the formation. The sound of rushing air was heard during the 3-to 4-second sighting.

August 18, 1964: Atlantic Ocean, 200 miles east of Dover, Delaware.

12:35 A.M. Major D. W. Thompson and first pilot First Lieutenant J. F. Jonke, on a U.S. Air Force C-124 transport plane, saw one round, blurred, reddish white object on a collision course with the C-124 from ahead and below. The airplane evaded the object. Sighting lasted 2 minutes.

September 4, 1964: Cisco Grove, California. The witness claimed to have seen an object come toward him. He saw two humanoid beings and two creatures he described as robots. Air Force conclusion: Psychological.

September 10, 1964: Cedar Grove, New Jersey. 7:09 P.M. P. H. DePaolo saw four white lights. They were seen to the north, going west for 45 seconds.

November 14, 1964: Menominee Falls, Wisconsin. 9:40 P.M. Dr. G. R. Wagner and two girls watched three dim, reddish lights fly through a 160-degree arc in 5–6 seconds.

November 19, 1964: Fourteen hundred miles east of Tokyo, Japan. One bright white flashing light was traveling from horizon to horizon in 20 seconds.

January 23, 1965: Williamsburg, Virginia. 8:40 A.M. Mr. T. F. Mains saw one mushroom-or lightbulb-shaped object, 75–80 feet high, 25-foot diameter on top, and 10-foot bottom diameter; metallic gray with a red-orange glow on the near side and a blue glow on the far side. The object made a sound like a vacuum cleaner. The witness's car's electrical system was affected as the object moved away at an altitude of 4 feet.

March 4, 1965: Corvallis, Oregon. 9:23 P.M. W. V. Harrison. Three lights rose from the ground, several seconds apart. The next day, an oily spot was found at the site.

March 8, 1965: Mount Airy, Maryland. 7:40 P.M. J. H. Martin, instrument maker for U.S. Bureau of Standards, watched six lights fly overhead slowly for 3 minutes.

April 4, 1965: Keesler Air Force Base, Mississippi. 4:05 A.M. Sighting made by U.S. Air Force Airman Second Class Corum and a weather observer; confirmation by college student R. Pittman not clear from available data. One 40-foot black, oval object with four lights along the bottom, flew in and out of the clouds for 15 seconds.

May 7, 1965: Oxford, Michigan. 7:30 P.M. M. E. Marshall spotted one light, like a satellite, split into two parts, one of which was copperish color, then two more joined up. One object may have been tumbling. Sighting lasted one minute.

July 6, 1965: Kiel, Wisconsin. 9:30 P.M. Mrs. E. R. Hayner reported one flashing light, like a satellite, which was seen for less than one minute. No further data was in the files.

July 25, 1965: Castalia, Ohio. 9:15 P.M. Amateur astronomer M. D. Harris, sixteen, watched as one bright blue star crossed 90 degrees of sky in 10–15 seconds.

August 4, 1965: Dallas, Texas. 9:30 P.M. Sighting made by J. A. Carter, nineteen. One light flew fast, straight and level for 12 seconds. No further data in files.

August 4, 1965: Tinley Park, Illinois. 11:35 P.M. Two unnamed fourteen-year-olds reported one light which moved around the sky for 16–17 seconds.

August 19, 1965: Cherry Creek New York. 8:20 P.M. Mrs. William Butcher, her son Harold, seventeen, and other children saw a large elliptical object, with a reddish vapor underneath, come close to the ground, then shoot straight up into the clouds a few seconds later. Radio was drowned out by static, and a tractor engine stopped. When the object was on the ground, a steady beeping sound could be heard. Afterward, a strange odor was noticed, and the next day, a purplish liquid, 2-/by 2-inch marks, and patches of singed grass were found at the site. A bull bellowed and tried to break its bonds.

August 30, 1965: Urbana, Ohio. 10:30 P.M. Sighting reported by M. A. Lilly, N. Smith, and T. Nastoff. One white ball, 5–8 feet in diameter and trailed by a 2-to 3-foot light, hit the road 100 feet in front of the witnesses' car, bounced, and flew away. Sighting lasted 3–4 seconds.

September 3, 1965: Exeter, New Hampshire. 2:00 A.M. Patrolmen Eugene Bertrand, Jr., and David Hunt, and Norman Muscarello watched as one large, dark, elliptical object with a row of red lights around it, moved slowly and erratically around houses and trees, while lights blinked in sequence. Farm animals were very noisy. Sighting lasted about one hour.

September 3, 1965: Damon, Texas. 11:00 P.M. Brazoria County Chief Sheriff's Deputy Billy McCoy and Deputy Robert Goode saw one triangular object, which was 150–200 feet long, 40–50 feet thick at the middle, and dark gray, with a long bright, pulsing, purple light on the right side and a long blue light on the left side. It came from a distance to 150 feet off highway and 100 feet in the air. Purple light illuminated ground beneath the object and the interior of police car. The driver felt heat on his left arm. Initial sighting lasted 5–10 minutes. Second sighting occurred later that night.

September 25, 1965: Chisholm, Minnesota. 9:55 A.M. Bett Diamon. Five orange lights in a row flew fast and made an abrupt turn during the one-minute sighting.

September 25, 1965: Rodeo, New Mexico. 10:00 P.M. Dr. George Walton, physical chemist, and wife saw two round white objects flying side by side, at 30–50 feet altitude, pacing the witnesses' car for 6 minutes.

October 4, 1965: Middletown, Ohio. Sighting reported by Tucker. Case missing from official files.

February 2, 1966: Salisbury, North Carolina. 11:15 P.M. Mr. and Mrs. L. J. Wise saw one silver, diamond-shaped object with several balls constantly in very fast motion around it, and much light. The object hovered over the trees for 3–4 minutes, while a dog barked, and then zipped out of sight. Sighting lasted one hour.

February 6, 1966: Nederland, Texas. 5:45 A.M. Mr. and Mrs. K. R.

Gulley reported one yellow, lighted object at 500 feet altitude, and a pulsating red glow on the lawn. The house lights went out, and high frequency bothered the witnesses' ears. Sighting lasted 5–10 minutes.

March 20, 1966: Miami, Florida. 12:15 A.M. U.S. Air Force Reserve Major K. C. Smith and an employee of NASA at Cape Kennedy spotted one pulsating light which varied from white to intense blue, made a jerky ascent, and then rapidly accelerated away to the north after 5 minutes.

March 22, 1966: Houston, Texas. 1:30 A.M. S. J. Musachia reported white flashing lights, and the air full of smoke. The lights lit up witness's apartment. Sound of "yen" heard up close during 4-minute sighting.

March 23, 1966: Temple, Oklahoma. 5:05 A.M. W. E. Laxson saw one large object, like a wingless C-124 transport plane—75 feet long, 8 feet high, and 12 feet wide—with a bubble canopy on top. It sat on the highway, a man dressed in military work clothes entered, and it rose after about 40 seconds.

March 26, 1966: Texhoma, Oklahoma. Midnight. Sighting reported by Mrs. P. N. Beer and Mrs. E. Smith. One flashing light buzzed their car from the front then hovered. Sighting lasted 10 minutes.

April 5, 1966: Alto, Tennessee. 11:55 P.M. W. Smith watched one oval object with a dark top that appeared cone-shaped when moving. It made a high-frequency noise during the 2.5-hour sighting.

April 5, 1966: Lycoming, New York. 3:00 A.M. Lillian Louis witnessed one vaporlike sphere hover and spin at low altitude, shooting its exhaust onto the ground below. Sighting of one minute.

April 16, 1966: Portage County, Ohio. 5:30 A.M. Dale Spaur and Wilbur Neff, among others, sighted a low-flying UFO that was bright enough to light the road underneath. They chased it for about 30 minutes, until it disappeared by climbing in the brightening sky. Air Force conclusion: Satellite and Venus.

April 30, 1966: Sacramento, California. 3:15 A.M. Anita Miller watched as one light moved around the sky for 2.5 hours.

May 7, 1966: Goodfellow Air Force Base, Texas. 9:55 P.M. Airman Third Class W. L. Whitehead watched one short, cylindrical object with pointed ends and a yellow light at one end and a blue light at the other, fly straight and level for 35 seconds.

June 6, 1966: Spooner, Wisconsin. 9:30 P.M. Dorothy Gray saw two domed discs with sparkling upper surfaces and square windows in their tops, revolving above a lake, apparently causing strange behavior of the lake water during the 25-second sighting.

July 10, 1967: Meridian, Mississippi. The witness said that his car coasted to a stop and the radio faded out. He saw an object of excessive size pass about 300 feet over his car. It disappeared by accelerating at an angle, disappearing into the low clouds.

August 21, 1968: Ottsville, Pennsylvania. Photographs of an object were taken as it flew in an irregular and jerky path. Air Force conclusion: Insufficient data for evaluation because the proper Air Force forms had not been filed.

September 15, 1968: Ocala, Florida 9:30 P.M. A light was observed doing aerobatics for 15 minutes. The light rose quickly and disappeared among the stars. Almost immediated a second, white light was seen under the haze above Ocala. The pilots of a light plane reported that the light came at them rapidly on a collision course, and the pilots thought it was a Sidewinder missile fired at them.

October 24, 1968: Minot Air Force Base, North Dakota. Thirty minutes after midnight until 4:30 A.M. A number of Air Force personnel, including the crew of a B-52, saw a light that was tracked by both ground-based radar and the B-52's on-board radars. Air Force conclusion: Ground-visual sighting was probably an aircraft (the B-52) *and* probably a star; the radar sighting was possibly a plasma; and the air-visual sighting was possibly a plasma.

November 23, 1968: Newton, Georgia. Witness encountered a brilliant light directly above the road as he rounded a bend in the road in sparsely settled territory. The light was about 200 feet ahead of him and 50–75 feet off the ground. The radio faded to static. The engine died. The light disappeared in a few seconds, going straight up, and the engine started by itself.

January 17, 1969: Crittenden, Virginia. 3:24 A.M. Roman K. Lupton was awakened by a sound similar to the hum of an electric motor that was in the process of going bad. Upon looking out the bedroom window, Lupton sighted several amber lights that were arranged in an elliptical fashion. It appeared to have a slow forward, up-and-down motion except when it made a left banking turn. Several of the neighbors heard the sound but no one else saw the object.

January 17, 1969 Bradenton, Florida 11:30 P.M. A fifteen-year-old boy watched several disc-shaped objects in the night sky. Air Force conclusion: Unreliable report.

GLOSSARY

AAF: Army Air Forces, the forerunner to the United States Air Force. Army Air Field.

AFOSI: Air Force Office of Special Investigation, originally known only as OSI.

AISS: Air Intelligence Service Squadron.

APRO: Aerial Phenomena Research Organization, a new defunct civilian UFO group.

ATIC: Air Technical Intelligence Center.

Condon Committee: The Air Force–sponsored study of UFOs conducted by the University of Colorado in the late 1960s.

FTD: Foreign Technology Division.

Flying disk: One of the first terms used to refer to UFOs.

Flying saucer: The term for objects believed to be spacecraft from other planets.

NICAP: National Investigations Committee on Aerial Phenomena, a new defunct civilian UFO group.

Project Blue Book: The last of the official Air Force investigations into UFOs.

Project Grudge: The second of the official Air Force investigations. It was the predecessor to Blue Book.

Project Saucer: The public name given to the official investigation known as Sign.

Project Sign: The first of three investigations. The code name was later changed to Grudge.

RAF: Royal Air Force, that is, the English Air Force.

Robertson Panel: CIA-sponsored study of UFOs completed in 1953.

UFO: Unidentified flying object. It is a generic term that refers to anything in the sky that can't be identified. It has come to be associated with the idea of extraterrestrial spacecraft.

BIBLIOGRAPHY

Air Defense Command Briefing, Jan. 1953, Project Blue Book Files.

Alberts, Don E. and Putnam, Allan E. *A History of Kirtland Air Force Base 1928–1982*. Albuquerque: 1606th Air Base Wing, 1985.

ATIC UFO Briefing, April 1952, Project Blue Book Files.

Baker, Raymond D. *Historical Highlights of Andrews AFB 1942–1989*. Andrews AFB, Maryland: 1776th Air Base Wing, 1990.

Binder, Otto. *What We Really Know about Flying Saucers*. Greenwich, CT: Fawcett Gold Medal, 1967.

———. *Flying Saucers Are Watching Us*. New York: Tower, 1968.

———. "The Secret Warehouse of UFO Proof." *UFO Report*,

Bloecher, Ted. *Report on the UFO Wave of 1947*. Washington, DC: author, 1967.

Blum, Howard. *Out There: The Government's Secret Quest for Extraterrestials*. New York: Simon and Schuster, 1991.

Blum, Ralph, with Blum, Judy. *Beyond Earth: Man's Contact with UFOs*. New York: Bantam Books, 1974.

"Brilliant Red Explosion Flares in Las Vegas Sky." *Las Vegas Sun*, April 19, 1962, p. 1.

Canadeo, Anne. *UFOs—The Fact or Fiction Files*. New York: Walker, 1990.

Catoe, Lynn E. *UFOs and Related Subjects: An Annotated Bibliography*. Washington, DC: Government Printing Office, 1969.

Citizens Against UFO Secrecy. "Conversation with Dr. Sarbacher." *Just Cause*, September 1985.

Clark, Jerome. *Emergence of a Phenomenon: UFOs from the Beginning through 1959*. Detroit: Omnigraphics, 1992.

———. *High Strangeness: UFOs from 1960 through 1979*. Detroit: Omnigraphics, 1996.

———. *UFOs in the 1980s*. Detroit: Apogee, 1990.

Committee on Science and Astronautics, report, 1961.

Cohen, Daniel. *Encyclopedia of the Strange*. New York: Avon, 1987.

———. *UFOs—The Third Wave*. New York: Evans, 1988.

Cooper, Milton William. *Behold a Pale Horse*. Sedona, AZ: Light Technology, 1991.

Creighton, Gordon. "Top U.S. Scientist Admits Crashed UFOs." *Flying Saucer Review*, October 1985.

Davidson, Leon, ed. *Flying Saucers: An Analysis of Air Force Project Blue Book Special Report No. 14*. Clarksburg, VA: Saucerian Press, 1971.

Department of Defense News Releases and Fact Sheets. 1952–1968.

Editors of *Look*. "Flying Saucers." *Look* (1966).

Edwards, Frank. *Flying Saucers—Here and Now!* New York: Bantam, 1968.

———. *Flying Saucers—Serious Business*. New York: Bantam, 1966.

———. *Strange World*. New York: Bantam, 1964.

Estes, Russ, producer. *Quality of the Messenger*. Crystal Sky Productions, 1993.

"Experts Say a Meteor Caused Flash of Fire." *Deseret News,* Salt Lake City, UT; April 19, 1962, p. 1.

Fact Sheet, "Office of Naval Research 1952 Greenland Cosmic Ray Scientific Expedition." October 16, 1952.

Fawcett, Lawrence, and Greenwood, Barry J. *Clear Intent: The Government Cover-up of the UFO Experience*. Englewood Cliffs, NJ: Prentice-Hall, 1984.

Final Report, "Project Twinkle." Project Blue Book Files, Nov. 1951.

"Fireball Explodes in Utah." *Nevada State Journal*, April 19, 1962, p. 1.

First Status Report, Project Stork (Preliminary to *Special Report No. 14*). April 1952.

"Flying Saucers Again." *Newsweek*, April 17, 1950, p. 29.

"Flying Saucers Are Real." *Flying Saucer Review* Jan./Feb. 1956: pp. 2–5. Foster, Tad. Unpublished articles for Condon Committee Casebook. 1969.

Fowler, Raymond E. *Casebook of a UFO Investigator*. Englewood Cliffs, NJ: Prentice-Hall, 1981.

Fuller, John G. *The Interrupted Journey*. New York: Dial, 1966.

———. *Incident at Exeter*. New York: G. P. Putnam's Sons, 1966.

———. *Aliens in the Sky*. New York: Berkley Books, 1969.

Gillmor, Daniel S., ed. *Scientific Study of Unidentified Flying Objects*. New York: Bantam Books, 1969.

Good, Timothy. *Above Top Secret*. New York: Morrow, 1988.

———. *The UFO Report*. New York: Avon Books, 1989.

———. *Alien Contact*. New York: Morrow, 1993.

Gordon, Stan, and Cooper, Vicki. "The Kecksburg Incident." *UFO*, Vol. 6, no. 1 (1991): 16–19.

Hall, Richard. *Uninvited Guests*. Santa Fe, NM: Aurora Press, 1988.

———. ed. *The UFO Evidence*. Washington, DC: NICAP, 1964.

———. *UFO* (Jan. Feb. 1991): 30–32.

Hanrahan, James Stephen. *History of Research in Space Biology and Biodynamics at the Air Force Missile Development Center 1946–1958*. Alamogordo, NM: Office of Information Services, 1959.

———. *Contributions of Balloon Operations to Research and Development at the Air Force Missile Development Center 1947–1958*. Alamogordo, NM: Office of Information Services, 1959.

Haugland, Vern. "AF Denies Recovering Portions of 'Saucers.' " *Albuquerque New Mexican*, March 23, 1954.

Hippler, Lt. Col. Robert H. Letter to Edward U. Condon. January 16, 1967.

History of the Eighth Air Force, Fort Worth, Texas. (Microfilm) Air Force Archives, Maxwell Air Force Base, AL.

History of the 509th Bomb Group, Roswell, New Mexico. (Microfilm) Air Force Archives, Maxwell Air Force Base, AL.

Hynek, J. Allen. *The UFO Experience: A Scientific Inquiry.* Chicago: Henry Regency, 1975.

Hynek, J. Allen, and Vallee, Jacques. *The Edge of Reality.* Chicago: Henry Regency, 1972.

Jacobs, David M. *The UFO Controversy in America.* New York: Signet, 1975.

Jung, Carl G. *Flying Saucers: A Modern Myth of Things Seen in the Sky.* New York: Harcourt, Brace, 1959.

Keel, John. *UFOs: Operation Trojan Horse.* New York: G. P. Putnam's Sons, 1970.

————. *Strange Creatures from Space and Time.* New York: Fawcett, 1970.

Keyhoe, Donald E. *Aliens from Space.* New York: Signet, 1974.

Klass, Philip J. *UFOs Explained.* New York: Random House, 1974.

————. *The Public Deceived.* Buffalo, NY: Prometheus Books, 1983.

Knaack, Marcelle. *Encyclopedia of U.S. Air Force Aircraft and Missile Systems.* Washington, DC: Office of Air Force History, 1988.

Library of Congress Legislative Reference Service. *Facts about UFOs.* May 1966.

Loftus, R. *Eye-Witness Testimony.* Cambridge, MA: Harvard University Press, 1979.

Lore, Gordon, and Deneault, Harold H. *Mysteries of the Skies: UFOs in Perspective.* Englewood Cliff, NJ: Prentice-Hall, 1968.

Lorenzen, Coral and Jim. *Flying Saucers: The Startling Evidence of the Invasion from Outer Space.* New York: Signet, 1966.

————. *Flying Saucer Occupants.* New York: Signet, 1967.

————. *Encounters with UFO Occupants.* New York: Berkley Medallion Books, 1976.

————. *Abducted!* New York: Berkley Medallion Books, 1977.

Low, Dr. Robert J. Letter to Lt. Col. Robert Hippler. January 27, 1967.

Maccabee, Bruce. "The Arnold Phenomenon: Part I, II, and III." *International UFO Reporter.* Jan.–Feb. 1995–May–June 1995.

————. "Historical Interduction to Project Blue Book Special Report #14." CUFOS, 1991.

McCall, G. J. H. *Meteorites and Their Origins*. New York: Wiley & Sons, 1973.

McClellan Subcommittee Hearings. March 1958.

McCormack Subcommittee Briefing. August 1958.

Menzel, Donald H., and Boyd, Lyle G. *The World of Flying Saucers*. Garden City, NY: Doubleday, 1963.

Menzel, Donald H., and Taves, Ernest H. *The UFO Enigma*. Garden City, NY: Doubleday, 1977.

"Meteor Lands in Utah, Lights Western Sky." *Los Angeles Times*, April 19, 1962.

Michel, Aime. *The Truth About Flying Saucers*. New York: Pyramid, 1967.

Mueller, Robert. *Air Force Bases: Volume 1, Active Air Force Bases within the United States of America on 17 September 1982*. Washington, DC: Office of Air Force History, 1989.

National Security Agency. Presidential documents. Washington, DC: Executive Order 12356, 1982.

Neilson, James. "Secret U.S./UFO Structure." *UFO*, Vol. 4, no. 1 (1989): 4–6.

Olive, Dick. "Most UFOs Explainable, Says Scientist." *Elmira* (NY) *Star-Gazette*, January 26, 1967, p. 19.

Palmer, Raymond, and Arnold, Kenneth. *The Coming of the Saucers*. Amherst, MA: 1952.

Peebles, Curtis. *The Moby Dick Project*. Washington, DC: Smithsonian Institution Press, 1991.

————. *Watch the Skies!* New York: Berkley Books, 1995.

Press conference: General Samford. Project Blue Book Files, 1952.

Project Blue Book. (Microfilm) National Archives, Washington, DC.

Randle, Kevin D. "The Pentagon's Secret Air War Against UFOs." *Saga*, March 1976.

————. *The UFO Casebook*. New York: Warner, 1989.

————. *A History of UFO Crashes*. New York: Avon, 1995.

Randle, Kevin D., and Cornett, Robert Charles. "Project Blue Book

Cover-up: Pentagon Suppressed UFO Data." *UFO Report*, vol. 2 no. 5 (Fall 1975).

Randles, Jenny. *The UFO Conspiracy*. New York: Javelin, 1987.

"Rocket and Missile Firings," White Sands Proving Grounds, Jan.– July 1947.

Ruppelt, Edward J. *The Report on Unidentified Flying Objects*. New York: Ace, 1956.

Russell, Eric. "Phantom Balloons Over North America." *Modern Aviation*, February 1953.

Sagan, Carl, and Page, Thornton, eds. *UFOs: Scientific Debate*. New York: Norton, 1974.

Sandreson, Ivan T. *Uninvited Visitors*. New York: Cowles, 1967.

———. *Invisible Residents*. New York: World Publishing, 1970.

Saunders, David, and Harkins, R. Roger. *UFOs? Yes!* New York: New American Library, 1968.

Scully, Frank. "Scully's Scrapbook." *Variety*, October 12, 1949, p. 61.

———. *Behind the Flying Saucers*. New York: Henry Holt, 1950.

Sheaffer, Robert. *The UFO Verdict*. Buffalo, NY: Prometheus, 1981.

Simmons, H. M. "Once Upon a Time in the West." *Magonia*, August 1985.

Smith, Scott. "Q & A: Len Stringfield." *UFO* Vol. 6, no. 1 (1991): 20–24.

"The Space Men at Wright-Patterson." *UFO* update.

Special Report No. 14. Project Blue Book files, 1955.

Spencer, John. *The UFO Encyclopedia*. New York: Avon, 1993.

Spencer, John, and Evans, Hilary. *Phenomenon*. New York: Avon, 1988.

Status Reports, Grudge—Blue Book, Nos. 1–12."

Steiger, Brad. *Strangers from the Skies*. New York: Award, 1966.

———. *Project Blue Book*. New York: Ballantine, 1976.

Steiger, Brad, and Steiger, Sherry Hanson. *The Rainbow Conspiracy*. New York: Pinnacle, 1994.

Stevenson, William. *Intrepid's Last Case*. New York: Villard, 1988.

Stone, Clifford E. *UFOs: Let the Evidence Speak for Itself*. CA: the author, 1991.

————. *The U.S. Air Force's Real, Official Investigation of UFO's.* Private report: the author, 1993.

Story, Ronald D. *The Encyclopedia of UFOs.* Garden City, NY: Doubleday, 1980.

Stringfield, Leonard H. *Situation Red: The UFO Siege!* Garden City, NY: Doubleday, 1977.

————. *UFO Crash/Retrieval Syndrome: Status Report II.* Seguin, TX: MUFON, 1980.

————. *UFO Crash/Retrieval: Amassing the Evidence: Status Report III.* Cincinnati, OH: the author, 1982.

————. *UFO Crash/Retrievals: The Inner Sanctum Status Report VI.* Cincinnati, OH: the author, 1991.

————. "Roswell and the X-15: UFO Basics." *MUFON UFO Journal,* No. 259 (November 1989): 3–7.

Sturrock, P. A. "UFOs—A Scientific Debate." *Science,* no. 180 (1973) : 593.

Sullivan, Walter. *We Are Not Alone.* New York: Signet, 1966.

Sumner, Donald A. "Skyhook Churchill 1966." *Naval Reserve Reviews,* January 1967: 29.

Swords, Michael D., ed. *Journal of UFO Studies, New Series, Vol. 4.* Chicago: CUFOS, 1993.

Technical Bulletin. "Army Ordnance Department Guided Missile Program." Jan. 1948.

Technical Report. "Unidentified Aerial Objects, Project SIGN." Feb. 1949.

Technical Report. "Unidentified Flying Objects, Project GRUDGE." August 1949.

Templeton, David. "The Uninvited." *Pittsburgh (PA) Press,* May 19, 1991, pp. 10–15.

U.S. Congress, House Committee on Armed Forces. *Unidentified Flying Objects.* Hearings, 89th Cong., 2nd Sess., April 5, 1966. Washington DC: U.S. Government Printing Office, 1968.

U.S. Congress Committee on Science and Astronautics. *Symposium on Unidentified Flying Objects.* Hearings, July 29, 1968. Washington, DC: U.S. Government Printing Office, 1968.

Vallee, Jacques. *Anatomy of a Phenomenon.* New York: Ace, 1966.

————. *Challenge to Science*. New York: Ace, 1966.

————. *Dimensions*. New York: Ballantine, 1989.

————. *Revelations*. New York: Ballantine, 1991.

"Visitors From Venus." *Time* January 9, 1950, p. 49.

War Department. *Meteorological Balloons*. (Army technical manual) Washington, D.C.: Government Printing Office, 1944.

Webber, Bert. *Retaliation: Japanese Attacks and Allied Countermeasures on the Pacific Coast in World War II*. Corvallis, OR: Oregon State University Press, 1975.

Wheeler, David R. *The Lubbock Lights*. New York: Award Books, 1977.

Wilkins, Harold T. *Flying Saucers on the Attack*. New York: Citadel, 1954.

————. *Flying Saucers Uncensored*. New York: Pyramid, 1967.

Wise, David, and Ross, Thomas B. *The Invisible Government*. New York: 1964.

Zeidman, Jennie. "I Remember Blue Book." *International UFO Reporter*, March–April 1991: 7.

INDEX